MW01027988

MONTE CRISTO

Looking from Pride of the Mountains Mine across tramway long span toward Mystery Hill.

MONTE CRISTO

by

PHILIP R. WOODHOUSE

with

ROBERT L. WOOD

THE
MOUNTAINEERS

Dedicated to the Monte Cristo miners,
whose years of toil provided this colorful legacy

Mountaineers Books is the publishing division of The Mountaineers,
an organization founded in 1906 and dedicated to the exploration,
preservation, and enjoyment of outdoor and wilderness areas.

MOUNTAINEERS 1001 SW Klickitat Way, Suite 201, Seattle, WA 98134
BOOKS 800.553.4453, www.mountaineersbooks.org

Printed in the United States of America
Distributed in the United Kingdom by Cordee, www.cordee.co.uk

16 15 14 13   1 2 3 4 5

Cover photograph: *Monte Cristo circa 1919*

Library of Congress Cataloging-in-Publication Data
Woodhouse, Phillip R   1938-
  Monte Cristo.
  Bibliography: p.
  Includes index
  1. Monte Cristo, Wash.—History. 2. Frontier and
pioneer life—Washington (State)—Monte Cristo.
I. Wood, Robert L., joint author. II. Title.
F899.M66W66   1979   979.7'71 78-71665
ISBN 0-89886-071-7

ISBN (paperback): 978-0-89886-071-9
ISBN (ebook): 978-1-59485-827-7

CONTENTS

AUTHOR'S NOTE

During the years since *Monte Cristo* was first published in 1979, I have given many lectures, video presentations, and slide shows on the subject. Always I have been asked what Monte Cristo is like "today." I hope these observations will provide a better understanding of what can be seen and experienced at the old mining town in the 1990s and, perhaps, beyond.

It is no longer possible to drive to the town site due to extensive washouts between Barlow Pass and Monte Cristo, and there are no plans to repair the road. Reaching the area requires a four-mile hike or mountain-bike trek along the old road. While this takes more effort, it allows the traveler the opportunity to get closer to nature and to search out the traces of the old railroad along which trains once rumbled and whistled through this valley on the way to the gold fields. Visitors should park at the end of the Mountain Loop Highway pavement at Barlow Pass, then proceed around the county gate onto the grade which once shook under the weight of the Everett and Monte Cristo Railroad's eighty-ton locomotives. Caution must be used on a perilous detour high up on the bank around one of the washouts. Bicyclists must be prepared for this. Otherwise, the grade is gradual and the scenery becomes even more grand the farther one goes. About a mile from the gate on the old road, the Twin Bridges remain standing for the crossing of the Sauk River.

Upon reaching the end of the road, those who have visited previously may notice that something is missing: the old Boston-American Mine cookhouse, which served as the Monte Cristo Lodge for many years, is gone. It was burned when a chimney fire ignited the

7

tinder-dry shingles that covered its sides. Several of the small cabins still line the edges of the old parking lot, and the railroad turntable frame continues to beckon energetic visitors to rotate it—which can still be done after all these years by the strong of arm and resolute of heart. Scattered about the area are many artifacts that harken back to the mining days: pulleys, ore cart wheels, gears, and axles, all lying in a confusing jumble.

The town is an excellent departure point for the many hikes available in the area, and less has changed once away from the more visited environs of the valley floor. The mountains and meadows of Glacier Basin, Silver Lake, and Twin Lakes are as inviting as ever, and the mine remnants still stand as a testament to the folly of man's futile efforts to change the face of the land. Those who choose to journey toward Glacier Basin may observe something new when passing through the upper town site along Glacier Street. Several trees have been festooned with the bright ribbons and signs that identify them as "witness trees," which are used to define the corners of land parcels that have been surveyed. Here they mark lands previously owned by a corporation which were purchased by a nature conservation group and turned over to the U.S. Forest Service. The valley is now surrounded on three sides by the Henry M. Jackson Wilderness Area, and many hope that the entire area will eventually fall within its bounds. The trails in the area are still maintained in passable condition, and the place remains a spectacular area to visit, with splendid peaks soaring four thousand feet above and sparkling streams dancing in the meadows below.

The future of Monte Cristo may take any one of many paths. About one hundred of the patented mine claims and town-site lots remain in private hands, as do other parcels of land in the valley. A group of landowners and other interested parties calling themselves the Monte Cristo Preservation Association has been maintaining the road and many trails in the area, although recent floods created a major setback to their efforts. It is doubtful that mining will resume at Monte Cristo due to the adjacent wilderness area and difficulty of access; however, a national emergency that requires the acquisition of the precious metals locked up in these mountains could change that. Only time will tell.

Philip R. Woodhouse
June, 1996

PREFACE

The data upon which this book is based were not originally compiled for the purpose of writing the history of Monte Cristo. Rather, I began collecting information about the town to satisfy my own curiosity and to answer questions which arose in my mind after numerous visits to the area. What little had been written on the subject appeared to be over simplistic or, in many cases, erroneous. I became deeply impressed by the accomplishments the early miners had achieved in tackling the wilderness from which they sought to extract wealth. I found giant wheels on high mountain ridges, tunnels dug in remote, inaccessible locations, and the remains of buildings that had been lashed to steep valley walls with cables.

None of the material that was readily available explained how these feats had been accomplished or by whom. Obviously a large amount of money and energy had been expended by the men involved in developing the area. When I began to locate information which answered my questions, I gained great respect not only for the achievements themselves but also the attitude with which they had been executed. In the 1890s concern was nonexistent about the environmental impact of a venture like Monte Cristo, and "studies" were not carried out to determine whether or not a project was feasible. If the miners required a structure or piece of machinery, they built it, within a time period that was so short it makes the schedules of today's construction seem ridiculous by comparison.

During the early days at Monte Cristo, financing was not a problem. Because the nation was experiencing a "boom" economy, men could be found who would finance any cause which seemed even remotely able to succeed. The total amount of money which was invested in Monte Cristo will never be known because many of the records have been lost. But samples of the projects which were required to establish Monte Cristo as a mining enterprise can give one some insight into the expenses incurred. For example, the railroad cost almost $2,000,000, and the purchasers spent nearly $400,000 to acquire the first four mine claims. Hundreds of thousands more dollars were expended on the tramways, concentrator, smelter, mine buildings, and the Monte Cristo townsite itself. How much wealth did all this investment wrench from the hills of Monte Cristo? Again, the exact figures are lacking, but an educated guess, based on the available data, indicates it did not exceed $1,000,000. If the total wealth of all the mines in the entire region is taken into account, the production probably did not exceed $1,500,000.

When enough of the facts and figures were available to reveal a continuum of activity throughout the years that Monte Cristo was a producing mining community, I began to realize that others would be interested in the Monte Cristo story. This book was, therefore, written to satisfy the curiosity of anyone who is fascinated by the area's history and by the indomitable spirit of the adventurous people who made that history.

I owe a deep debt of gratitude to many people who aided and encouraged me during the compilation of data and the writing of this book. The list is too long to be included here, but is incorporated in the credits at the back of this volume. I do, however, wish to express my special thanks to Robert L. Wood, who contributed a great deal of time (as literary editor of this book) in leading this novice through the difficulties of writing a history of such complexity.

PHILIP R. WOODHOUSE

CHAPTER I

1889

THE GLITTERING MOUNTAIN

In the mid-1800s what is now western Washington was virtually an untouched region. Like a dark green carpet, the virgin forests blanketed the lowlands and extended up deep valleys into the Cascade Mountains, unbroken except for the meager clearings made by man. The fir, hemlock, cedar, and spruce comprising the forests grew to enormous size, causing a pioneer to exclaim: "The bodies of the trees are so large that one cannot see more than a hundred yards in any direction." In fact, they towered more than 200 feet skyward and stood so close together very little light filtered to the forest floor—a world of dank twilight and perpetual gloom. This, combined with the characteristic gray weather of the Puget Sound region, instilled a sensation of awe and fear in the hardiest settlers and adventurers who dared to enter this uncharted land in Washington Territory.

The impediments presented by the forests were both augmented and alleviated by the numerous rivers that rose in the snowfields of the Cascades. The streams rushed through steep-walled canyons and, gathering tributaries along the way, poured out onto the lowlands, where they carved meandering beds as they sought sea level at Puget Sound. Although they were barriers to the progress of the pioneers, the rivers also served as avenues of commerce. The products wrested from the new land could be floated down them to market, needed trade goods shipped upstream to the nearly isolated settlers.

One such avenue, the Skykomish River, was used as the route of entry into what was to become Snohomish County. The trappers and hunters came first, seeking the furs found in abundance along the river's banks. They were quickly followed by the prospectors, whose search

11

for minerals led them farther upriver into the foothills and canyons of the mountains. Thus a small number of tenuous footpaths and horse trails were established to connect the newly built trading centers of Snohomish City and Gunn's Place (Index) with the mining claims and logging camps tributary to the river.

In 1859 several Steilacoom men organized a syndicate to construct roads in the area, and they sent Ed Cady and a man named Parsons up the North Fork of the Skykomish River to locate a route over the Cascades in order to provide access to the Columbia River Basin. The men began the trip late in the season, and early snowfall prevented their crossing the crest of the mountains. The route they blazed appeared to be satisfactory so far as it went, however, and Cady discovered, upon consulting with the local Indians, that this was the route the natives had used for years in the course of trading with the people who lived in the eastern part of the territory.

Under Cady's direction, construction of the trail began early in 1860. The route led over Cady Pass, then down the Wenatchee River, and into the Columbia Basin. Later that same year the trail was extended northward to the Kettle River in British Columbia, where some mining was in progress. Shortly thereafter Scott's Place or Scott's Camp (later called Galena) was established in the dense forest at the confluence of Silver Creek with the North Fork of the Skykomish. This small camp became an important way station on the new cross-mountain route as well as a center to serve incipient mining activities in the Silver Creek region.

The way now open, prospectors and speculators poured into the virgin country to seek fortunes and stake claims in the unmapped wilderness. In 1874 men filed claims on the North and South Forks of Silver Creek, several miles upstream from Scott's Camp. About fifty were recorded that summer and fall, the first by L. T. Ireland. No central authority existed in those early days to control or record the filing of claims; consequently, local prospectors created their own mining districts to bring control and order to the process. On October 15, 1874, a number of miners met at Silver Creek, where they organized, defined, and established the Skykomish Mining District and agreed upon laws governing it. Jay G. Kelly was elected president, H. L. Pike designated secretary.

Between 1874 and 1880, the town of Mineral City grew at the junction of the North and South Forks of Silver Creek, and in 1880 the Silver City Townsite and Mining Company purchased many of the original fifty claims at the creek's headwaters. Because a horse trail had not been constructed through the narrow, heavily timbered canyon, all material had to be packed in and out of Mineral City on the men's backs. Minor prospecting and development work continued along Silver Creek until 1882, when Elisha H. Hubbart hacked a foot trail to Mineral City and relocated the Anna claim, along with the Trade Dollar and the Morning Star. Interest was rekindled and prospecting continued at a lively pace through 1890.

By late spring, 1889, no one had ventured north of the headwaters of Silver Creek to seek his fortune in the untouched land lying beyond that mountain spur. In fact, nobody suspected that an unknown valley north of Mineral City was about to change the mining history of the Cascade Mountains. But the stage was set, the way open, for the events that were to follow.

Joseph Pearsall was typical of the Mineral City prospectors. He had considerable knowledge of the geology and mineralization of the area and, as others before him, had come to Silver Creek to seek wealth in the Cascades. One day in the spring of 1889—probably in late May or early June—Pearsall traced a promising mineral outcrop up the side of Hubbart's Peak east of Mineral City. The climb was steep and treacherous, but during the afternoon he reached the ridge crest that separated Silver and Troublesome Creeks, near the summit of Hubbart's Peak. From his lofty perch, near 5,500 feet in elevation, he could look across the Cascades, whose peaks and valleys resembled the rising and falling swells of the ocean, frozen forever in their places.

With a pair of field glasses, Pearsall scanned the country adjacent to his eyrie. Examining the wall of a prominent peak to the north, he observed bands of red streaking the mountain from base to summit. He recognized the brick-red color as belonging to a material called iron hat or gossan. This color, of primary importance to the area's prospectors, was caused by oxidation of the rich sulphide ores upon their contact with the atmosphere and was an indication of the wealth lying hidden beneath the cap of gossan. While Pearsall reflected on the possibilities of prospecting this new area, his attention was attracted to a red-gold glitter—the reflection of the afternoon sunlight from one of the ledges. Scanning further with his field glasses, he observed that virtually the en-

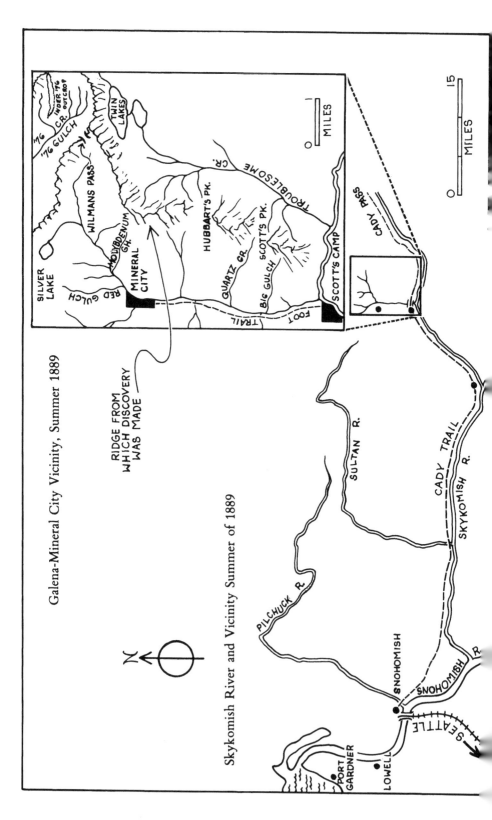

Galena-Mineral City Vicinity, Summer 1889

Skykomish River and Vicinity Summer of 1889

RIDGE FROM
WHICH DISCOVERY
WAS MADE

tire ledge from valley floor to mountain summit glittered and sparkled in the late summer sun.

Pearsall's heart leaped with excitement, because he recognized almost immediately that this material was probably galena, the sulphide ore of lead, stained red-gold by the gossan on the vein's surface. This was a find of great importance, since the majority of the galena in this region was argentiferous—that is, it contained silver, the metal, rather than gold, that was of primary interest to the area's prospectors. As Pearsall contemplated the significance of the discovery, he plotted a path toward the region to the north. Upon further observation, he located a pass in the spur between Silver Creek and the new valley, and he proceeded to plan his entrance into the mysterious realm to sample its riches.[1]

Ascending the headwaters of Silver Creek, Pearsall crossed the pass and entered into a district never before experienced by white men. He descended into the unnamed canyon which was walled in by mountains that rose almost 4,000 feet from the valley floor, his attention constantly riveted upon the glistening band streaking the opposite mountainside. The way was brushy, but not disagreeably so, the traveling easy and rapid compared with making one's way through the dense forest and underbrush at the lower elevations of Silver Creek.

As he crossed the valley floor, where a brook bubbled merrily from the snowfields, Pearsall began to appreciate the magnitude of what he had discovered. After a short ascent of the talus slopes at the base of the canyon's north wall, he reached the glittering band and collected specimens of the material. He then discovered, to his delight, that what he had supposed was true. He was standing at the base of an entire mountain of galena! His spirits soaring, he recrossed the creek and ascended the canyon's south wall, with his sample in hand. Once again he stood in the pass, whence he could view his find in the revealing light of the afternoon sun. His ecstacy knew no bounds as he descended the headwaters of Silver Creek toward Mineral City in the gathering twilight.

At Mineral City, Pearsall met Frank Peabody, a prospector friend, and beside the evening campfire he related, in confidence, his experiences of the previous days. Since Peabody was about to leave for Seattle, Pearsall gave him some of the ore samples to have them assayed for their metallic content. Because Peabody knew many men of means in the area and was a persuasive talker, the prospectors hoped that a "grubstake" could be arranged to allow further exploration of the new area.

Shortly after arriving in Seattle, Peabody chanced to meet John MacDonald Wilmans, a long-time friend whom he had known in his earlier days in Arizona Territory. What luck this was! Here was, in fact, a man with financial assets. Although Mac Wilmans (as he was known to his friends) was only 31 years old, he had already made and lost several fortunes in mining and business ventures. He could truly appreciate the importance of the little sample of ore Peabody had carried from Mineral City. Together they had the sample assayed, and they judged the results to be very favorable.

Consequently, Wilmans decided to accompany Peabody to Mineral City to view the "promised land" himself. Traveling north, the men acquired horses at Snohomish City and set out on the Cady Trail toward Scott's Camp. Along the way they met Pearsall, who was delighted by the fortunate turn of events and decided to go with them back to the site of the discovery. Reaching Scott's Camp, they had to abandon their mounts and backpack all their necessities as no horse trail yet led up Silver Creek. The going was rough, and Wilmans wasn't feeling too well after the long day's hike up Silver Creek to the pass from which the valley could be viewed. But from this hard-won vantage point he could clearly see the vein cutting the mountain from top to bottom like an incredible sequined veil, and he is reported to have exclaimed: "Boys, the world is ours!"

The men camped that evening on the ridge and built a large fire which did little to dispel the bitter chill of the alpine night. The next day, Wilmans, who was exhausted, suffered the first stages of a severe cold. Because he felt very ill, he remained with Peabody while Pearsall once again descended into the canyon to obtain more samples. By the time the latter returned, Wilmans was running a fever, and he was sicker than he had been that morning. Despite his illness, he did manage to impart his name to the place where he had spent the night, and to this day old maps show Wilmans Pass on the ridge between Silver Creek and the new valley.

The trio, ore samples in hand, began the trek back to civilization on the third day after leaving Scott's Camp. Walking fifteen miles a day, they finally reached a point thirty miles downstream where transportation could be obtained to ease the remainder of the journey. By the time they reached Seattle, Wilmans was quite miserable, but not sufficiently so to be committed to bed, and he proceeded to have the ore assayed. Because the samples showed well in both silver and gold, he decided to give Pearsall and Peabody a grubstake of $150 to return to the valley and locate as many claims as possible, gather more samples, and report back as to their findings. In addition, the men agreed that Pearsall and Peabody would each be entitled to one-eighth of whatever the property earned, with Wilmans receiving the remaining three-fourths. The two prospectors' shares were each bonded for the sum of $7,500, thus they were assured of receiving at least that amount for their efforts. The venture was to be kept strictly confidential to prevent news of the find leaking into the community and possibly triggering a ''gold rush.'' Such an event might very well cause a stampede into the remote area, and that of course would not be to the economic interests of the men presently involved.

Newly outfitted, Pearsall and Peabody headed back into the mountains. Meanwhile, Wilmans, realizing the necessity for additional capital in the venture, related the discovery in confidence to two Seattle friends. Thomas Ewing and George W. Grayson were wealthy mining investors of some experience, and for this guarded information Wilmans extracted the sum of $75.

Still quite feverish, Wilmans embarked for San Francisco on his way to Arizona. His condition did not improve, and the trip was cancelled. Instead, he went home to Park City, Utah, leaving word that Pearsall and Peabody were to report to him there as to what they had achieved. Wilmans then wrote to his older brother, Fred, his oft-time partner in mining ventures, about his experiences and findings in Washington Territory, and discussed the possibility of his brother's involvement in the new venture.

Meanwhile, Pearsall and Peabody had returned to the valley and staked two claims along, and adjacent to, the outcrop with the glittering paystreak. Because the first one was located on July 4, the property was named Independence of 1776, but this was quickly shortened to Independence of '76, and finally to '76. The name was also given to the creek and the valley through which it flowed. The second claim, located the next day on an outcrop parallel to the '76, was named Glacier. Shortly afterward, their supplies nearly exhausted, Pearsall and Peabody recorded the claims at Snohomish City, then made their way back to Seattle. Upon arriving, they sent a report to Park City, where Wilmans was waiting.[2]

Fred Wilmans, older brother of Mac Wilmans, one of three brothers eventually in-volved in the financing and promotion of the mining enterprizes in the new-found region.

Although the information was extremely encouraging, Wilmans had not fully recovered from his bout with the Cascades and he decided it would be more prudent if his brother made the trip to Seattle. As a consequence, Fred Wilmans arrived in the city in late August, 1889, and immediately arranged for a second locating trip into the '76 region. Amidst the first color of early fall, he made his way up the Cady Trail with Pearsall and Peabody to Scott's Camp, where the horses were left.

Once again backpacking was the only mode of transport. Ascending the foot trail along Silver Creek, the men climbed toward Wilmans Pass and, crossing over, descended into '76 Gulch.

Because the two major ore outcroppings had been located by Pearsall and Peabody on the first expedition into the area two months earlier, they decided to stake claims higher up the mountainside, on the same veins, in order to obtain rights to as much of the surface lead as possible. The first such extension to be located, on August 29, 1889, was the Ranger, situated well above the '76 claim. The upper locating points of the Ranger were almost at the top of the ridge, nearly 2,500 feet above the floor of '76 Gulch.

While assisting in the location, Pearsall noticed what appeared to be a pass just above him. His natural curiosity aroused, he climbed the short but steep pitch to this col, then discovered he could easily walk out onto a glacier. After taking a few steps beyond the col, Pearsall gazed 1,700 feet down into a cirque of incredible splendor. The bowl was ringed by jagged mountains which rose skyward thousands of feet, and the center of the basin was occupied by a small, tree-covered knoll. The remainder of the cirque was largely treeless, consisting of grassy, heather-strewn meadows traversed by a braided stream that sparkled in the sunlight. At the basin's northwestern, or outlet, end a timbered ridge less than a mile long rose about 500 feet above the floor. Between this ridge and the opposite wall the stream gathered its many channels and flowed past several small emerald isles, then out of the valley to points unknown.

Pearsall scanned the far wall of the basin with his field glasses. He was astounded to discover, from the ridge where he now stood, the same glittering galena in the red streaks of gossan as he had seen earlier that year from Hubbart's Peak. This could mean only one thing: the veins he was now surveying were continuations of those in '76 Gulch, and he concluded they passed completely through the ridge. By this time Peabody and Wilmans had arrived and, sharing his view, were thunderstruck by their discovery. What thoughts must have raced through their minds at that moment! If these veins were, in fact, continuous through the mountain, it did not require pencil and paper to estimate the enormous quantity of galena hidden beneath their feet, not to mention the amount represented by the vein on the basin's opposite side, which they could trace visually for thousands of feet up the mountainside. Profoundly impressed, they quickly decided to abandon for the

The ridge of mountains which separates '76 and Glacier Basins. Wilmans Peak is left of center, with '76 Gulch in the foreground. Immediately to the right of Wilmans Peak is the gap over which Glacier Basin was first glimpsed. Looking Northeasterly.

moment activities in '76 Gulch in favor of devoting their energies to exploring and locating properties in the new basin.

The men traveled down the glacier to a ridge between the basin and another glacier—a field of ice about one mile long which terminated to the southeast in a blue-green lake. Descending snowfields from this ridge, they passed between a rock pinnacle and the south wall of the basin, then picked their way down a steep gully to the bottom at a point just behind the central knoll. A short walk brought them to the outcrop of ore that cut through the timbered ridge and ran up the mountainside to the east. They could now see the steep, forbidding wall of the ridge dividing the basin from '76 Gulch; the red streaks were quite apparent on this wall, displaying approximately the same angle as the veins on the other side in '76 Gulch. This meant that what they had concluded on the ridge top was, no doubt, true—the veins of argentiferous galena extended through the mountain and continued into the peak on the other side of the basin. Awestruck by this discovery, as well as by the scenic grandeur, the men set about the task before them and staked three claims—the Pride of the Mountains, Pride of the Woods, and the '89—on the major vein crossing the basin. This occurred on August 29, 1889, the same day they located the Ranger, and thus defined the vein from the face of the timbered ridge to a point far up the mountain.

While working at their prospects, the men named the prominent features about them. The mountain spur separating the basin from '76 Gulch, over which they had just passed, was called Wilmans Peak after the two brothers. The hanging glacier they had crossed suggested the name Glacier Basin for the valley and Glacier Creek for the stream flowing from it.

The rugged southwest wall of Glacier basin. Wilmans Peak is at the far right, with Wilmans Glacier left of center. Wilmans, Pearsall and Peabody crossed this glacier on their descent into the basin in late August, 1889.

The prospectors spent the night in the basin, and they were probably the first white men who ever slept there. The next morning they climbed the rock slide where the timbered ridge joined Wilmans Peak. After a brief, 500-foot ascent, they stood at yet another high pass from where they could see many miles down a valley to ranges of unknown, unnamed mountains. The canyon floor lay about 2,000 feet below them. Reasoning that '76 Creek must flow into this river at some point, they began to descend the rocks toward the stream. About 700 feet below the pass, the familiar gossan showed up once again on the side of the timbered ridge. Here, on August 30, 1889, the men located the Baltic and Mystery claims along this extension of the vein which ran through Glacier Basin.

As the prospectors continued down the rock and talus slope, a beautiful waterfall came into view at the northern end of the timbered ridge below which they were descending. At this point Glacier Creek thundered 300 feet into the lower valley. The men quickly applied the name Glacier Falls to this phenomenon as they continued their descent toward Glacier Creek. After following the stream about a mile, they came upon a major confluence, where two creeks of about equal size rushed together. Because they were able to see up into '76 Gulch from this point, they realized this was '76 Creek, and they need only follow it upstream to return to their original properties. However, a question that had been gnawing at Pearsall and Peabody from the day of discovery now began to beg ever harder for an answer: Where were they? They realized, of course, that '76 Creek and Glacier Creek joined to form a river. But what river was this at whose headwaters they stood? With evening approaching, they abandoned the question for the moment. After slashing their way through the brush up '76 Creek, they reached the familiar ground in '76 Gulch, where they spent the night.

On August 31, Pearsall, Peabody, and Wilmans once again set about the task of locating properties in '76 Gulch, which they had left two days earlier. The '74 and '75 were staked on that date as lower extensions of the original '76, as was the Emma Moore, which was situated parallel to, and north of, the '74. This completely claimed the entire visible outcrop of the major veins in the area as well as the projected extension of the outcrop beneath the talus and '76 Creek.

Because their prospecting tasks had been concluded, and the first indications of winter were in the air, the men left '76 Gulch and began their

The Newly Discovered Area at Close of 1889

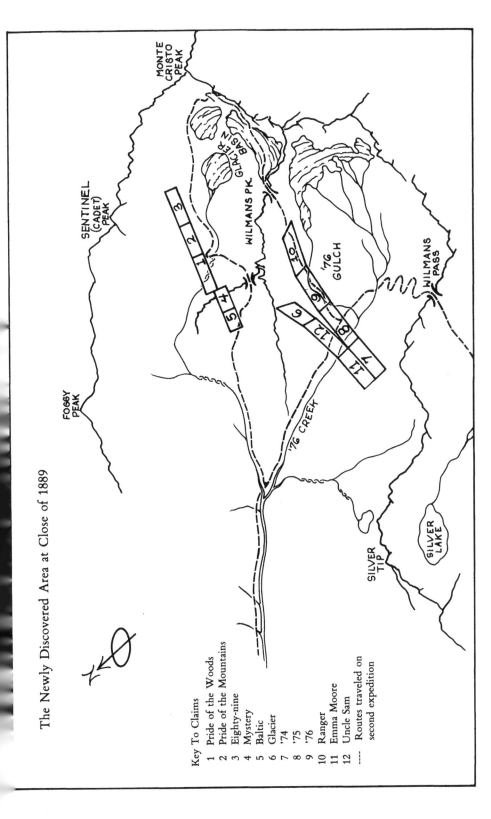

Key To Claims
  1 Pride of the Woods
  2 Pride of the Mountains
  3 Eighty-nine
  4 Mystery
  5 Baltic
  6 Glacier
  7 '74
  8 '75
  9 '76
  10 Ranger
  11 Emma Moore
  12 Uncle Sam
  ---- Routes traveled on
        second expedition

homeward journey, samples in hand. Pearsall and Peabody now decided
to part company with Wilmans and follow the river to its mouth, while
he returned to Seattle via the Wilmans Pass-Cady Trail route. And
follow the river they did, hacking through the brush, sometimes
wading or swimming in the stream itself, as circumstances demanded.
The river flowed almost directly north through virgin country. Their
food supplies almost depleted, Pearsall and Peabody were forced to subsist on raisins plus whatever blueberries and salmonberries they could
find along the way. Seven days after leaving Wilmans at their camp in
'76 Gulch, the exhausted men stumbled upon a farmhouse in the
bottomland of the now broad valley. To their amazement they learned
that the river whose headwaters they had discovered was the Sauk, a
major tributary of the Skagit, and they were only nine miles south of
Sauk City and the Skagit itself. The valley they had descended was
brushy and rugged, but of a moderate grade, and possibly suitable for a
trail into the area. Moreover, the Skagit was navigable during high water
by steamboat all the way to Sauk City. Their discovery was complete.[3]

Upon reaching Seattle, Wilmans had the new samples assayed before
he returned to Park City, where he related the events of the trip to Mac.
Pleased by the outcome, the brothers elected to terminate their business
at Park City (it was almost completed anyway), move to California, and
wait until spring before returning to the Cascades, whereupon they
would devote their full energies to this new venture. During the winter
they sold their holdings and properties in Utah and invested the funds in
a California sheep ranch. Each purchased land to provide a financial
cushion should the mining venture in Washington prove disappointing.

CHAPTER II

1890

MONTE CRISTO

When the spring of 1890 brought its blush to the Pacific slope of the Cascades, Fred and Mac Wilmans prepared to return to the mountains which held their hopes and dreams, locked in stone, at the headwaters of the Sauk River. Securing a large force of men and enough supplies to last the summer, the brothers headed north to the new properties. Upon arriving in Snohomish City, they started up the Cady Trail and soon had a taste of early spring in the Cascades. The firm and solid trail of the previous dry summer and fall had been reduced to an almost impassable quagmire by melting snow and torrential rain. The spring of 1890 was, in fact, unusually stormy, and on their first attempt to reach the new camp the men were stopped twelve miles short of their goal. The snow remained much later in the Cascades than they had anticipated, and the deep, packed drifts impeded movement toward '76 Creek. Only by constant and exhaustive effort did they finally reach the camp in April, while storm after storm raked the foothills and mountains in an unceasing rampage.

Although the men reached '76 Gulch with their packs, most of the supplies required for the summer's work remained at Scott's Camp. Because he had suffered a severe back injury in a mining accident during his youth, Fred stayed in '76 Gulch to supervise activities, while Mac and another man began the herculean task of packing supplies from Scott's Camp into '76 Gulch via Wilmans Pass. At the same time, a small force of men began cutting a horse trail along the footpath route. For two months Mac and his companion made the round trip a number of times between '76 Gulch and Scott's Camp. The trip down was comparatively easy, but the return journey the second day was not. Heavily bur-

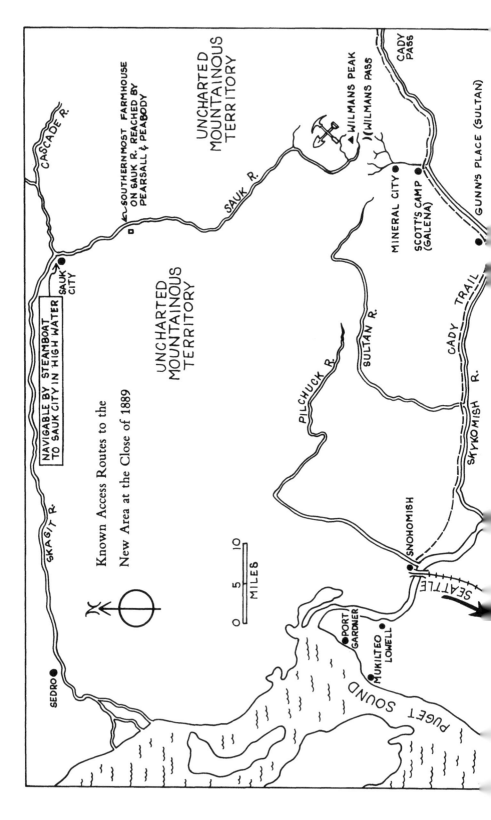

Known Access Routes to the

New Area at the Close of 1889

NAVIGABLE BY STEAMBOAT
TO SAUK CITY IN HIGH WATER

SOUTHERNMOST FARMHOUSE
ON SAUK R. REACHED BY
PEARSALL & PEABODY

UNCHARTED
MOUNTAINOUS
TERRITORY

UNCHARTED
MOUNTAINOUS
TERRITORY

CASCADE R.

SKAGIT R.

SAUK R.

SAUK
CITY

SEDRO

WILMANS PEAK
(WILMANS PASS)

CADY
PASS

GUNN'S PLACE (SULTAN)

MINERAL CITY

SCOTT'S CAMP
(GALENA)

CADY TRAIL

SKYKOMISH R.

SULTAN R.

PILCHUCK R.

SNOHOMISH

SEATTLE

PORT
GARDNER

MUKILTEO
LOWELL

PUGET SOUND

0 5 10
MILES

dened, they would slowly make their way up Silver Creek to Wilmans Pass, then down to '76 Gulch, where the crew in the meantime constructed the first building. The fifteen-by-fifteen foot log structure, with its stone fireplace, became known as the " '76 Cabin," and stood for many years. During the evenings the men relaxed by sitting around the campfire, when they read or discussed their dreams and ambitions—and predicted, of course, an exciting future for their discoveries.

Grandiose though their schemes may have seemed, and however far their flights of fancy carried them, they always had to face one sobering fact: regardless of the amount of wealth in the hills, it was worthless unless transported to market and turned into hard, cold cash. As Mac and his helper could attest by this time, they needed transportation, and on a large scale. To accomplish this, they would have to interest other capital in order to finance the necessary facilities. But access to the remote area was so difficult the average capitalist would be skeptical, at best, about supporting the venture. What was needed was a name for the camp—one that would not only capture and fire the imagination of men far and near but also exude riches by its very utterance. Thus the conversation around the evening campfires inevitably drifted to the subject of what to call the place. During one such rambling discussion, Fred Wilmans mentioned that the title of a book he carried—*The Count of Monte Cristo* by Alexander Dumas—brought to mind visions of great wealth, along with a sense of mystery. All the half-dozen or so men present had read the book, and after talking about the name for some time everyone agreed to call the new camp Monte Cristo in honor of that fictional master of intrigue and fortune.[1]

Although they had solved the name question, the more pressing problem—lack of transportation—continued to plague them, while Mac and his partner made their two-day treks to Scott's Camp to bring up needed supplies. After Fred Wilmans had been in '76 Gulch about a month, his old back injury flared up severely enough to render his stay impossible, and he left for the family ranch in California, leaving Mac to run the entire operation.

The horse trail into '76 Gulch was finally completed two months after it was begun, and the job of transporting goods from Scott's Camp to Monte Cristo could now be borne by beasts of burden. After the cabins were completed, the men set about tasks more directly related to mining: discovery of new veins, tracing surface outcrops of known ones, and blocking out already traced ore veins which showed promise. The valley was beginning to appear and sound like a real mining camp as additional cabins were built and the concussions caused by "giant powder" exploding thundered through the mountains.

Early in the summer of 1890, Frank Peabody decided to stake his own claims in the Monte Cristo area, and together with C. W. Shepp he located properties in '76 Gulch. This independent venture required operating capital, but Peabody was not too successful in obtaining the required funds. Finally he reached an agreement with Mac Wilmans which provided that Peabody quitclaim his one-eighth share of the Wilmanses' holdings for the bonded sum of $7,500. This satisfied both parties, and cut Peabody loose from the Wilmans brothers to seek his fortune in his own way. During the summer, Peabody and his partner claimed seven properties in the '76 Gulch area.

During the spring of 1890, Pearsall and Wilmans located more claims, adding new names to the Monte Cristo district. On May 12 they staked the Ibex No. 1 and Ibex No. 2; on May 17, the Clara and West Seattle; on May 22, the Sentinel. And thus it continued into the summer months, with men fanning out into the hills around '76 Creek to seize the wealth which lay before them for the taking. Before the year ended at least thirteen more claims were located and added to the Wilmanses' properties. In addition, development of the earlier claims proceeded—the veins were blocked out and faced up, and a considerable amount of ore piled on the dumps, awaiting a solution to the transportation problem. Because heavy machinery could not be hauled into the area, the work proceeded by hand. The blasting powder holes were drilled by the age-old method which employed two men: the "shaker man" held the drill and rotated it in the hole, while the "steel driving man" drove it into the rock with a sledge hammer. This was strenuous, time-consuming labor, and the tunnels were pushed into the veins no faster than a few feet per week. Heavy machinery, such as compressors, air drills, and steam engines, was sorely needed; but without the means of transporting the items into Monte Cristo they were only a dream in the summer of 1890.

Attempting to keep the Monte Cristo find secret was like trying to hold water in a sieve, and in June the third party to enter the area descended the steep wall of '76 Gulch. The group, led and grubstaked by C. H. Packard, included Andrew Lochrie and Knut Anderson. These men, no less ambitious than the Wilmans party, set about their tasks immediately. They began locating claims that were parallel to and extensions of the ones already staked by the Wilmans group.

News of gold and silver travels like the wind—it stirs up a storm with no apparent effort. As word of the discoveries at Monte Cristo spread, the storm began to sweep across the Pacific slope of Washington, when prospectors and would-be prospectors set their sight on this new area. Mining men who had established good reputations in western Washington traveled to Monte Cristo to look at samples and report on the activity that was supposedly uncovering so much wealth in Snohomish County. Their accounts were perhaps typified by the comments of a man whose zeal was pronounced, although his spelling not the best: "I care not how inexperienced one may be, he is inflated with enthusiasm and admiration when he beholds the rich mineral girdle which nearly envelopes a mighty mountain, and which can be diserned and followed with the naked eye a mile distant." On August 1, 1890, the *Snohomish Weekly Sun* carried a report from the Idaho Mining and Milling Company, of which Joseph Pearsall, the discoverer of the Monte Cristo lode, was a prime member, along with H. M. Shaw, J. Rightman, and a man named Whitey. In the report, Shaw stressed the importance of Snohomish City to the new mining areas, and urged the local businessmen to invest their capital in a smelter, lest the industry pass them by. On August 29, the same newspaper published an interview with L. W. Getchell, who was considered one of the most experienced mining men in the region. Getchell stated that the Monte Cristo discoveries far surpassed the richest mining districts that he had seen in New Mexico, Nevada, or California.

On the same date, the *Seattle Journal* made an almost identical comment:

> California, Nevada, Colorado, Arizona and Montana can testify to the wonderful impetus given to them by mining discoveries. The great excitement caused by the discovery of gold in Australia will be remembered. Compared with recent discoveries in this state, however, these finds are but pygmies. Experienced mining men have no hesitancy in saying that the new find is the largest and the richest that has ever been made and that one hundred dollars to one dollar will be taken out in comparison with the others.[2]

The rush was on, but while other men hurried to Monte Cristo,

Joseph Pearsall was about to step away. Although he was the discoverer
of the property, and entitled to one-eighth of the Wilmanses' holdings,
he was an independent person who enjoyed the thrill of discovery more
than the profit to be subsequently gained. He was known to his friends
as a "human mountain goat"—a man who climbed to search where
lesser men dared not go, and so he wished to remain. Furthermore,
Pearsall was involved in the Idaho Mining and Milling Company,
which had large holdings in the Silver Creek district and elsewhere, and
he lacked sufficient time to devote to both ventures. He therefore
divested himself of all interests in the Monte Cristo district for the sum
of $40,000. The transaction was recorded on August 20, 1890, and re-
leased him to devote his full efforts to the future discoveries of the Idaho
Mining and Milling Company.

After completion of the horse trail and establishment of the cabin in
'76 Gulch, Mac Wilmans felt the time had arrived to introduce his co-
investors to this mountain paradise. He returned to Seattle and contacted Ewing and Grayson, who were sharing the bill for the development work. They were impressed with Monte Cristo and the improvements that had been accomplished. Ewing elected to remain with the
venture, though on a reduced scale, but Grayson was getting up in years
and had already invested $800 in the enterprise. His experience told him
that the transportation problem was the critical issue, and massive
amounts of capital would be required to build roads into this remote
area. He reasoned that eventually the necessary funds would be attracted
to Monte Cristo, but by the time they were he would be too old to enjoy the fruits of his investments. Therefore, Grayson decided to back
out of the Monte Cristo venture before he was drawn more deeply into
it. Ewing, in part, agreed with Grayson, and on September 24, 1890,
Ewing and Grayson quitclaimed their interest in twelve of the major
claims to the Wilmanses. Grayson additionally deeded most of his holdings in the minor claims as well. Ewing elected to keep some shares in
the event Monte Cristo surprised the skeptics and became an El Dorado.
Mac paid Grayson the $800 due him, and gave Ewing an equivalent
amount for his shares. Ewing stayed at Monte Cristo, while Grayson
returned to the city, to remain on call as a consultant for the Wilmanses' future enterprises.

Meanwhile, C.H. Packard grubstaked three men—James Lillis,
Oliver McLean, and Ben James—who joined his venture, and together

they began locating claims in both '76 Gulch and Glacier Basin. Among the notable ones staked that year by Packard were the Sidney in '76 Gulch, and the Philo, Rantoul, and Whistler in Glacier Basin. Before the summer was over, the Packard group had recorded more than ten claims in the Monte Cristo Mining District.

About July 1, Mac Wilmans left the camp and returned to his California home to be with his wife on the occasion of the birth of his second child. Because his first, a boy, had succumbed to disease in Arizona Territory some years earlier, Mac looked forward with great anticipation to the new arrival. "She was welcomed by all," he wrote in his memoirs, "and thrice heartily welcomed by her parents." After he had seen to the well-being of his wife and the infant girl, he returned to Monte Cristo, where the crews were busy developing the ledges and improving the general life style in the raw camp. Work continued steadily into the fall, when the crisp nights turned the vine maple a fiery red, in stark contrast to the nearby evergreens.

As winter approached, the snow level on the mountainsides reached steadily lower. Consequently, the parties in Monte Cristo made plans to abandon the camp for the season and seek warmer and more comfortable climes until spring returned. Leaving the area in a timely manner was a matter of survival as well as comfort, for Wilmans Pass stood at 4,800 feet elevation, and the miners faced the very real danger of becoming isolated in the Monte Cristo area throughout the winter if the snow came too soon. This fact, combined with the enormous effort required to pack supplies into the camp that spring and summer, brought a resolution from Mac—upon his return in the spring, he would investigate the feasibility of a low-altitude trail into Monte Cristo via the Sauk River from Sauk City on the Skagit.

Monte Cristo was again left to the snows of winter when the adventurers fled to the comforts of their homes.

During the summer of 1890, while preliminary development work was under way in the Monte Cristo region, seemingly unrelated events occurred in western Washington which were to have a profound impact on the mining enterprises in the Cascades. The Northern Pacific Railroad had reached Puget Sound in 1886 by following a circuitous loop through the southern part of the state from Spokane to Pasco, thence north to Tacoma by way of the Yakima River. In the late 1880s, Jim Hill's Great Northern pushed steadily westward, with intentions of pressing directly west from Spokane to a new port on the sound. Because this would create a more direct route to the Pacific markets for the Great Northern, the Northern Pacific decided to build a second line, also directly west from Spokane, to compete with the shorter road the Great Northern planned. The Northern Pacific had tentatively elected to cross the Cascade Range in the northern part of the state, descend the Skagit River valley, and reach tidewater at Fidalgo Island near Anacortes.

Charles Colby and Colgate Hoyt, who were members of the executive committee of the Board of Directors of the Northern Pacific, decided it would be to their advantage to acquire a great amount of land at that tidewater terminal, establish an industrial city there, and reap handsome profits upon the arrival of the railroad on their property. The men arrived in the Puget Sound region early in 1890 and began buying the logged-off tracts on the tideflats of Fidalgo Island near Anacortes. But their plan leaked, and acreage that had been selling for $1.50 to $5.00 suddenly jumped in price to $500 to $1,000 per acre.

Greatly disappointed at this turn of events, Colby sought the advice of Henry Hewitt, Jr., a friend whom he had known from earlier financial dealings with the Wisconsin Central Railroad in Wisconsin. Hewitt had moved to Tacoma some years earlier, invested in timber, and had become one of the wealthiest men in the Pacific Northwest. Colby invited Hewitt to accompany himself, Angus McDougall (inventor of the whaleback-type ship), Henry C. Davis (private secretary to President Oakes of the Northern Pacific Railroad), and John Plummer on a trip to Alaska to discuss the situation. Hewitt knew Washington well, particularly its land and timber resources, and could prove to be invaluable as an advisor to Colby's venture; but, unknown to Colby, Hewitt had plans of his own, which also included a new city.

Hewitt was well aware of the enormous quantity of timber upstream on the Snohomish and Skykomish Rivers, and he had rented a boat, sounded Port Gardner Bay at the mouth of the Snohomish, and found it deep enough to dock large ocean-going vessels. He had consulted with the present owners in the vicinity of Port Gardner—the Rucker brothers, W. G. Swalwell, and Frank Friday—and suggested to them that it would be an excellent location for a major seaport and lumber center. Hewitt had invested in some of the land himself, and they had made big plans for the future.

Hewitt seized the opportunity afforded by the Alaska trip to convince Colby of the wisdom of constructing the proposed industrial city on the peninsula at the mouth of the Snohomish River. The harbor was deep, fresh water plentiful, and large amounts of land already logged. Best of all, Hewitt argued, everything could be purchased for about $30 per acre. Besides, it made no sense to run the railroad so far north to cross the Cascades. It was more logical, he continued, to cross the mountains directly west of Spokane, which would bring the railroad down the Skykomish, not the Skagit, and the city would be located at the only acceptable tidewater terminal. Furthermore, if the Northern Pacific did not come down the Skykomish, the Great Northern almost certainly would.

These arguments sufficiently convinced Colby and party, that by the time of their return to Puget Sound they were ready to look the proposition over and decide on the new location. The Colby group examined the area, and the men were duly impressed. As a bonus, should they select that site, all the existing owners in the immediate locale of Port Gardner, who owned some 800 acres, agreed to contribute half of their properties in order to get the project started.

Colby and his companions then returned east to discuss the possibilities with their associates. In mid-September of 1890, Colby authorized Hewitt to begin quietly purchasing acreage on the peninsula. While Colby suggested that no more than $800,000 be spent, the ultimate amount was left up to Hewitt. Late in September, he commenced buying land around Port Gardner, and in less than ninety days had acquired over 6,000 acres. Prices tended to rise while he bought, but he was still able to keep the average cost per acre within his original estimate of $30.

As 1890 drew to a close, a new planned industrial city was about to rise at the mouth of the Snohomish River. The total population of Snohomish County at this time was only 8,514 people, with the largest concentration, 1,933, living in Snohomish City. Port Gardner appeared to be a strange place to establish an industrial city. But, unlike the mountain weather which caused suspension of the Monte Cristo operations, the winters on Puget Sound were comparatively mild, and plans for the city rapidly took shape. Before another year passed, the two ventures—Monte Cristo and the industrial city—would become inextricably intertwined.

LaRoche Photo

The site upon which the new city was to rise at the mouth of the Snohomish River. Although largely logged off, a great amount of cleanup work was in order.

CHAPTER III

1891

ADVENT OF EASTERN CAPITAL

Early in 1891, Henry Hewitt, Jr. traveled to New York City to meet with Charles Colby and Colgate Hoyt to finalize formation of the company that would manage the recently purchased land. Although skeptics anticipated another "boom and bust" failure by the year's end, the men hoped to avoid the fate of "planned cities" previously established on Puget Sound—communities that had been doomed due to lack of employment in the locales where they had been built. The new land company would take a different approach. Simultaneous with platting the city at the mouth of the Snohomish River, it would establish industries to support the people who would comprise the city's population. In fact, no lots would be sold until the factories had been built or were at least far enough advanced that their construction would provide jobs for the residents. The men also prepared a set of building code minimums to prevent a town of tents or shacks from rising on the land. If specified types of buildings were not built upon certain designated commercial lots within a stipulated time, stiff penalties would be levied. The first industries were to be a steel barge works (patterned after one on the Great Lakes) to manufacture whaleback-type ships; a nail factory; a brick works; a sawmill; a paper mill, and various wharves to handle the anticipated shipping into and out of Port Gardner Bay.

While the plans took form, Colby sought a suitable name for the city and the land company. One evening during dinner at Colby's house, his nine-year-old son, Everett, asked for more dessert. This prompted Hewitt to quip that here was a lad who wanted only the best for himself, just like they wanted for their enterprise. He then casually suggested that the firm be called the Everett Land Company. Colby was

35

taken with the idea, and all present agreed. The city would be named Everett. Colby appointed Hewitt president of the company because of his knowledge of the area. Upon his return to Washington, Hewitt began the task of platting and subdividing the city.

Meanwhile, Colby and Hoyt attempted to interest other investors in the Everett Land Company and its supporting companies. Both men were well thought of in New York financial circles, therefore new money was not difficult to come by. One man in particular—the financier John D. Rockefeller—proved to be an invaluable source of capital. He had invested with Colby and Hoyt on previous occasions, and was an acquaintance and fellow church communicant of both. Rockefeller and Hoyt rode the elevated railroad downtown to work each morning, and the latter took advantage of the opportunity to interest this very wealthy man in the Pacific Northwest properties, which he described in the most glowing terms. Coincidentally, Rockefeller was in need of just such an outlet; for, at 52 years of age, he was on the verge of a nervous breakdown, and unable to satisfactorily control his $10,000,000 annual earnings by himself. He reasoned that here was an excellent opportunity to use the energy and expertise of Hoyt and his associates to manage a portion of his money. With their own funds involved in the ventures, Colby and Hoyt would more than likely be prudent in the handling of the companies, and this would assure the safety of other investors' assets as well. Reasoning thus, Rockefeller committed a sizeable amount of his financial resources to the Everett Land Company and its attendant companies.

Mac and Fred Wilmans returned in the early spring of 1891 to the Pacific Northwest to renew the mining activity at Monte Cristo. The snow was still too deep in the Cascade Mountains to attempt an entry into the district, but immediate resumption of work at the mines was not their purpose. The summer of 1890 was still fresh in their thoughts, and the difficulty of access remembered as the major impediment to the area's development. With the two months' backpacking from Scott's Camp to '76 Gulch etched in his memory, Mac took the preliminary steps to establish a low altitude wagon road up the Sauk River from Sauk City, on the Skagit, to the Monte Cristo claims. He set a crew of men to work building a path suitable for wagons drawn by oxen, horse, or mule teams. The methods used were typical highway construction techniques of the day—where the forest floor was sufficiently firm, the

LaRoche Photo

Early buildings in the new city of Everett, c.a. 1891.

men left it undisturbed, except to clear away logs and brush. The route twisted and turned to circumvent as many trees as possible, thus reducing the amount of work required; but not all could be avoided. The trees that had to be removed were generally sectioned and split, then utilized as "puncheon"—the type of surface built when a boggy or swampy stretch of land had to be crossed. Two large, rough-cut timbers were laid parallel with the direction of the road, one on either side, across which split planks were placed to form the corduroy surface that would bear the weight of loaded wagons. Trestles and bridges also had to be employed at several places along the right-of-way.

During the previous summer, Mac and Fred had become aware of another need of the new camp. Although log cabins were fine for habitation, mines and associated structures required lumber, an almost nonexistent product in Monte Cristo. Clearly, the first major item to be hauled over the wagon road would be a sawmill—the complete works, consisting not only of the saws but also the steam engine and boiler to drive them, together with all the connecting belts, pulleys, and shafts.[1] So urgent was the need, however, that the dismantled mill, loaded on

many wagons drawn by teams of oxen and mules, followed closely
behind the construction crews. The road was pushed up the Sauk while
winter slowly released its grip, the workmen making such progress as
weather and terrain permitted.

As spring phased into summer, the storms diminished in ferocity and
men fought their way into Monte Cristo via Silver Creek and Wilmans
Pass. The valleys were still buried under deep snow, however, and the
men realized that a great deal of damage had been done during the
winter. Avalanches had destroyed most of the buildings and cabins constructed the previous summer. One exception was the Wilmanses' first
cabin. Located away from the more vertical slopes, it remained standing. Obviously the mining camp could not be situated in the steep-
walled valleys of '76 or Glacier Creeks, for nothing built by man could
withstand the tons of snow which came down the mountainsides each
winter. Fortunately, at the junction of the two creeks, where the Sauk
River originated, the terrain was less precipitous and distant enough
from the avalanche paths to allow a townsite to be established without
fear of yearly destruction. Consequently, land was cleared on the low
ridge between the two creeks, with the most level portion, just above
the junction, set aside for the sawmill. This was also the point at which
the wagon road would enter the area, which further strengthened the
conviction that this was the proper location for the town.

While the road was slowly built up the Sauk, other problems arose.
The construction required more capital than originally expected, and
Mac and Fred became somewhat embarrassed for money. They were
drawing funds against their financial cushion, the ranch in California;
clearly the situation required quick corrective action. Because 1891 was
a boom year, financing for any worthy cause was readily available for
the asking. In the late spring, Mac and Fred closed a deal with Edward
Blewett, a well-known mining investor, whereby he purchased a
quarter share in twenty-three of the more important Wilmans properties for the sum of $9,000. This gave them some working capital.
Shortly thereafter, on June 16, the Honorable Hiram G. Bond, judge
and investor from New York, and Leigh Hunt of the *Post-Intelligencer*, a
Seattle newspaper, together bought a quarter share in the same properties for the sum of $25,000. This action, as Mac stated in his reminis-
cences, put the Wilmanses ''on easy street.'' Bond and Hunt soon purchased a quarter of Blewett's interest for an undisclosed amount, thus

giving them a still greater ownership in the major Monte Cristo mine claims. They also acquired a substantial portion of the Rainy group on July 23. This made them, after the Wilmans brothers, the largest land holders in the Monte Cristo region. Together with their associates, Blewett, Hunt, and Bond brought a new dimension of thought to Monte Cristo. Blewett's mining experience, Bond's financial background, and Hunt's financial and journalistic training made the trio a team to be reckoned with.[2]

On Friday, May 22, 1891, the *Snohomish Weekly Sun* heralded the next phase of the Monte Cristo venture when it printed a commentary by Frank Brooks, a mining man from Leadville, Colorado, who stated, in part:

> ...I find the mountains...belted with mineral claims rich in lead and carrying high volumes of gold and silver. The principal need of this country at present is the means of transportation. There is no way of getting in except over a miserable trail [that], when I passed over it, was in horrible condition. From what I could learn, steps are being taken to build a wagon road from Sultan City into the district. There is one from Snohomish to Sultan, but for heavy traffic it would require considerable repairing. The great need is for a railroad. The character of the veins or ore in that district require and justify the building of a railroad into it.

Bond had visions of a railroad up the Sauk parallel to the wagon road. In fact, before the latter was completed, he had a team of surveyors working on the right-of-way. This team was headed by M. Q. Barlow, an engineer with an excellent reputation in the Northwest. He was thoroughly familiar with the peculiarities of the weather on Puget Sound and in the Cascades, and was well aware that the mountains were noted for heavy winter snows and violent spring runoffs.

By late June the wagon road up the Sauk was nearly completed, and hopes ran high in Monte Cristo as the sawmill came closer to reality. Enterprising men poured into the area. A.J. Agnew established a general store—the Monte Cristo Mercantile Company—in a log cabin on some of the first cleared land in the new townsite, several hundred feet up the slope from the creeks. A post office was secured that year, and Owen McDevitt appointed postmaster.

The arrival of part of the Sauk road crew in Monte Cristo was a major event, greeted with great celebration. The wagon road at this time was not sufficiently completed—the last seven miles was merely a horse

One of the earliest buildings to be located in the new townsite of Monte Cristo. A.J. Agnew's Monte Cristo Merchantile Company Store was located in this humble log cabin while its proprietor awaited a sawmill to provide lumber for a more suitable facility. Wilmans Peak is seen in the distance.

trail—to permit all parts of the sawmill to be hauled to the townsite. While lighter loads, and some of the smaller components of the machinery, could be unloaded from the wagons and packed on horseback, the major items, such as the boiler and steam engine, had to wait until completion of the road. Consequently, the chief mode of construction continued to be log cabins.

The railroad right-of-way progressed well. One day Barlow climbed part way up the side of the Sauk Valley, about four miles below Monte Cristo, to establish a survey point. Noticing a small spring bubbling from the mountainside some distance above, he visually traced the stream's course down the rocks and observed that it did not appear to flow into the Sauk River. Where, then, did it drain? His curiosity aroused, Barlow climbed higher and discovered why it did not empty into the Sauk. Deeply etched into the side of the canyon was a low pass, through which the little brook coursed into a different river system. The tall timber hid the gap from casual view, and one could locate it only by chance, as he had. Barlow did not, at the time, fully appreciate the significance of his find because he did not know what river had its headwaters at this spot. This was still an unmapped region, and he had a job to do in the Sauk Valley which precluded exploration of the newly discovered area. Barlow charted the pass on his survey sheets, and named it, appropriately enough, after himself. He then continued his task of establishing a right-of-way down the Sauk Valley.

A few days later, Fred Anderson and F. M. Headlee, who had been prospecting along the headwaters of the Stillaguamish, came upon a small, low pass at the head of one of the creeks tributary to that river. Crossing it in thick timber, they wound up in the Sauk Valley. The men reported their find to the Wilmans-Bond group in Monte Cristo, thinking that it might be of interest to them. When Barlow learned of this event, he quickly ascertained that the discovery he had charted earlier was none other than this pass into the Stillaguamish Valley. This fact cast a new light on the entire transportation project.

Deposits of silver and copper had been discovered on the Stillaguamish River about ten miles below Barlow Pass, and a town, Camp Independence, was rising at that spot. If trains could be run up and down the Stillaguamish, the trade from this new community would greatly enhance the revenue of the railroad company. Furthermore, the miners could use this shorter route to Puget Sound and not have to rely

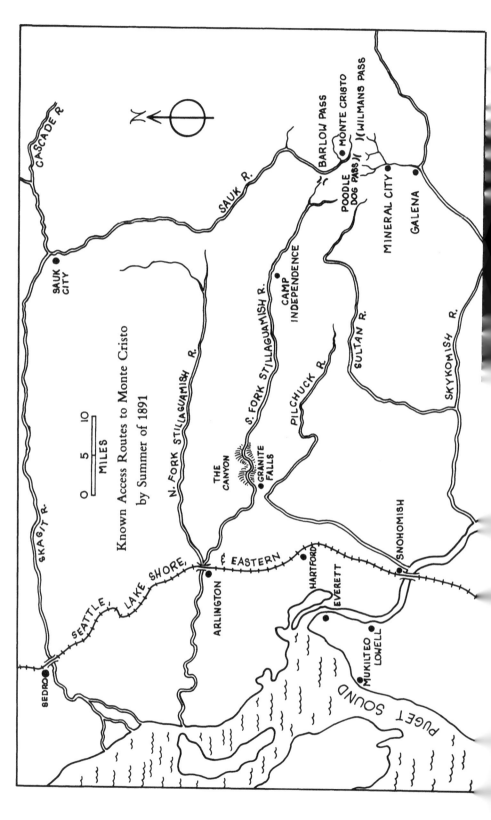

Known Access Routes to Monte Cristo by Summer of 1891

on the vagaries of the Skagit River for steamboat transportation to Sauk
City. Another possibility had been considered—running the line down
the Sauk to the headwaters of the North Fork Stillaguamish, then down
that river to join the Seattle, Lake Shore and Eastern at Arlington. But
this would mean high fees for trackage rights or freight haulage on that
line to Seattle.

The Wilmans-Bond group directed Barlow to survey the feasibility
of a route over Barlow Pass and down the South Fork Stillaguamish past
Camp Independence (later Silverton), and on to the Seattle, Lake Shore
and Eastern Railroad. What Barlow found in his survey was very encouraging. Therefore, Wilmans-Bond decided to abandon the Sauk in
favor of the Stillaguamish route.

While Barlow surveyed along the Stillaguamish, the Wilmans-Bond
people pursued another possibility brought about by this change of
events. The Everett Land Company's new industrial center was rising
at the mouth of the Snohomish River, but one industry not planned for
the city was mining, with its accompanying smelters and railroads. The
Stillaguamish route would, however, make Everett the logical terminus
for the Monte Cristo line and thus a natural place to establish a smelter.
The mining group therefore contacted Henry Hewitt, Jr., and discussed
the possibilities of financial backing for the railroad and smelter. About
the same time, discoveries of iron ore were made by other prospectors in
the Mount Pilchuck area near Granite Falls, and these too were made
known to Hewitt. He was skeptical, but took note of the work previously accomplished, and the fact that the mining enterprise was already surveying its own railroad. He sent two engineers into the mountains to check on the wealth supposed to exist at Monte Cristo. Although their report was never made public, several months later the
Everett Herald explained the conditions thus:

> The gorges on the sides of which the mineral veins are exposed are in
> some places 3,000 feet deep. It is, on the whole, an exceptional situation,
> where nature, with her glacial plowshare, has cut the mountain with
> deep furrows, leaving exposed upon their broken sides her deep buried
> mineral treasures. Nature has, in fact, done the mining, and what
> remains for man is to take the ores and reduce them. [Everett Herald, May
> 5, 1892]

The report was favorable, to say the least, therefore Hewitt contacted

Colby and Hoyt and told them of the discovery. When the news reached New York, it electrified the financial people. Everett would become the Pittsburgh of the West.[3]

Although they were elated by this news, Colby and Hoyt were not about to rush into something so large without corroborative data on the mineral potential of the Cascade Mountains. Consequently, they contracted the services of Alton L. Dickerman, a mining engineer of national repute, who had done much of the geological work at the Gogebic mines in northern Michigan. Accompanied by Mac Wilmans, Dickerman toured the Monte Cristo area during the late summer of 1891. He was impressed by what he saw at the camp—although no more than 300 feet of exploratory tunneling had been completed, the glaciers that carved the canyons appeared to have done much of the development work by exposing the veins. Dickerman collected samples, probed the few short tunnels, and traced the outcrops, taking copious notes of his observation.

Upon receiving his first verbal report, Colby and Hoyt arranged a deal with the Wilmans-Bond group, whereby $50,000 was paid to hold an option on four claims at Monte Cristo—the Pride of the Mountains, Pride of the Woods, '89, and Galore. Dickerman's final written report, while not outright skeptical, was somewhat reserved, for with only 300 feet of underground work accomplished, he could only speculate on the continuity of the veins at depth. If, indeed, they passed completely through the mountain and beneath the level of the creeks, Monte Cristo would prove to be one of the greatest mineral discoveries of all time. On the other hand, if large-scale tunneling indicated a lack of vein continuity below the surface, the district could turn out to be a great failure. But Colby and Hoyt had samples in hand which attested to the area's wealth, and the pessimism in Dickerman's report seemed very distant when assays came in showing high values of lead, silver, copper, and gold. Dickerman was asked to join the group as chief mining engineer, but he refused. Instead, he elected, perhaps wisely, to remain on a consulting basis. In his mind, sufficient development work had not been accomplished to prove conclusively the value of the find at Monte Cristo.

Meanwhile, the Wilmans-Bond group consolidated its holdings in three mining companies—the Monte Cristo, the Pride of the Mountains, and the Rainy. The first two were capitalized for $10,000,000 each, the latter for $5,000,000. The Wilmans brothers (Fred, Mac, and Steve, a younger sibling who had recently entered the venture), together with Hiram Bond, Ed Blewett, and Leigh Hunt, held a majority of the stock in the companies. Development work continued at the mines, with the most promise shown in the Glacier Basin area at the four claims on which Colby and Hoyt held their options—the Pride of the Woods, Pride of the Mountains, '89, and Galore. All lying along the same vein, they showed the most continuous surface outcrop in the area. This lead could be traced for a mile over Mystery Hill (named for the Mystery mine on its face) and up Cadet Peak (after the Cadet located near its summit, and formerly called Sentinel Peak). The outcrop varied from one to thirty feet in width, and dipped at an angle of seventy degrees where it passed through Mystery Hill, but became more horizontal, changing its dip to thirty degrees, on the side of Cadet Peak above Glacier Basin. Tunnels were drilled at several levels along this vein, and the ore slowly blocked out.

With the completion of the low altitude wagon road, such as it was, heavy machinery could be shipped into the Monte Cristo camp, and the badly needed compressors, air drills, and aerial tram systems were ordered. The entire sawmill, however, had not yet made the trip. According to an article in the *Port Gardner News* on October 16, 1891, the Monte Cristo Mining Company was "making arrangements to ship a lot of machinery" to its mines about November 1. The items would be "shipped by boat from Seattle, via Mount Vernon to Sauk City, thence hauled to the mines." Included was a cable that weighed more than ten tons, to be "used for constructing a tramway railroad for bringing the ore down the mountains for shipment."

The article commented further about the surveying then in progress along the Stillaguamish River for the Monte Cristo railroad. The pace of development at Monte Cristo was beginning to accelerate as more money became available, and better access to the area was achieved.

Coincident with the increased tempo in the mountains, Everett was now a beehive of activity. New construction was going on everywhere in the city at the mouth of the Snohomish River. In fact, investors queued up in lines to buy lots for $1,000 each, and they paid still higher prices for the choice commercial properties. The nail factory neared completion; so also the steel barge works. Associates of Colby and Hoyt watched these events with great interest, and "sugared the wine" by investing heavily in the industries and townsite, thus quickening the boom to a feverish pitch.

A group of Snohomish City citizens began one project destined to have major impact on Monte Cristo. The thought had occurred to some of the town's more enterprising businessmen that even if the Great Northern built down the Skykomish River, it nevertheless might bypass their community. To prevent this happening, they organized the Snohomish, Skykomish and Spokane Railroad, with the intention of building from Snohomish City up the Skykomish to meet the Great Northern when it built over the mountains from eastern Washington. This would assure the town's future as a major railway junction between the Seattle, Lake Shore and Eastern and the Great Northern.

On the other hand, Henry Hewitt, Jr. realized the importance of the project to Everett, and he quietly purchased a majority interest in the Three S Company—as it was popularly called—in mid-1891. His purpose was to assure the selection of Everett as the tidewater terminus of the Great Northern, or whatever railroad built down the Skykomish River; for, without this, the great port of Everett, serving the rich oriental trade, would be an unattainable dream. Therefore, on October 2, 1891, construction began at Snohomish City of an extension of the Three S to Everett. The work was contracted to be completed within 120 days, and it progressed rapidly across the lowlands to the river, just opposite Lowell, about three miles from Everett. However, the necessary bridge over the Snohomish River was not completed in 1891, and the project was left unfinished.

During the year the center of activity in the mountains shifted from '76 Gulch to the townsite, and travelers entering via Silver Creek found it easier to cross the divide through a lower pass near Silver Lake. At 4,300 feet, this trail eliminated about 500 feet of altitude gain from the trek, and allowed men to descend the Sauk Valley wall directly above Monte Cristo. This pass, at the head of a small gully just above the Poodle Dog claim, was given the name Poodle Dog Pass, by which it is still known today.

So, gradually, Wilmans Pass was abandoned in favor of the lower, shorter route, and by the close of 1891 was little used except by those wishing direct access to '76 Gulch from Silver Creek. But Monte Cristo hummed with activity as development work continued. In fact, an accurate map was needed to keep track of the various properties in the

region. Consequently, the uncharted region was soon to be added to the
mapped areas of the world. During the summer of 1891, R.G.
Hoffman, a Seattle mining engineer, surveyed and took notes for the
purpose of drawing an accurate geologic map of the Monte Cristo area.

With a crew of fifty surveyors, Barlow was busy working on the
right-of-way for the Monte Cristo railroad along the South Fork Stillaguamish. The line was laid out to meet the Seattle, Lake Shore and
Eastern right-of-way near Lake Stevens, midway between Granite Falls
and Snohomish City, and by now it had become evident that the railroad would pass through Granite Falls. Because the promoters of
Everett had not made their intentions clear regarding the Monte Cristo
properties, the railroad's builders were uncertain whether they should
cross the Seattle, Lake Shore and Eastern and push on to Everett, or effect a junction with that line to provide access to the markets in Seattle.

However, clarification of the Everett group's interest in Monte
Cristo came like a thunderbolt just prior to Christmas, 1891. The
Colby-Hoyt syndicate exercised its options to purchase a portion of the
Pride of the Mountains Mining Company, which consisted of the Pride
of the Woods, Pride of the Mountains, '89, and Galore claims. The
filing with the country auditor listed "one dollar and other valuable
consideration" as the amount exchanged for the property. As a matter
of fact, however, the "other valuable consideration" amounted to
$375,000—$150,000 cash paid on December 10; $50,000 option
money; plus a bond for $175,000 to be satisfied from the earnings of the
mine at a later date. But this did not buy the company outright; it
purchased a two-thirds share, with the Wilmans-Bond group retaining
one-third in the form of stock holdings. This was an unheard of amount
to pay for virtually undeveloped mining property located in such a wild,
remote area as Monte Cristo. But during the boom year of 1891 nothing
seemed too far-fetched, and the best was yet to be announced. The Wilmanses' share of the transaction was $86,000 cash, a bond for $67,000
to be paid from mine earnings, and a large block of stock in the
company.

Winter snows closed the operations at Monte Cristo, but the activity
at Everett surged ahead unabated. With such a large investment in
Monte Cristo, the Colby-Hoyt syndicate had other plans to make.
Heavy equipment had to be hauled to the mines, and ore carried out,
smelted, and refined. This required more money, and plans were made

accordingly. By the close of 1891 it appeared that Everett, indeed, was destined to become the Pittsburgh of the Pacific, with Monte Cristo and other regions in the Cascade Mountains supplying the iron, lead, gold, copper, and silver ores to fuel the economy.

Miners on the side of Mystery Hill, enduring the inhospitable winter weather in late 1891. Note the lack of snow clothing, skis or snowshoes.

CHAPTER IV

1892

GETTING THERE

During the winter of 1891-92, the entire nation experienced a downturn in business activity. Workers were unemployed, businessmen became alarmed at the reduction of trade, sources of capital dried up. But, somehow, this generally gloomy outlook appeared to have bypassed the Everett and Monte Cristo enterprises. Plans for the new industrial city, with its promise of mineral wealth from the nearby mountains, forged ahead with no lack of optimism or capital. If the boom years of 1890 and 1891 were leading to the bust of 1892 elsewhere in the country, it certainly was not evolving that way in Everett.

In fact, if one were to believe the *Everett Herald*, the future looked very bright. The newspaper's first issue, dated December 17, 1891, extolled the virtues of Everett and Snohomish County, with special emphasis given to the future of mining: "Over in the Cascades, not more than fifty miles from Everett, are more minerals within a radius of ten miles than any other place the world can show....The mines contain everything—gold, silver, copper, lead, iron, and in plenty." Nor was the impact of impending railroad construction through the region overlooked:

As a consequence there is a great stir in the mineral section, and already preparations are being made for the building up of a big town there....A good idea of the richness of the state in a mineral way can be learned from an account of the five districts referred to—Silver Creek, Monte Cristo, Sultan Basin, Troublesome Creek and Silver Gulch district—from which J. N. Scott...has come direct....

According to Mr. Scott, who has done a great deal of mining in his time and has spent two years among the five districts named, the great difficulty will be, when the railroad and mines are in operation, that the output will be far above the demand. There is no limit to the minerals he says....Adjoining the Silver Creek district on the north is the Monte Cristo district, of which so much has been printed of late. In it are large deposits of galena—among the largest that have ever been found, says Mr. Scott....It is predicted that with the advent of the [rail] road dollars will roll out of the mining district by millions, in the shape of gold, silver, copper, lead, iron and other minerals. [*Everett Herald*, December 17, 1891]

Moving swiftly to exploit the Monte Cristo mining region, the Colby-Hoyt syndicate quietly arranged for development of the mines, but when news of the anticipated activity leaked to the public, rumors ran rampant in Everett, Monte Cristo, and all points between. No less than five smelters would be built in Everett! Stories about immense wealth discovered in the mountains were circulated every day. This all added to the optimism and tales of grand changes to come.

On July 7, 1892, Colby-Hoyt announced that it was seeking sixty acres of land on which to build a smelter in Everett. The city's newspaper billed it as a "monster plant, capable of supporting a good sized town of itself." The site was not decided immediately, but it would be on the peninsula's northeast or downwind side to prevent the sulphurous fumes from fouling Everett's air. As a matter of fact, the smelter's location depended heavily upon the ultimate placement of the railway to Monte Cristo. The smelter was to be one of the largest on the west coast, handling not only the Monte Cristo ores but also imports from overseas and eastern mining regions. New construction was everywhere; optimism and high hopes were enjoyed by all.

By mid-August the long-awaited smelter site had been established on a hillside just east of the northern tip of the Everett Peninsula. Gravity could thus be utilized to transport the ores from the bins at the upper levels through the various processes required on the successive lower levels. This location would also allow delivery of ore via the Seattle and Montana Railroad from the wharves on Port Gardner Bay, or by the Everett and Monte Cristo Railway from the Cascade Mountains. The complex would consist of several structures—sulphide mill, 50 by 50 feet; two roasters (to remove arsenic), each 32 by 100 feet; ore bunkers, 105 feet square; sample building, 40 by 60 feet; furnace house, 50 by 95 feet, and an engine house, about 75 by 75 feet. The dust chamber would

The plant of the Puget Sound Reduction Company (Everett Smelter). This view is from Steamboat Slough looking Westerly.

run east from the furnace for 182 feet, then south 178 feet to the stack. A local firm, the Electric Brick and Tile Company, was awarded the contract for the bricks, all 1,400,000 of them, to be delivered on demand.

On November 17, the syndicate predicted another ninety days' work would see the smelter in full operation. The side tracks were in place, and the workers had completed the headquarters, assay office, and buildings to house the furnace, engine, boiler, blower, and ore. Work was in progress on the roasters, dust chambers, and the stack. Machinery had been ordered from Wisconsin, California, and Ohio. William C. Bulter was to be superintendent; Alton L. Dickerman, mineralogist; E. L. Bailey, cashier, and C. H. Taylor, auditor.

By the end of 1892, Everett was beginning to look like an industrial city, what with the construction of the smelter well under way and other enterprises nearing completion. Moreover, the city had been linked to two railroads. Concomitant with these developments, the social year in Everett was brought to a close with a gala Christmas party at the Monte Cristo Hotel, which had been built by the Colby-Hoyt syndicate as the city's showplace. The ladies of the town, dressed in silk and diamonds, and led by Mrs. Butler, formed a receiving line at the entrance to the hotel's ballroom. A grand time was had by all, especially Henry Hewitt, Jr., who reasoned that Everett, with its ability to produce such a sophisticated event, had come of age, and the major hurdles were in the past. In the myopic view from the ballroom, the future for 1893, and beyond, looked bright indeed.

The big difficulty, of course, was transportation—how to get the ore from Monte Cristo to Everett. At the beginning of 1892 the Colby-Hoyt people had concluded, like the Wilmanses had two years earlier, that transportation was the foremost problem facing them, and their greatest efforts were to be directed toward its solution. The wagon road up the Sauk River, begun the previous year by the Wilmans brothers, had never been completed. In fact, the last seven miles below the townsite was nothing more than a horse trail. Clearly, they needed a railroad. The syndicate therefore advanced funds, pending final arrangements, to the Wilmans-Bond enterprises, which were already working to establish the right-of-way up the Stillaguamish. The Everett people hoped to construct the line before the year ended.

With the advance, Colby-Hoyt exercised a certain amount of control to assure that the money was used in the most frugal manner to accomplish the goal. One of the first tasks these overseers undertook was to review the railroad's proposed location to determine, from the standpoint of expense, whether or not too much liberty was being taken with the route. They quickly concluded that the right-of-way, as proposed, was too costly. Barlow had surveyed, most of the way, a route along the side of the mountains, some distance above the river, but this necessitated expensive blasting along the hillsides and bridging the creeks (as opposed to building trestles). He had also plotted a circuitous loop just above Granite Falls rather than running the road directly down the narrow canyon through which the South Fork Stillaguamish plunged for five miles. Barlow argued that this design avoided the destructive effects of late winter and spring washouts common in the Pacific Northwest. But his defense fell on deaf ears, and he was ordered to run the line by the most direct and economical route down the canyon to Granite Falls. Local people attempted to warn the eastern investors of this folly, but they were told, in reply, that the Stilla-

The new Monte Cristo Hotel in Everett nearing completion. This was the finest establishment in town and played host to all the notables who passed through Everett on their way to Monte Cristo.

guamish was nothing more than a trout stream compared to certain eastern rivers along which they had built and, considering their vast experience in rail construction, they could see no reason to be concerned. This arrogance was to cost the Colby-Hoyt-Rockefeller interests dearly over the years.

If the railroad were to be completed before the year ended, as planned, the company needed immediate access to the entire Stillaguamish Valley. A small army of workers set to work to build a puncheon wagon road, similar to the one begun by the Wilmanses, from Getchell—a small town on the Seattle, Lake Shore and Eastern Railroad—to Monte Cristo. The road would run along the South Fork Stillaguamish, cross Barlow Pass, then follow the Sauk River. Once this was completed, railroad construction could be initiated at many points along the right-of-way, and heavier machinery hauled into Monte Cristo on the road itself.

Due to the availability of work in the area, and the lack of it elsewhere, laborers and the unemployed poured into the region seeking jobs. They arrived from all walks of life, with packs on their backs, the approaching depression having taken its toll elsewhere. By March 10, three engineering parties were engaged in the final locating of the railroad up the Stillaguamish as far as the snow permitted, while a crew of seventy-five men worked on the wagon road. The total number of workers projected to be employed on this and the Great Northern route when work began in earnest was ten thousand. Monte Cristo and its companies were becoming big business.

The Everett and Monte Cristo Railway Company, capitalized at $1,800,000, was incorporated in the middle of March. Officers of the new company were: President, George S. Brown; Vice President, Robert D. Murray; Secretary, Francis H. Brownell; Treasurer, Henry A. Schenck; and Assistant Treasurer, Schuyler Duryee. The line was now totally out of the hands of the Wilmans-Bond group and controlled by the eastern capitalists. The railroad would be built through the narrow Stillaguamish Canyon between Granite Falls and Government Marsh, a flat six miles upstream. Six tunnels had to be blasted through the headlands which projected from the canyon's wall to the river's banks, the longest extending 833 feet. By the end of March work on three of the tunnels had already commenced.

The construction crew was busy clearing and grading the right-of-way near Granite Falls when the men discovered, while blasting along the Stillaguamish, a vein of rich calcopyrite or copper-bearing ore. The resultant claim, located two miles above the town, was appropriately named Wayside, and destined to become not only a producer of copper but also the deepest mine in Washington, with a shaft descending 900 feet, the lowest point 450 feet below sea level. One could not help but make rich discoveries in the Cascades; dig almost anywhere, the wealth was at hand. Or so it appeared.

The Colby-Hoyt syndicate had not yet decided whether the railroad would, one, cross the Seattle, Lake Shore and Eastern; two, pass around Lake Stevens and descend directly into Everett; or, three, join with the line at the town of Hartford. The surveys made from Lake Stevens to Everett indicated the grade was too steep, necessitating a large loop to the north to make the slope acceptable. However, during the week of April 18 an event occurred that decided the future course of events for the railroad—the purchase by the Everett and Monte Cristo Railway Company of the extension of the Snohomish, Skykomish and Spokane, or Three S Railroad, that had been building from Snohomish City to Everett. This meant that a junction with the Seattle, Lake Shore and Eastern at Hartford would require leasing trackage rights to only seven miles of that line. The Monte Cristo trains would complete their trip to Everett by returning to their own tracks at Snohomish City. Rumors continued for several years that the railroad was to be built directly into Everett, but it never was, although several additional surveys were carried out. The route remained as established in early 1892.

By the middle of May, Barlow's men were five miles below Barlow Pass, digging a survey line through four to six feet of snow. The winter, true to form, was reluctant to give way in the mountains. Barlow's people were followed closely by the crew constructing the wagon road, which already had a stage line running over its existing length. However, the frequent spring rains delayed accomplishment of the work along the railway, often washing out grading already completed or preventing the men from working efficiently during the downpours.

A new rumor now began, one that was to last many years—that the Monte Cristo road was to be extended across the Cascades into the Okanogan country. This never happened, although surveys were made. Nevertheless, the rumor died hard, and almost outlived the railroad. The idea was popular with townspeople and folks who lived along the line because, if true, it would place them on a major cross-state railroad, thus bolstering the local economy enormously. But it remained only a rumor, though a persistent one.

F.E. Finney, the manager of the Everett and Monte Cristo, arrived in Everett in his private railway car on June 8. He proceeded to inspect the progress along the road, which consisted of "alternate stretches of cutting through ridges of rock and trestling over the intervening gullies." As the chief railroad consultant for the Colby-Hoyt syndicate,

A surveying crew checking the work of the graders three quarters of a mile beyond Barlow Pass on the railroad right of way. This was the summer of 1892, and the rails had not yet reached to this point on the line.

Finney had built other lines backed by them in the past, including the Wisconsin Central. While in Everett, he conferred with James Hill regarding the location of the tracks through Everett and the placement of the depot. He was pleased with the activity along the right-of-way and within the townsite of Everett.

About the same time that Finney arrived, a major contract was let for construction of three Howe truss bridges to span the most important crossings of the Stillaguamish River. The first one was a "deck span" where the train ran over the top of the truss; the other two were "through spans," with the train running through the girder. The first, located at mile 10.3, would be 150 feet long and designated Number 14. The second, Number 18, was located at mile 15.3 and consisted of two sections, each 126 feet in length. The third, Number 33, at mile 24.6, was a single girder of 126-foot length, and was located about four miles below Silverton (formerly Camp Independence). All mileages were measured from Hartford Junction along the right-of-way.

On June 23, the *Everett Herald* quoted T. Tonneson, assistant engineer on the railroad, with regard to the problems of construction in the Stillaguamish Canyon:

> That canyon is one of the most difficult places to build a railroad I ever saw. It is about five miles long with almost perpendicular walls, and the road through it has six tunnels from 300 to 800 feet long. On the 800 foot tunnel they are in 80 feet at one end and 100 feet at the other, and it will be finished inside of four months. The others are all pretty well along. The grading from Hartford to the Stillaguamish is progressing rapidly and will be finished in July. When that section is ready, tracklaying will begin. The canyon is swarming with prospectors and location notices are posted up in all directions.

The mountain snows were now melting rapidly, and construction once again was under way on the Sauk wagon road, which had been abandoned seven miles below Monte Cristo the previous year. The Wilmanses hoped to push the road into their camp as soon as snow conditions permitted, in order to haul the remainder of the sawmill's components up the valley and commence milling operations. Although some work was being done at the mines, the snow was still too deep for any serious labor to begin. Construction of the other wagon road, along the Stillaguamish, progressed well, and by late May it had been advanced to within ten miles of Monte Cristo. Coincidentally, men and supplies poured into the valley via the stage line operated over the road. In fact, according to one report, a hundred teams passed over it daily, "freighting railroad supplies, mining materials, merchandise and outfits for the settlers." The townsite even boasted a lodging house—a log cabin, known as the Monte Cristo Hotel, operated by the Monte Cristo Mining Company. The establishment offered the only accommodations in the valley.

While construction of the railroad moved along smoothly, it was not without excitement. In early July a small forest fire raged out of control and engulfed the engineering camp of O. W. Jasper, destroying all the crew's belongings. Fortunately, the notes and charts, together with all but one instrument, were saved from the holocaust.

An incident that highlighted the human conflicts involved in the project was reported in the *Everett Herald* on July 21. Most of the laborers employed on the railroad were Italian immigrants, and many spoke little if any English. One day two choppers were cutting a tree immediately above where a crew of Italians was working on the railroad's right-of-way. The tree did not fall as planned; instead, it rolled down the embankment onto the laborers, injuring two. One of the woodsmen hurried down to help and to apologize for what had occurred, but the Italians misinterpreted what was happening. Thinking they were being attacked, a laborer grabbed a rifle and headed toward the logger. Upon seeing the irate fellow approach, the unarmed axeman fled down the right-of-way, his pursuer close behind. He arrived at a surveyor's camp and leaped inside the tent, only to discover the civil engineer's wife alone. He quickly explained and she ordered him to hide. When the Italian burst into the tent, gun in hand, he was confronted by the woman, now also armed with a rifle. Neither could understand the other's language well, but after they had stared at each other a minute or so, the fellow lowered his weapon and, following a brief parley, returned to his companions. The woman had come from Chicago only a few weeks prior to the incident, but she proved herself equal to the challenge of the "wild West."

The railroad's development reached a major milestone in late July when the Three S road—extending from Everett to Snohomish City— joined with the Seattle and Montana tracks, which ran up the shore of Puget Sound from Seattle. This created a loop around the Everett Peninsula, along which many industries, including the smelter, were located. Thus the time was "not far distant" when the riverside all along the Snohomish would have "added to its daily noise the rumble of the...car wheels,...the toot of the engine whistle and the clang of its warning bell." In Snohomish City, at the other end of the Three S, connection was about to be made to the Seattle, Lake Shore and Eastern, which would allow a direct link between Everett and the Monte Cristo line's junction at Hartford.

On July 23, the first of three locomotives destined for the Monte

Cristo railway left Seattle (via the Seattle, Lake Shore and Eastern) to assist in tracklaying at Hartford. An 80-ton, 10-wheel Mogul, with 22- by 26-inch cylinders, manufactured by Cooke Locomotive and Machine Company in Paterson, New Jersey, had been shipped to Seattle, then assembled in the Northern Pacific roundhouse by W. S. Boyd of the Cooke Company, and run to Hartford. The name plate on the smoke box bore the number "1." A second engine, of identical type, was being put together by Boyd and would follow within a week.

Meanwhile, the laying of track had been delayed until the rails arrived. They were being transported on two sailing vessels—the *Abner Coburn* and *Annie H. Smith*—by way of Cape Horn, and were expected to arrive shortly in Everett. About 5,000 tons of iron had been ordered, and operation of the railroad was predicted by Christmas of 1892, with no one having any serious doubts but that this deadline would be met.

Work on the six tunnels in the Stillaguamish Canyon was also proceeding. By August 25, the longest, Tunnel No. 1, had been bored 550 feet, leaving only 283 feet remaining. Completion was expected by late September, as about eight feet could be excavated in a day. The other five tunnels were either finished or close to completion. Eight hundred men were working along the five-mile stretch of the canyon alone, with the entire line employing over 2,000 workers.

A seventh tunnel, located seven miles below Silverton, was being dug through sand and dirt for 500 feet and was referred to as a "mud tunnel" because of the absence of rock to blast. The sand was of good cement quality, and used to make concrete elsewhere along the line. This bore was expected to be ready for rails on October 15.

One day in mid-September, while working inside with his men, the shift foreman heard a hissing sound emanating from the digging face. He had heard such a noise before on previous jobs, and immediately announced it was time to break for lunch. After clearing all the men, he took a lantern and went to the face to investigate. As he had suspected, they had tapped a vein of sand and water that was under extreme pressure, and the sibilant sound was made by this quicksand shooting into the tunnel. Having confirmed his suspicions, he turned to leave. He was walking toward the entrance, some 250 feet distant, when the hissing abruptly magnified into a roar. He dropped the lantern and ran toward the opening. The roar behind him changed to thunder. He exited, turned, and clawed his way up the steep embankment just as tons of mud and broken rock shot out the entrance. A large pit, 40 feet deep by 150 feet across, formed on the hill above as the land subsided into the rapidly filling hollow below.

By the middle of September only three shift foremen remained in the tunnel construction camp. Offers of double and triple pay were refused by the workmen because "a perfect Niagara of mud and water" had made the labor so disagreeable the men would not work at any price. This was one job that nobody wanted. Faced with this opposition, the railroad elected to build a temporary shoo-fly around the obstacle. This necessitated a 25-degree curve—too sharp to be acceptable even on a mountain railway such as this, but under the circumstances the company had no choice. Not much work had been completed above Silverton, although the crews were busy grading toward Barlow Pass, and the projected date for completion of the railroad was still set for the year's end. But in Everett the long awaited shiploads of rails had not yet arrived.[1]

To keep the construction camps free of the usual problems caused by liquor, the Snohomish County Commissioners banned the sale of alcohol along the railroad and posted signs which warned of the penalties awaiting those caught in this act. However, the prohibition was not always strictly enforced, and that fact caused the local people on one occasion to assert their indignation at the flaunting of the law by taking matters into their own hands. A man named Monnohan operated a saloon and dance hall of ill repute just north of Granite Falls near the railroad right-of-way. One September day, having lost all patience with him, a large group of residents, many of them armed, descended upon his establishment, forcibly ejected him and his help, and warned him to seek employment elsewhere. The mob then demolished everything breakable in sight: windows, mirrors, chairs, and tables. After venting their rage in this manner, they attached a large charge of dynamite and destroyed the building. Having thus settled one problem, the crowd marched to another local business which catered to the same trade, and advised the proprietor to be gone within 24 hours or suffer the same fate. He left.

On November 2, the *Abner Coburn* arrived in Everett with the badly needed steel and iron for the railroad. The vessel, a full-rigged three master carrying six topsails and three skysail yards, presented a handsome sight in port. The voyage had required 174 days, 40 of those to round Cape Horn. The ship carried 2,500 tons of rails, and 500 tons of steel wire for the nail works. The railroad iron consisted of 1,684 rails (enough for 20 miles of track), 5,890 fish plates, 120 kegs of bolts and nuts, and 890 kegs of spikes. Labor problems in unloading notwithstanding, the material was rushed to Hartford Junction where the crews were waiting to begin track laying.

Construction of the Monte Cristo road could now get under way in earnest. Four of the six tunnels had been finished, and the grading was almost completed to Silverton. The four Howe truss spans had been pre-cut in Granite Falls and waited for rails to be laid so that work trains could haul the timber to the bridge sites for installation. Everything appeared to be on schedule. The shoo-fly was being graded around the ill-fated Tunnel No. 7, because the railway company had given up hope that a passageway could be dug at that location. An open cut, 104 feet deep, was considered, but never attempted.

In late November, 1892, an early winter storm slammed inland from the coast, wreaking havoc on the western slope of the Cascades. All the major rivers flooded. The Snohomish River delta became a vast sea, and on the lowlands the tracks of the Great Northern and the Three S were submerged.

The railroad builders now received their first taste of what had been forecast by Barlow and other local people earlier that year. The Stillaguamish, channeled into its narrow canyon, rose to an alarming height. As one newsman commented, the river was "as fickle as the weather." When the skies were bright and calm, the stream was very quiet, but during severe storms it became a raging torrent. The grade of the railroad had been thought to be far above the high water mark, but the Stillaguamish now flowed *through* Tunnel No. 6, and demolished the log cribbing. The flood also destroyed the trestle work that had been erected in the river bed for the purpose of constructing the three Howe truss bridges. In addition, a large stretch of grading above Granite Falls was washed away while men watched helplessly or ran for their lives. Even at the higher elevations, away from the narrow canyon's torrents, the work did not escape unharmed. Part of the wagon road was under water and all its bridges were gone.

The storm abated as quickly as it had come, leaving behind its legacy of destruction. Repairs were immediately started to put the wagon road in shape, to enable supplies to reach the beleaguered crews along the railway. Obviously the latter could not be completed in 1892, but while much of the line lay in ruins, plans were still afield to construct the cutoff between Hartford and Everett, and the rumors were resurrected that the Everett and Monte Cristo was to be extended across the Cascades to eastern Washington.

Now all the company could hope to accomplish in 1892 was to regrade through the Stillaguamish Canyon and push the road as close to Silverton as possible. Sleighs could then haul supplies over the snow from the terminus to Monte Cristo, thereby allowing the mines to operate throughout the winter, thus assuring that a large amount of ore would be present on the mine dumps when the trains arrived in the spring. In fact, the miners had already begun stoping in the Pride of the Mountains, and a considerable quantity of ore had been brought out.

Early in 1892, Monte Cristo received the distinction of becoming one of the world's charted places. R. G. Hoffman, who had taken extensive notes and surveys the previous summer, completed his detailed map of the region. About the same time, the New York investors gained control of the majority of the mining properties shown on the map. However, the Wilmans brothers, Ed Blewett, and associates retained stock in the new companies, although Hiram Bond sold his holdings and withdrew from the venture. The Colby-Hoyt syndicate intended to run the mines as a large-scale operation and wasted no time moving in that direction. In March, approximately six months after exercising its options on the Pride of the Mountains Mining Company, the syndicate incorporated the Monte Cristo Mining Company, with officers designated as follows: President, Joseph L. Colby; Vice President, Fred W. Wilmans; Secretary Pro Tem, William C. Butler; Treasurer, Edward Blewett. Trustees were Joseph L. Colby, Fred W. Wilmans, James H. Hoyt, Edward Blewett, and Alton L. Dickerman. The Rainy Mining Company also changed its officers, and the names were almost identical with those of the Monte Cristo Mining Company. Clearly, the Colby-Hoyt people now controlled the major mines of Monte Cristo, with the Wilmanses serving as subsidiary partners.

During this period about sixty men labored in the mines doing assessment work, and piled ore on the dumps to await the tramways and railroads which would transport it to market. The wagon road up the Stillaguamish had been completed over Barlow Pass and the last four miles, along the upper Sauk, were under construction. The Sauk River trail was abandoned, the sawmill machinery returned to Sauk City and started on its way toward the Stillaguamish Valley road. In Monte Cristo, stumps were removed to make way for the anticipated building boom when the mill arrived. The final locating of the railroad was made at Monte Cristo, with the depot, turntable, and engine house sites all situated on the flat where '76 and Glacier Creeks joined to form the Sauk River.

The wagon line from Getchell to Monte Cristo was completed by August 11, with the sawmill machinery comprising part of the first freight to travel the entire distance.[2] The road was billed as the best in Snohomish County, and four-horse teams hauled loads weighing up to four tons over the route on a regular basis. A week after the road's completion, the long-awaited sawmill was in operation, turning out 10,000 board feet of lumber daily. As fast as the trees could be cut and skidded to the town, they were reduced to lumber to feed the hungry market close at hand. One of the earliest projects was a structure built to house the mill itself, one that would withstand the ravages of the winter soon to come.

With more people swarming into the area, "the country was full of miners and prospectors." Consequently, lumber was quickly cut for a boarding house to accommodate the mining company's workers. Another establishment opened about this time, when Jacob Cohen started the Pride Hotel. This building, named after the Pride claim in Glacier Basin, was among the town's first structures built of sawn lumber.

The mill also cut timbers for a mammoth concentrator to be erected on Glacier Creek above Monte Cristo. Realizing that the majority of the ore locked in the mountains was not high grade but lower quality "concentrating" ore, the Colby-Hoyt people announced the pending construction, with contracts let almost immediately. The cost was to be about $250,000, and they created the United Concentration Company to handle the assembly and operation of the facility as well as the aerial tramways that would carry the ore to it.

The Wilmanses had not sold or shared all their interests in the Monte Cristo properties, but had retained ownership of a number of claims on the flanks of Wilmans Peak. The brothers formed two firms to handle operations at these locations. The Wilmans Mining Company consolidated the properties in '76 Creek; the Golden Cord Mining

Company included those along Glacier Creek. The areas owned by the first company were high above the valley floor, and consisted largely of the Comet and Monte Cristo properties, lying 5,000 feet or more above sea leyel.

A tramway 10,000 feet long was needed to haul the ore down. A man named Parsons, representing the Hallidie Tramway Company of San Francisco, came to Monte Cristo in August to discuss details with the Wilmans brothers. The tram was to be in two parts. The upper section, a single span over a deep gully, would be a Bleichert type, with two anchored steel carrying cables on which the buckets would hang from wheels. A continuous loop of lighter steel line, or traction rope, linked by clutches to the cars, would be employed to control their speed up one carrying cable and down the other. At the lower terminal of the single span, down which 700 feet of elevation was lost, a transfer station would be located on the ridge near an outcrop, 100 feet high, called the "Old Man of the Mountain Rock." The ore would then be transferred to a Hallidie patent tram similar in construction to a modern ski lift, with the buckets fastened to a single steel rope which both supported and moved the loads. This would carry the ore to the valley floor and deposit it behind the new concentrator, where it would be prepared for shipment.

The Wilmanses also planned to build a transfer bunker and bunkhouse for the Comet mine claim. The site chosen for the buildings—the only level spot on the mountainside—was shaped like the prow of a ship, and protruded from the side of Wilmans Peak. An advertisement for employment at this mine might well have read "sleepwalkers need not apply," because the first step from the precipitous location was a 300-foot cliff.

The Wilmans brothers were not the only ones constructing tramways during the summer of 1892. The Colby-Hoyt syndicate began building a small system that would run from the Mystery mine claim to the vicinity of the Monte Cristo townsite. This tram was never completed, nor did it carry any ore, because its construction was halted by the onset of winter snows and was not resumed the next spring.

Despite the business downturn, demand still existed for mining stock in the east. Late that summer, John MacDonald Wilmans decided to take his family east to visit relatives and peddle stock in the Monte Cristo companies. Mac left Fred and Steve in charge of the Monte

Cristo properties. He also carried their stocks, and would attempt to sell them.

Upon reaching New York, Wilmans went directly to see Colby, who bought $35,000 worth at $1.36 per share. Mac was carrying about 300,000 shares in all, and he wired back to his brothers, telling them of the sale. The reply from Fred and Steve was very emphatic—he was not to sell their stock for less than $2.00 per share. Suspecting his brothers had struck something big, Mac sold another, previously promised block for $12,800, and removed the balance of the stocks from the market.

Colby informed him that he was prepared to purchase all the remaining stocks at the $1.36 per share price, but Mac was unwilling to go against his brothers' wishes and refused. He returned to San Francisco a short time later. The general economy of the country continued its downturn, and it became impossible to sell the stocks anywhere, at any price. The Wilmanses lost $250,000 by not selling when the opportunity had presented itself.[3]

Meanwhile, Joseph Pearsall, the discoverer of Monte Cristo, was back in the area, locating new properties for the Pearsall Mining Company. Despite the developments already undertaken, he was convinced that some "rattling good mines" were still "up there," waiting to be found. True to form, this human mountain goat staked the claims on the ridge top behind Wilmans Peak, above the glacier he had crossed when first entering Glacier Basin in 1889. All the properties were prefixed by the word "iron." Among them were the Iron Town, Iron Dale, Iron Clad, Ironton, Iron Crown, Iron Knight, and Iron Man. The mines never did produce, largely becaue of their remoteness, but Pearsall enjoyed the sport and adventure of discovery.

The tramway equipment for the Wilmans Mining Company arrived from San Francisco in late September, and was rushed to the mines. The Hallidie Company estimated the installation time at one month. Winter, however, soon played its part in closing down operations in the area, especially those at the higher elevations, such as the Comet bunker at 5,400 feet, from which the tram was to be built.

Work at the mines progressed well. On September 1, Jennings S. Cox, assistant superintendent of the operations at Monte Cristo, wrote a letter to William C. Butler, in which he detailed the previous week's activity and indicated that the majority of the work had been done in the Mystery and Pride mines on Glacier Creek. Little effort had been expended in the '76 Gulch mines because the men found less ore as they tunneled deeper. Drilling was still done by hand, and the longest tunnel to date was the upper Mystery at 77 feet in length. It had been driven only eleven feet that week.

On October 6, the *Everett Herald* quoted Alton L. Dickerman, who had just returned from Monte Cristo, as stating that the mines had been purchased almost sight unseen with little development work to prove their worth. He emphasized, however, that they were increasing in value with every foot of depth gained in the tunnels. Dickerman further asserted that all the mines showed much greater quantities of ore in the tunnels than they did at the surface outcrops. The mining companies were now in a position to operate summer and winter, and when the tramways and railroads were completed they would be ready to ship ore on a huge scale. He closed by stating that Monte Cristo had the potential to become one of the greatest mining camps in the United States.

The companies planned for a force of about 40 men to remain in Monte Cristo during the winter of 1892-93. This comparatively small number was sufficient to maintain crews at the Pride of the Woods, Rainy, and '76, who would develop the mines as much as possible before major work began anew in the spring. No attempt was made to employ a large number, because supply during the snowy months was uncertain, at best. William Thorne remained in Monte Cristo as foreman, and he stockpiled the necessary provisions prior to the onset of cold weather.

The snows came, heavy and deep, closing all access to the region for long periods throughout the winter. The men were supplied periodically, although with great difficulty. While the blizzards slowed or stopped other activity, Thorne's men continued to work in their splendid, self-imposed isolation. Now, for the first time, the miners viewed the mountains in their winter raiment, noting the awesome power of the avalanches, the dazzling beauty of the white mantle that followed in the wake of each storm.

CHAPTER V

1893

DEPRESSION

Not much contact was had during the winter with the forty or so miners working the Monte Cristo properties under the leadership of William Thorne. Supply trips into the snowbound region were few, but the men took their isolation in stride, what with plenty of work to be done and little time to reflect upon their situation. No communication or travel in the mountains was possible without snowshoes, and the men used them occasionally "to visit the outside world." On April 20, Thorne arrived in Everett, accompanied by Peter Noreen, one of his crewmen. The men had broken the bonds of their "prison" by walking thirty miles over the deep snow. They stated that when they left, five feet remained in the townsite, with more at the mines.

Less than four years had passed since Joseph Pearsall discovered Monte Cristo, but the region was coming of age. On February 27, 1893, the Monte Cristo Mining Company of Washington, anticipating a building boom, filed a plat of the Monte Cristo townsite. This was not done in Washington but 2,000 miles distant, in the common pleas court of Cuyahoga County, Ohio. The plat was filed as a matter of record and copies were quickly sent to Brown and Brownell, Colby-Hoyt's attorneys in Everett, for registration with the Snohomish County Auditor in Snohomish City.

The plat resembled a pistol, with the barrel, represented by the main street, pointing down valley toward the Sauk River. The Monte Cristo theme was not forgotten in assigning street names: Dumas, the main thoroughfare, honored the author of the book for which the town had been named; Mercedes recalled the Count of Monte Cristo's sweetheart. Other avenues, such as '76 or Glacier, reflected local features.

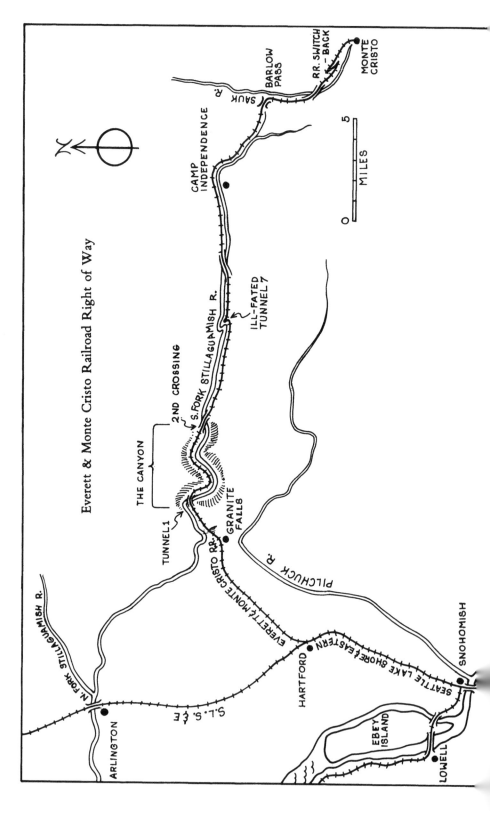

Everett & Monte Cristo Railroad Right of Way

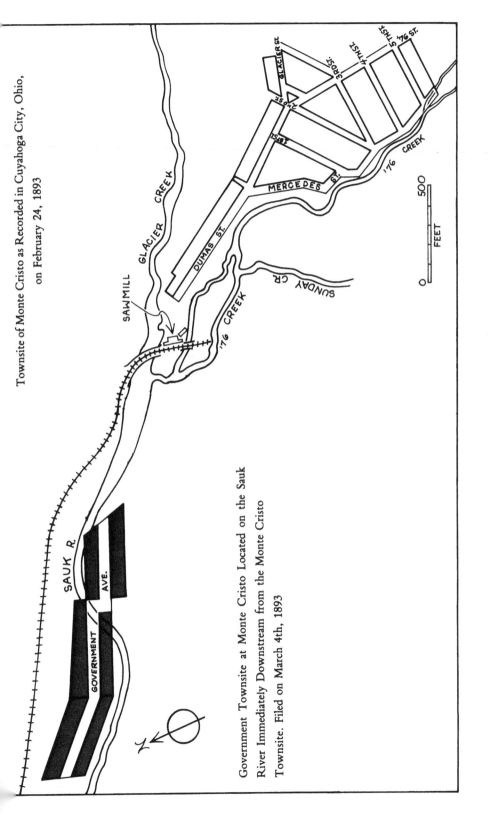

Townsite of Monte Cristo as Recorded in Cuyahoga City, Ohio, on February 24, 1893

Government Townsite at Monte Cristo Located on the Sauk River Immediately Downstream from the Monte Cristo Townsite. Filed on March 4th, 1893

The cross-streets were numbered 1st, 2nd, 3rd, 4th, and 5th. All 236 lots were immediately made available for sale at the company offices in Everett and Seattle.[1]

Another Monte Cristo townsite was mapped and submitted on March 4 to the Washington state court for incorporation. Situated just below the junction of '76 and Glacier Creeks along the Sauk River, it had been organized by a group of local men, represented by prospector F. M. Headlee, one of the discoverers of Barlow Pass, now an attorney-at-law. The new plat was filed as a government townsite, one of only two in the state of Washington, and its 91 lots were quickly put up for sale. Thus, two Monte Cristos had been located adjacent to each other in the Sauk Valley.

Meanwhile, Pennsylvania capitalists completed purchase of 22 claims in the vicinity of Goat Lake, which lay in the valley immediately north of Monte Cristo. The easterners planned to build a road down Elliott Creek to connect with the Sauk River road, a distance of four miles, and commence development work on several claims that summer. They were very secretive, however, and no one knew much about their activities.

The Monte Cristo Development Company, organized the previous year to buy land and exploit properties, centered its activities in the Silverton-Sultan Basin area. The firm owned 25 claims on the opposite side of Marble Pass, above Silverton. Because it planned a long aerial tramway to transport the ore to the railroad for shipment to Everett, the company watched with great interest the disappearance of the snow and the progress in construction of the Everett and Monte Cristo Railway. By July 3 the ground was clear enough that the work could begin.

On June 1, Jennings S. Cox, assistant superintendent of the Monte Cristo Mining Company, wrote to Thomas Weir, general superintendent, outlining the company's properties and current state of development. Cox detailed the work accomplished on each claim of every mining company owned by the Colby-Hoyt syndicate in western Washington. He described tunnels on almost all the properties, though most were exploratory rather than productive in nature. Virtually all the mining attempts in '76 Gulch had met with disappointment because ore quality dropped sharply when the tunnels increased in depth. The glittering mountain had sparkled only on its surface.[2] The real values were found in the Pride group of claims and the Rainy properties on

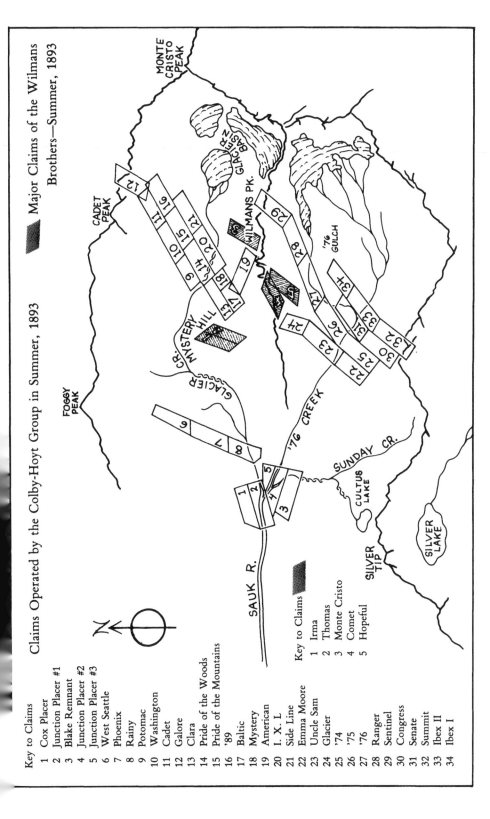

Claims Operated by the Colby-Hoyt Group in Summer, 1893

Major Claims of the Wilmans Brothers—Summer, 1893

Key to Claims

1 Cox Placer
2 Junction Placer #1
3 Blake Remnant
4 Junction Placer #2
5 Junction Placer #3
6 West Seattle
7 Phoenix
8 Rainy
9 Potomac
10 Washington
11 Cadet
12 Galore
13 Clara
14 Pride of the Woods
15 Pride of the Mountains
16 '89
17 Baltic
18 Mystery
19 American
20 I. X. L.
21 Side Line
22 Emma Moore
23 Uncle Sam
24 Glacier
25 '74
26 '75
27 '76
28 Ranger
29 Sentinel
30 Congress
31 Senate
32 Summit
33 Ibex II
34 Ibex I

Key to Claims

1 Irma
2 Thomas
3 Monte Cristo
4 Comet
5 Hopeful

Glacier Creek. Eighteen hundred tons of ore had already been piled on the dump of the Pride of the Woods No. 1 tunnel, and other mines had similar amounts ready to ship.

During the winter of 1892-93, the snow had done considerable damage to the company's sawmill, rendering it inoperable. In late June, however, a new mill was being readied for shipment to Monte Cristo as soon as the wagon road had been repaired. Within two weeks, the mill was in place and ready to begin operations. But the solution of a problem regarding the tramway was not so easily come by. Snow slides during the winter had destroyed 12 towers which the United Concentration Company had built on its tram line between the townsite and the face of Mystery Hill. Obviously towers could not be placed at just any location, however desirable, because the avalanche paths had to be avoided. The company therefore concluded that its efforts were leading to an inadequate tramway system, one incapable of transporting the quantities of ore projected. The time had come to contact experts in the field and let them handle the job, but much of the season when work could be done had already passed; if the tram were to be completed before the winter snows came, construction would have to proceed at maximum speed.

Weir reflected this urgency in a letter, dated June 21, that he wrote to the Trenton Iron Company, builders of the Bleichert patent trams, wherein he requested they send a mechanical engineer to Monte Cristo immediately. The man had to be capable of making specifications and price quotes on the spot. In reply, the New Jersey firm wired that their engineer, William Hewitt, was at Weir's disposal and would start west the moment he received further instructions. Weir telegraphed back for Hewitt to proceed to Everett at once, where he would be met and escorted to Monte Cristo.

The Trenton Iron Company had elected to bid on the tramway system, and by June 24 William Hewitt was on his way west. He stopped at Missoula, Montana, to confer with Alton L. Dickerman about requirements for the trams, then continued on to Everett. About a week later, Hewitt was in Monte Cristo surveying the site of the tramways. He had only a few days to submit his estimate. About this time the plans for the concentrator, as submitted, were found to be inadequate to handle the syndicate's projected milling operations. Two firms, the Chicago Iron Works and Frazer & Chalmers, were requested

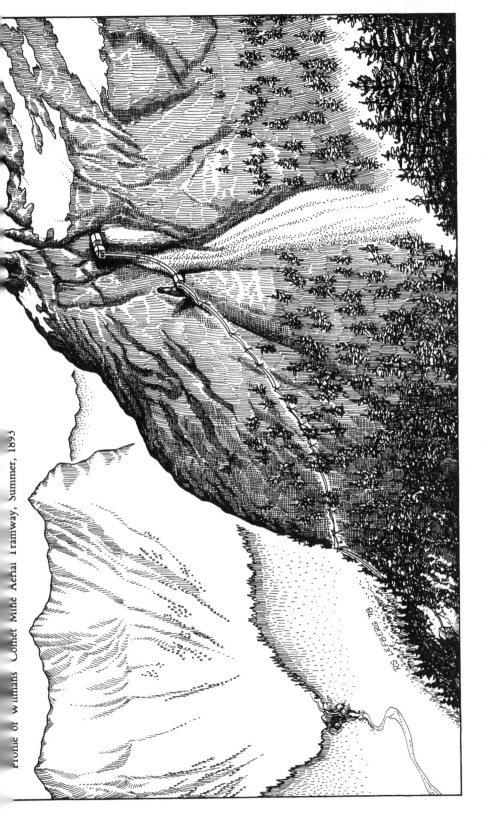

Profile of Willmans Comet Mine Aerial Tramway, Summer, 1893

RS LEEBERG '78

to resubmit their proposals, following a thorough consultation with Weir and Dickerman. A month later the suggestions of Frazer & Chalmers had been accepted, the machinery for the concentrator ordered, and the sawmill was cutting the timbers for its own shelter. The carpenters were on the site assembling the new plant as fast as the lumber could be manufactured. The tramway had been completed from the Comet bunker, 2,700 feet above the town, and the Wilmans Mining Company began transporting ore down from that lofty place.

The plans for the United Concentration Company's trams, to be built by the Trenton Iron Company, were approved by the head office in New York, and work was quickly begun on the lines. A letter from Weir to the Trenton Iron Company accompanied the plan view and profiles of the tramways; succeeding letters described more data transmittals, discussed the location of the tension station on Mystery Hill and the terminals at either end of the lines, also stressed the importance of shipping material at an early date to facilitate construction before the first snow. Weir also sent a "bill of lumber," which specified the materials needed to erect towers to support the lines, to Bryan and Flynn, who had contracted to provide the necessary timbers.

Of special concern to the mining company was the long, 1,200-foot span over Glacier Basin. Such trams usually employed a patented interlocking wire rope for the carrying line because if a strand broke it would not unravel and jam the ore buckets. But in the 1890s, due to technical limitations, this type of cable could be produced only in 500-foot lengths. If it was used for the Glacier Basin span, several couplings, of larger diameter than the cable, would be required. The company's experts were fearful that an ore bucket might jump the carrying line, thus causing the cable to jam between the wheels and frame. Normally, a car so disabled could be dragged to the nearest tower and the trouble corrected. But with no access for 1,200 feet, it could be pulled only to the first cable-joint where it would jam because the coupling was too large to pass between the frame and the wheels. This would necessitate lowering the entire carrying cable to effect a repair. For this reason, the company stipulated that couplings were not to be used on the large span. An impasse apparently had been reached, but an alternate choice was selected at the last moment—a new type interlocking wire rope, just introduced, that could be produced in lengths sufficient to permit continuous, unbroken cables to cross Glacier Basin.

Herman Siewart Photo

The aerial tramway from the Comet Mine of the Wilmans brothers is visible as a series of X-shaped towers descending the side of Wilmans Peak just above the terminal building. The ore has travelled 10,000 feet upon reaching this point, and has descended 2600 feet of elevation. Many hundreds of tons were shipped down the slender cables. The smokestack of the concentrator and the surface tram can be seen in the foreground.

The remainder of the tram was equipped with the standard interlocking cable. The loaded bucket side of the long span had to have a heavier cable (one inch diameter) and counterweights to maintain a 20,000 pound tension; the unloaded bucket side required lighter (seven-eighths inch) cable and counterweights to maintain 11,000 pounds of tension. In addition to housing the counterweights, the station on Mystery Hill also contained an air brake system and winding wheels to control the speed of the descending ore buckets as they dropped the 2,000-foot vertical distance to the receiving terminal. An eight-horsepower gasoline engine built by Fairbanks-Morse drove a two-stage Curtis air compressor to supply air for the brake system. The engine also powered a small dynamo to provide power for station lights, needed because a snowshed completely covered the facility.[3]

By mid-August the concentrator building was in an advanced stage of construction, with installation of the roof under way. The United Concentration Company was negotiating for a 100-lamp dynamo to be installed at the mill and run by the 200-horsepower Corliss steam engine. This would provide enough power for lighting part of the town along with the mill.

Despite the ghastly economic picture throughout the rest of the country, the depression did not appear to be hindering the Monte Cristo enterprises. One side effect of the panic, however, had become painfully evident to mining men everywhere—the price of silver was rapidly plunging downward. The United States had vainly attempted to stabilize the market throughout the world, but the value of the metal continued to decrease. The big question was: What would the price of silver be when the Monte Cristo mines were ready to ship? Much of the ore contained silver as its principal value. Manager Rust of the Tacoma Smelter noted that the silver repeal bill, just passed by Congress, had improved the outlook for the metal's future worth. But he did not think that the United States could "undertake to carry the silver of the world."

After an extended trip to the east, Alton L. Dickerman returned to Monte Cristo, where he spent ten days inspecting the progress of the Colby-Hoyt syndicate's mines. He then made a lengthy statement to the press—published by the *Everett Herald* on November 9—indicating that he was pleased with the state of affairs in the mountains. He noted that Monte Cristo was a "veritable bee hive" of activity and said that

Profile of Pride-Mystery Mine Aerial Tramway

R.S. LEFBERG. '78

Looking up the aerial tramways toward Mystery Hill. The right hand system lowered ore from the Mystery #3 tunnel located in the face of the hill. The left hand tram brought down the output of the Pride of the Mountains Mine located on the opposite side of Glacier Basin. The troublesome long span was located on this line where it crossed the basin beyond the hill. This long tram was capable of carrying 230 tons of ore in a ten-hour day.

when the concentrator was completed and the mines fully equipped, the output would be enormous. Dickerman predicted that 3,000 men would be employed when production began on a large scale, and he noted that this would assist the smelter in Everett "to run successfully at its projected capacity." He went on to forecast that the mines would "rival the Comstock in production and send down silver enough to pave the streets of Everett." In fact, Washington would be "the most active and prospering mining state in the union for the next decade." Much remained to be done at Monte Cristo, however, before Everett's streets could be paved with silver.

The tramway construction proved to be difficult because the heavy winding equipment, engines, and other fittings, made mostly of cast iron, were hauled by teams of oxen or horses to remote places on the top of Mystery Hill or the back side of Glacier Basin. For example, the

The Monte Cristo concentrator of the United Concentration Company seen here during the winter of 1893-94. The roof has just been completed and the window frames are yet to be installed. Mystery Hill, lined with trees, is in the distance.

largest wheels used on the Pride of the Mountains tram—the ones located at the tension station high atop Mystery Hill—were almost eight feet in diameter, just under 17 inches in width. Made of solid cast iron, they weighed several tons each, and two were mounted on a common five-inch diameter shaft. The brake flanges were five inches wide, circled by equally wide straps, between which were mounted pads made of oak. This assembly controlled the speed of the traction cable, to which the loaded ore cars were clutched as they made their way down the steep slope to the collector terminal in the valley.[4] However, despite the difficulties involved, construction of the trams and concentrator progressed well, and C. F. Rand, secretary of the Puget Sound Reduction Company, was pleased with the preparations when he visited Monte Cristo in mid-September.

Early in November, J. S. Bartholomew, who had been residing in LaConner, journeyed to the settlement with the intention of establishing a newspaper to be called the *Monte Cristo Mountaineer*. Along with his journalistic duties, Bartholomew became one of the town's leading citizens, serving as the first justice of the peace, and occupying other civic posts. He began publication of the paper on November 30. During the same week, the Sunset Telephone Company examined the community with an eye toward setting up an exchange to serve the remote area. In addition, Monte Cristo was placed on a new mail route, with the railroad acting as the star carrier.

The community still suffered from a shortage of lumber in late 1893, and many businesses and homes were utilizing tents or log cabins until more suitable accommodations could be built. One such business, located in the government townsite, dispensed whiskey from a tent and, lacking a bar, served the liquor on a nearby stump. This established the name of the place—"The Blazing Stump"—and when a permanent building was constructed, the name was transferred. Thus the infamous Blazing Stump Saloon was born.

More and more, Monte Cristo began to take on the appearance of a permanent settlement, as the raw edge of the frontier was replaced by an atmosphere of respectability. The village now had between 25 and 30 school children and was assigned School District No. 70 of Snohomish County. Miss Mae Stewart was engaged to be the first teacher. By the close of 1893, the first Presbyterian Church had been established, and a constable's and justice of the peace's offices opened.

Lacking machinery for the task, large pieces of equipment, such as these wheels, were transported with the use of animal power to their remote locations. Many of the trails were steep and precipitous and would defy the use of machinery on them.

But all this activity in the Monte Cristo basin during 1893 was not without its counterpart in Everett (where work on the smelter progressed) and also along the railroad right-of-way between the two communities. Work on the railway continued throughout the winter of 1892-93. In fact, a few days after the new year (1893) began, the tracks were in place as far as the first crossing of the Stillaguamish River, about three miles above Granite Falls. A second sailing vessel, the *Annie H. Smith*, had arrived in Everett with the final cargo of iron, and the material to complete the line was now on hand. Although the track-laying crews closely followed the receding snow, the spring of 1893 proved to be cool and stormy, and it became clear that the projected opening date of May 1 would not be met. However, the workmen reached the second crossing of the Stillaguamish by the end of March, and the bridge carpenters assembled the two 126-foot through span Howe truss bridges at that point. Work advanced rapidly, considering the quantity of snow that still lingered in the area. Only one river crossing remained, and the railroad was expected to reach Silverton shortly. At the same time, the company strung telegraph lines in order to maintain regular communication with progress at "the front," as the upper end of the railroad was called. Meanwhile, construction of the new depot in Everett was under way. The station measured 32 by 44 feet, and was equipped with all the latest appointments. The coaling bins, farther up the track, were constructed next, in anticipation of regular service over the line.

The railroad announced a new schedule on April 27, calling for trains to run to the end of ballasting at "the front." The first scheduled ones operated between Hartford Junction and the upper end of the Stillaguamish Canyon at Government Marsh, where a wye allowed the locomotive to be turned around.

By this time the wagon road was clear of snow only to Silverton, where about 300 Monte Cristo residents who had wintered elsewhere were stranded. They had been returning to their homes, but upon arriving in Silverton had discovered that the way was blocked by four feet of snow beyond that town. The heavy winter snows had, in fact, dealt harshly with structures already in place along the railroad. On May 11, the *Everett Herald* quoted Henry Pennycook, who had been in charge of a camp seven miles below Monte Cristo, as stating that 36½ feet of snow had fallen during the winter—29 of that since late Jan-

Work crew transporting ballast rock in the canyon of the Stillaguamish. Locomotive #3 is seen a mile above tunnel number one. Notice that the rock has been hand-stacked on flatcars. The use of machinery was very limited at this time.

uary—and that the depth in the camp was still seven feet, although only 42 inches remained at Silverton. He reported that on January 19 the temperature had dropped to 22° below zero, snow began falling and did not cease until nine feet had accumulated. During one storm ''pretty well on in March'' nearly six feet fell in four days.

> The weight of snow broke the stringer in the bridge over our camp, and the stringers in the bridge at the forks of the Sauk were broken in three places. We have had one Chinook wind, which was blowing when I came down last Thursday. They are hauling goods to Silverton on sleighs, and have been packing on ponies to the Hoodoo mine, three and one-half miles above Silverton, all winter. Traveling is all done on snow-shoes or on Norwegian ski.
>   A strange fact about the snow is that hardly any fell on the Sauk, just across the ridge, but all the heavy snow fell on the Stillaguamish. I

think the reason is that all the storms came from the southwest, and the mountains between the Stillaguamish and the Sauk shut the clouds in like a wall. [*Everett Herald*, May 11, 1893]

On June 8 the railroad reached a point seven miles from Silverton. With the snow now gone, the men laid rails swiftly, attempting to

The Monte Cristo townsite in early summer of 1893. The Monte Cristo Merchantile Store is the cabin on the right. In the distance smoke rises from the sawmill's boiler. The railroad had not yet arrived.

reach Monte Cristo at the earliest possible date. In addition, one crew of workmen repaired winter damage to the wagon road while another up ahead strung telegraph lines in order to establish early communication with the mining camp.

As the railroad approached, with its promise of fast, cheap transportation, Silverton witnessed a flurry of activity. The rails were spiked into place in the town on June 29, and the citizens "celebrated the event in the evening with salutes of giant powder that awoke the echoes of the everlasting hills." Perhaps they had anticipated the Independence Day festivities; but by July 4 the tracks were one and a half miles beyond Silverton, and the telegraph had reached Monte Cristo. Work on the railroad above Silverton progressed swiftly, and on July 13 the company announced that, beginning Monday, July 17, a passenger train bound for Silverton would leave Everett every morning at 9:30 A.M. In addition, freight was hauled regularly over the wagon road from Silverton to Monte Cristo.

August 5 was a milestone, of sorts, for Monte Cristo. On that day the townspeople heard their first locomotive whistle. The railroad had reached a point within a mile of Barlow Pass, thus was only five miles distant, and the prospect of its completion created a great deal of excitement. By August 10, the tracklayers were just a mile below Monte Cristo, working on a switchback 2,000 feet long that had to be constructed because the grade up the canyon was too steep to make a direct approach. A week later the tracks were laid into Monte Cristo, with the final ballasting in progress about a mile below the town. Shortly afterward the company began work on a switchback spur line between the townsite and the concentrator, about 1,000 feet farther up Glacier Creek. Completion of the spur would permit hauling the concentrator's heavy machinery by rail to the front door, greatly facilitating its installation, and later the concentrated ore could be transported directly to the smelter.

Thus, only four years after Joseph Pearsall, the "human mountain goat," discovered the district, a railroad connected it with the outside world. The line—officially the Everett and Monte Cristo Railway—was accepted from Henry and Balch, the contractors who had built it, and the company announced plans for a daily train to run from Puget Sound to Monte Cristo.

On Wednesday, September 6, 1893, the first scheduled passenger train left Everett for Monte Cristo. The railroad was put to immediate use, and business proved brisk along the entire route. On September 7, the company ran an excursion train in order that everyone who wished could see the mountain grandeur. More than 150 persons took advantage of the opportunity to glimpse this remote place which had become

Herman Siewart Photo

Locomotive number three backs slowly down the canyon of the Stillaguamish with a passenger and combination car just below tunnel number five. This scene was viewed from immediately above the East portal of tunnel number four. Notice the workmen in the foreground who appear to be cutting timbers for placement in the tunnel. This photo was taken c.a. 1893.

almost legendary, and all were deeply impressed by what they saw. The train arrived shortly after the first snows of winter had frosted the peaks, accenting the mining camp's alpine setting. The journey bolstered the sagging morale of the visitors: they reasoned that with the railroad now a reality, the ore would soon begin moving to Everett and operation of the smelter could begin. This was good news to men who had been caught in the middle of the nation-wide depression and desperately needed jobs. What the tourists witnessed was a bustling Monte Cristo—the town and nearby mines together boasted an estimated 1,000 inhabitants, who were busy digging out the ore or assembling the tramways and concentrator to handle and process it.

With the approach of winter, however, numerous people living in Monte Cristo pondered whether to stay or leave before the cold weather arrived. Already the ground was covered by 20 inches of snow, and they were apprehensive about the railroad's ability to maintain service when the snow deepened. This, combined with the fact that many residents were still housed in tents or other temporary shelters, convinced quite a few to depart.[5] The railroad had anticipated the problem, however, and a steam-powered rotary snowplow, purchased in Paterson, New Jersey, was presently en route to Everett. The plow was a Leslie pattern rotary and reflected the latest design, as did all the railroad's equipment.[6] During the trip across the country, banners displayed on the plow's sides extolled the wonders of Everett and listed the various industries in the new city.

The Everett and Monte Cristo line had signed a track-usage agreement with another railroad, the Great Northern, that called for joint use of the former's tracks between Lowell and the junction with the Seattle and Montana line at the northern tip of the Everett Peninsula. The companies then installed new telegraph equipment along the Everett and Monte Cristo to facilitate handling of the heavier traffic over the road until the Great Northern completed its tunnel under the city of Everett, which would eliminate the trip around the peninsula. This was a severe blow to Henry Hewitt, Jr., but the fact was now evident—as it had been to many unbiased observers for some time—that the Great Northern did not intend to make Everett the western terminus of its line. Instead, it would continue over the Seattle and Montana route to Seattle, thus relegating Everett to the status of a way station.

During 1893, and concomitant with the building of the Everett and
Monte Cristo Railway, the Everett smelter—to be operated by the
Puget Sound Reduction Company—rapidly took on the appearance of a
completed plant as the construction proceeded on schedule. By the
beginning of February the main chimney and dust chamber had been
completed and the masons were busy placing the brickwork for the furnaces. The boilers were ready to be set in position, and the line shafting
was on its foundation. Men were working on the roasters (known as
the Brown-Allen improved O'Hara type) and the crusher building.
They were of the latest design; in fact, only about a dozen such roasters
were in use in the entire country. The Reynolds Corliss type steam
engine, with 18- by 42-inch cylinders, was in place and its flywheel set,
awaiting connection to the boilers. And, to provide easy access for the
workers, an electric street railway was under construction from Everett.

The company experienced difficulty, however, in obtaining brick for
the plant. Apparently the Electric Brick and Tile Company found it
hard to provide the quantities required by the accelerated schedule of
construction. But eventually the smelter was ready for business. The
plant was completed in mid-May, and the *Everett Herald* described it in
detail, noting that, by utilizing three furnaces, it could economically
handle 240 tons of free milling or arsenic/sulphur-contaminated ores
per day.

Only one thing was lacking: money. The plant, built under contracts
let the previous year, now required additional funds in order to
commence operations; but, by May, 1893, "money had crawled into its
hole." Financing was almost impossible to obtain because the
pessimism of 1892 had become the depression of 1893. This was a panic
due to lost confidence. Planned cities like Everett and enterprises such as
Monte Cristo were built on confidence that sufficient money would be
available to establish the industries and mines on a paying basis. Many of
the financial backers who had come to Everett because Colby, Hoyt,
and Rockerfeller had invested there, were becoming dismayed at the
lack of return on their money. They were skeptical about putting in
more funds and began to think of themselves as creditors, demanding a
return on the money they had already spent.

An Illustrated History of Skagit and Snohomish Counties, published in
1906, commented thus:

Hard times and hard weather seem to have drawn a wail from the people of the Sound in general, and we find those of Snohomish to have joined the general chorus. In February the ground was covered with two and a half feet of snow and the mercury dropped as low as twelve and fourteen below zero. This, with the hard times, made things rather dreary. The Tribune of April 20th laments in the following terms: "Hard times! Hard times! There is scarcely a town on the Pacific coast but what is crowded with idle men, men of all trades willing and ready to take any kind of employment they can get and at almost any kind of wages. There are to-day in Snohomish almost two men for every job of work there is to do, and all other towns in this vicinity are crowded with idle men, and still there are advertising schemers all over the country who are continually getting men to come here from the East.''

By the middle of June, the tracks of the Great Northern Railway had been completed across Stevens Pass to Everett. Consequently, the leaders of Everett—including Henry Hewitt, Jr.—planned a gala reception for James J. Hill, the railroad's president, who was scheduled to arrive on the first through passenger train from the east. He would be received in style at the Monte Cristo Hotel. The city fathers had fashioned a silver plate, set in velvet, with Hill's name inscribed, to be presented to him. The plate had been fabricated from the first silver brought down from the Monte Cristo mines, thus symbolized the link between the two ventures. However, Hill wired that urgent business prevented his coming west in the foreseeable future.

About this time business activity in Everett began to take a decidedly ominous turn, strikingly manifested by the new smelter, which stood idle because the Puget Sound Reduction Works could not raise the capital necessary to commence operations at the plant. During the week Hill had been scheduled to arrive, the Bank of Everett closed its doors. Two more of the city's banks were quick to follow, leaving only two of the original five banks open. Wage cuts in Everett and Seattle during the previous year had foretold this panic, and with the bank closures a reality, the local businessmen had no doubt it had arrived.

C.H. Taylor, Auditor of the Monte Cristo Mining Company, expressed dissatisfaction with the management of the Everett Land Company in a letter to Joseph L. Colby, the mining company's president. He stated, in part:

There is a vast amount of grumbling here about the unaccountable methods of the Everett Land Co., and I cannot avoid hearing some of it. Unless something we looked for comes very shortly, to make property saleable here at the high prices originally placed upon it, some of the people now here will have to leave, I think. The great Northern Ry. which was to make a boom, has been completed and has not caused a ripple.

And leave they did—not only because they could not afford the high-priced property but also because they had lost their jobs or their businesses had failed. What the investors had bestowed upon Everett, they could, and did, as easily take away. Construction in Everett, as elsewhere, came to a grinding halt.

The general economy went from bad to worse. By mid-August, the Northern Pacific Railroad was bankrupt (both Colby and Hoyt were on the executive committee of that line), and the Everett Land Company was sliding deeper into debt. Hewitt wanted to wait out the depression and resume business when times were not so hard, but the investors with money in the land company, and allied firms, had a different view. Hewitt had signed contracts with landowners in the area (including the Rucker brothers), requiring him to build a city, but with his financial resources now depleted, he could not comply.

Upon completion of the Everett and Monte Cristo Railway, business in the mountains rose to new heights of accomplishment; but in Everett the hard, cold facts of the depression had a crushing effect. By this time the bankruptcy of the Everett Land Company was no secret. Half the population of Everett had departed to seek employment elsewhere, and many left unpaid mortgages behind. The New York capitalists were alarmed and issued bonds for the sum of $1,500,000, at eight per cent interest, against the land company. They hoped thereby to raise enough money to allow the several industrial enterprises in Everett to resume or begin operations, and thus jolt the economy off dead center. John D. Rockefeller, who also had invested money in Everett, graciously purchased the majority of the bonds. He was, in fact, one of the few men in the country at that time with the means to buy such bonds, and this transaction gave him controlling interest in the Everett companies.

On October 19 the first load of ore arrived at the smelter. Although the mineral was transported on an Everett and Monte Cristo car, it did not come from Monte Cristo but had been shipped from east of the Cascade Mountains. The Puget Sound Reduction Company announced that the smelter would be started for a trial run upon the arrival of more raw material already contracted for. During the first week in November, the boilers were fired up, and while the furnaces had not been lit, the machinery was put in motion for the crushers to begin pulverizing the ore to prepare it for the assayers and the smelting process. Although several weeks would pass before the workmen lit the furnaces, the sound of the machinery in operation after such a long delay heralded new prosperity and gave hope for the city's future. On the surface, it appeared that the economy was improving, however sluggishly. While the operation at the smelter caused rejoicing in Everett, many people still looked to the Monte Cristo mountains for their salvation. The situation did look brighter there. The concentrator building had almost been completed, except for the windows; the tramways nearly assembled from the Pride and Mystery mines, and the railroad completed to the concentrator. The Wilmanses' tramway from the Comet mine was finished, and about 100 tons of ore had been shipped down it to the concentrator.

But as the year of depression drew to a close, the rotary plow had not arrived in Everett. The snow on the railroad became a severe problem, and many residents of Monte Cristo began to flee the town and its raging blizzards for the more temperate shores of Puget Sound. The snow continued to fall, and many workers, and owners too, who had remained in Monte Cristo began to worry about the ability of the railroad to maintain the line through the winter. Snow at the switchback below the town was seven and one-half feet deep by the year's end, with no snowplow to clear the tracks. Fearing isolation and possible starvation, a number of people departed for the lowlands, leaving only a skeleton crew to handle essential construction and maintenance.

D.B. Ewing Photo

One of the thrills of winter travel on the railroad was watching a rotary snowplow at work. The rotor could be turned in either direction allowing snow to be cast left or right as the situation demanded. Driven by its own steam engine, it was pushed ahead of a standard locomotive. The action is seen from the car following the locomotive on the Everett and Monte Cristo Railroad.

CHAPTER VI

1894

PRODUCTION BEGINS

Although many of Monte Cristo's inhabitants had left to reside elsewhere during the winter of 1893-94, the fear which prompted the exodus—visions of a railroad blocked by heavy snows, and the resulting isolation—failed to materialize because the company was able to cope with the snowfall without major incident. Then, during the first week of January, the ability to handle deep drifts and avalanches was greatly enhanced when the rotary snowplow arrived in Everett. The machine, painted a deep brown color, with the letters "E. & M.C. Ry. No. 1" printed in gold on its sides, was about the size and shape of a box car. The plow was not self-propelled but driven forward by an ordinary locomotive pushing from behind, while a boiler and steam engine located toward the rear supplied the power to turn the blades. The entire front was occupied by a steam-driven rotor designed to bite into the snow with its many cast iron knives and in one motion lift it high into the air and clear of the tracks. The company displayed the plow in Everett for a short time, then quickly rushed it to the mountains where the winter weather demanded its use.

T.J. McBride, the railroad's general manager, accompanied the maintenance train to Monte Cristo on its first run with the rotary, when snow up to four feet in depth was encountered, "much of it packed down hard and icy, but the plow ran through it with ease, hurling the snow high over the telegraph lines and poles and away from the track a hundred feet or more." The plow's performance in drifted snow was spectacular and efficient, but wherever avalanches had covered the tracks, men had to walk ahead with long iron rods to probe for concealed rocks or trees which, if struck, would often rip knives from the rotor, necessitating costly and time-consuming repairs. Nevertheless, the company anticipated it would experience "no trouble in keeping communication open between Everett and the big mining camp" during the winter.

With the trains running to Monte Cristo, work on the concentrator continued on schedule, and the United Concentration Company predicted that the plant would be ready in February. The heavy equipment was beginning to arrive and was immediately moved into the building and installed. By January 18 the structure had been completed and much of the machinery was in place. On the other hand, the winter snows brought to a complete halt attempts to finish the Pride of the Mountains and Mystery tramways. The danger of avalanches and the difficulties encountered when working in the deep, soft snow precluded work on these facilities.

The snowfall at Monte Cristo during January exceeded four feet, bringing the winter's total to nearly 18 feet. However, because the snow packed down, the depth on level ground was about three feet. Nevertheless, work in the townsite continued without interruption. As carloads of lumber arrived, new buildings began to rise on Dumas Street and at other locations in the town.

The efforts of the miners began to pay dividends when, in early January, the first carload of ore was shipped over the railroad from Silverton and delivered to the Puget Sound Reduction Company. Money raised by the sale of the Everett Land Company bonds in 1893 was applied to businesses in Everett, the smelter included, in an attempt to revitalize the stagnant economy. This allowed the reduction company to begin purchasing ore, and by the end of February the bins at the plant were full. One of the furnaces was fired up, and a sample run reduced the raw mineral to Doré bars, a mixture of gold and silver commonly referred to as bullion.[1]

The run was successful, resulting in 30 tons of bullion. This was shipped in March to San Francisco on the steamer *Umatilla*, for refining. Since the delivery of ore was sporadic at best, continuous operation of the smelter could not be sustained in early 1894, but the presence of the gleaming Dore bars on the Everett dock inspired local businessmen and workers alike. The depression appeared to have bottomed out; business should improve in the foreseeable future. The nail works had been started again, and the paper mill at Lowell was productive. Along with the bullion, the *Umatilla* also carried 47 tons of paper and 250 kegs of nails. Although this activity could not match the boom of 1891-92, it represented a start on the road back to prosperity.

With the smelter now prepared to handle the ore, the only hurdle that remained was to obtain sufficient quantity to enable continuous operation of the plant. To this end, the concentrator at Monte Cristo was completed early in February, and a trial run made of its machinery. The boilers were fired up, and the 200-horsepower Corliss-type engine thundered to life, rotating the transfer shafting, which in turn operated the various pieces of machinery through large flat belts. Everything worked well; therefore the United Concentration Company took delivery of the plant from the contractors, Frazer & Chalmers of Chicago, during the second week in February, opening the way for the Monte Cristo ore to move continuously to the smelter.

The concentrator was a double-section mill, with the sections capable of being operated together or independently, as desired. Each section could process 150 tons of mineral in a 24-hour period, giving the plant a total concentrating capacity of 300 tons per day. Thus the capacity of the plant could be tailored to the production rate of the mines. In addition, the sections could be slightly altered to handle different ores from the various mines, adding to the mill's versatility. Three tons of ore yielded approximately one ton of concentrates, with about an 85 per cent retention of the metallic value.[2]

The preparations for handling the ore were now complete—the railroad encountered no problems in keeping the line open, the smelter was proven and ready, and the concentrator had been finished. Only one link in the system remained to be accomplished—the aerial tramways, down which the ore was to be transported from the mines to the concentrator. But the weather did not cooperate insofar as tramway construction was concerned. More than ten feet of snow fell at Monte Cristo during February, raising the winter's total to almost thirty feet. Consequently, the depth of the snow plus the danger of avalanches precluded most labor that was not done in the immediate vicinity of the townsite.

Work at Monte Cristo, however, continued without interruption. During April, C.E. White of the Fidelity Trust and savings Bank of Everett announced he would construct a building on Dumas Street which would house a store and a bank. Numerous other buildings and additions appeared as fast as the lumber supply and weather permitted.

Fred Wilmans returned to Washington on March 6 from California. After conferring with Colby in Everett, he traveled to the Wilmanses' properties at Monte Cristo to take charge, and he predicted that ore from the Comet mine would begin moving down the tramway to the concentrator within two months. By the middle of April, the Wilmanses had nine men at work on the side of Wilmans Peak, and operations began shifting to a summer schedule. However, heavy snows in early May delayed operations, and as late as the middle of the month six to seven feet of snow remained in Monte Cristo, with about fifteen feet still on the ground at the upper mines.

The late snows, combined with the generally moderating temperatures, spawned massive avalanches which swept away everything standing in their paths. One of several avalanches that roared down Wilmans Peak destroyed an 80-foot-high tramway tower. According to J.W. Mercer of the Monte Cristo Mining Company, the slide "covered an area of about forty acres and moved down the mountain some 2,000 feet."

> After the avalanche had stopped in its devastating course he walked over to it and gave it pretty close examination. In places there were great fissures from 8 to 10 feet wide down which he could look a distance of seventy-five feet. The tremendous force of such an immense body may be better imagined than described. It moved with a terrible and awe inspiring roar carrying great trees and boulders before it. One miner was carried down with it but managed to escape with nothing more than severe bruises. From a little experience the miners learn when to expect slides, as for instance after heavy rains, and take the precaution to keep out of danger. [*Everett Herald*, May 17, 1894]

Although snow was still a hazard to be avoided in the mountains, at Granite Falls a different kind of problem arose. The village was a major stop on the Everett and Monte Cristo Railway and had a long, curved platform to facilitate handling freight and passenger traffic. But in 1894 a town was not considered "on the map" if it lacked a station. Therefore, Granite Falls greatly desired a depot, and to this end the city's leaders drew up a petition that was signed by 150 local voters. They did not simply ask the railroad for a depot; the understanding was that they would offer something in return. At this time the Everett Land Company was seeking to capture the title of county seat from Snohomish City, and was attempting to enlist support among other communities in Snohomish County to achieve this goal. The issue was hotly debated, and it had become evident that the future location of the county's government would soon be put to a vote. The "something" which Granite Falls residents offered in return for a depot was to pledge their solid block of votes in favor of moving the county seat to Everett. The ensuing vote called for the move but legal challenges prevented it occurring until 1897. Granite Falls received its depot, although the significance of its role in the controversy remains unknown to this day.

Meanwhile, in Monte Cristo the United Concentration Company decided to replace the destroyed tramway tower and quickly put the tram system in operation. To assist in this and other tasks, a $75,000 loan was floated on the company's properties, and the money used to cover the costs of tramway repairs and new machinery. Coincidentally, the gradual recovery of the silver market spurred activity at the mining camp. The investors in the Monte Cristo properties had been awaiting an upswing in silver prices, and they repaired the necessary equipment in order to take advantage of the increased market value when it occurred. For this reason part of the loan money was used to replace the towers on the Mystery and Pride tramways. By late June, the final tower had been replaced with a huge pole weighing an estimated 20 tons, set 15 feet into the earth, and measuring 40 inches in diameter at the base and 16 inches at the top. This spar rose 102 feet from the ground, and was heavily guyed to prevent snowslides from uprooting it. Clearly, the United Concentration Company expected it to last.

While work progressed feverishly on the trams, the Wilmans brothers announced plans to construct a second aerial line from the Golden Cord properties on the north side of Wilmans Peak to the concentrator. Work was begun immediately, with towers to be constructed when the receding snows permitted. Wasting no time, the Wilmanses also put the Comet mine tramway in operating condition, and by May 24 they were once again sending down ore.

While on a tour of the western states, the Honorable J. Sloat Fassett, senator from New York, made the following comments after observing this work:

> I have been actively interested in mining for fifteen years, and I looked forward to my Monte Cristo trip with critical intentions. I had heard of the district from, I might say hundreds, who had either visited it or had

some direct or indirect interest. I returned with the conviction that it is a stupendous undertaking and that its most enthusiastic admirers have not overstated the conditions. The natural difficulties are great but capital and engineering skill have overcome them. . . .

I found machinery in readiness to handle ore in quantities that would surprise the world. To use a western expression, it is an attractive proposition. If the open season is used for energetic development these mines will make all connected with them happy. With the camp in full operation, there is not a ton of ore that will not pay a profit on the working. It is a low grade ore, and needs to be handled with economy and sagacity, and that large quantities shall be reduced, but the quantities are there and accessible. All the principal mines are bullion producers. I estimate that the camp will be good as a revenue proposition, even if it is only run to the full capacity of the present concentrator. The mines can now send down 1,000 tons of ore a day, but the full glory of Monte Cristo will not be realized until the camp is producing 5,000 tons a day, and that is well within the possibilities. Even at that rate the supply—one must say the visible supply—is inexhaustible. [*Everett Herald*, May 31, 1894]

Although great strides had been made, Monte Cristo remained an outpost of civilization surrounded by almost limitless wilderness. This fact was emphasized on June 5, when the tracks of a full-grown bear were discovered on Dumas Street. A number of men armed themselves and set out to kill the beast. While they were following the spoor, an eagle soared overhead and screamed vigorously, as though defying their efforts. The animal was lucky and the men returned to town empty-handed. Not so fortunate, however, was another bear that chanced upon one of the mines a month later:

At the breakfast table at the cabin of the Glory of the Mountains mine one morning last week the miners heard a series of very queer sounding grunts, and Clement B. Coffin set down his coffee cup and stepped out to reconnoiter. He was considerably astonished to see a full grown black bear standing quietly about 100 feet distant. Stepping inside he got his telescopic rifle, dropped the sights down to zero, and aiming behind the brute's foreleg, pealed away and shot him through the heart. The bear trotted off, about fifty feet before he dropped and died. He weighed about 400 pounds. [*Everett Herald*, July 12, 1894]

By June 7, Monte Cristo had assumed the appearance of a producing mining camp, with the Wilmanses having already transported 800 to 900 tons of ore down Wilmans Peak, while more arrived each day. To take advantage of the recovering silver market, Alton L. Dickerman, Colby-Hoyt's consulting engineer, had been given almost unlimited power to rush the development of the syndicate's mines at maximum speed.

The miners at Monte Cristo readied their equipment for the shipment of ore. The main cable of the Golden Cord tramway, begun a short time earlier, was stretched on July 12. The Mystery and the Pride of the Mountains trams neared completion, and test runs were made to prove

Meyer Photo

The Mystery/Pride cookhouse located in the lower end of Glacier Basin on the side of Mystery Hill. This one building prepared meals for over eighty men working two shifts. The two Xs on the snow in the distance mark the spot where several men were seriously hurt or killed in an avalanche earlier in the year. At 4300 feet elevation in the Monte Cristo area the snow commonly piled to the smokestack on the roof of the building, requiring extensive digging to keep access to the doors open.

the mechanisms and make the final adjustments. On July 19 the remainder of the material for the Golden Cord tram was unloaded in Everett from the steamer *City of Puebla* for shipment to Monte Cristo. This meant that four aerial lines would soon be carrying ore to the concentrator, and operation of the project on a massive scale could begin.

Luck seemed to favor the venture at the Pride of the Mountains mine, for the discovery of a rich, six-foot ledge of ore coincided with the completion of the big aerial tramway stretching over Glacier Basin, across Mystery Hill, and down to the receiving terminal just up valley from the concentrator.

Meanwhile, the United Concentration Company contracted for the installation of an 150-lamp dynamo to be installed in the concentrator and run by the Corliss engine along with the mill machinery. This dynamo would provide sufficient electricity to illuminate the concentrator, the aerial tramway receiving terminal, the covered ground tram between the two, and the crusher building. The excess power would provide lighting for part of the town as well.

Problems were encountered in the operation of the Mystery and Pride of the Mountains tramways. They were not, however, caused by any fault of the mechanisms, but by the lack of telephones ''to make signals for running the trams.'' The Monte Cristo Mining Company had borrowed two telephones from the Wilmans Mining Company, but had been asked to return them. A few days later the communications problem was solved, however, when previously ordered telephones arrived from Seattle, and soon the big tramway from the Pride of the Mountains was in operation. Joseph Colby, who was on hand when it started, gave this account:

> We are now tramming ore down from the Pride of the Mountains, and the sweetest music my ears have heard in two years was the dropping of the ore upon the griddle as it came down from the mine. This week will see the tramway fully established and in running order from the Mystery mine and next week the ore from the vein will be going into the concentrator. [*Everett Herald*, August 2, 1894]

The ''griddle'' he referred to was a coarse screen or ''grizzly'' which separated that ore fine enough to be sent directly to the concentrator from that which had to be run through a coarse crusher to reduce its size before further processing. The ore, so long on the mine dumps, was finally being transported to the concentrator.

Everett was now in deep financial trouble. The bonds floated by the Everett Land Company in 1893 to obtain money for the restoration of the economy were coming due, and no money was on hand to make payment. Rockefeller, who had purchased the bulk of them, was alarmed at this turn of events. He realized that direct action was necessary to protect his interests in the Pacific Northwest. In desperation, Hewitt attempted to raise the money by selling the Everett Land Company's water and electric works, as well as its street railway system, to the city government at a substantial loss, but the voters defeated the proposal. The eastern promoters of the Everett Land Company then threatened to sue Hewitt in an attempt to recoup their losses.

Hewitt was summoned to New York to face Rockefeller, who had decided he could no longer trust him to handle his interests. Moreover, Rockefeller had decided not to create additional panic by forcing the Everett Land Company into bankruptcy. As Hewitt stood helplessly by, Rockefeller quietly assumed his personal debts, took his stock in the land company, and made Joseph Colby president. Hewitt was allowed to retain a few parcels of land and $14,000 cash, enough to support him for one year. Thus, the "father of Everett" returned to Washington stripped of his position and possessions.

But the Pacific Northwest enterprises were not the only ones Rockefeller was investigating, for the depression had served to highlight the quality of his ventures—differentiating those having substance from those which did not. Reports filtering back to Rockefeller from his far-flung empire in early 1894 indicated that something was amiss and the trust he had placed in many of his co-investors was unwarranted because his money had not earned the return it should have. In fact, Rockefeller soon realized that he needed someone to handle his investments because he was too involved with the operation of Standard Oil to attempt to oversee his other diversified holdings. He therefore chose Frederick T. Gates, his private secretary and long-time friend, to handle this business. Throughout the spring of 1894, Gates checked into the Rockefeller interests in various parts of the nation, uncovering scandals ranging from malfeasance to outright fraud.

On August 1 Gates arrived in Everett, accompanied by Francis Brownell, attorney for the land company, to look into the affairs of Rockefeller's Pacific Northwest enterprises. The purpose of the trip was not announced, and a local newspaper presumed that he had come to "look into the various phases of the proposition." Gates quickly made it clear, however, that he would have full control to make any future decisions involving the Rockefeller investments at either Everett or Monte Cristo.

Less than a month later, Gates announced a reorganization of the Everett and Monte Cristo Railway Company which was to set a pattern for the restructuring of the other Rockefeller controlled companies. The new officers were: President, Frederick T. Gates; Vice-President, J. B. Crooker, of Minneapolis; Secretary, Francis H. Brownell; Treasurer, Schuyler Duryee; General Manager, T. J. McBride; General Freight and Passenger Agent, S. N. Baird. Six days later the *Everett Herald* noted: "The reorganization is understood to be in the Rockefeller interests." Indeed it was, as were the ones which soon followed; for, while Rockefeller was, by this time, the largest single investor in the Everett-Monte Cristo venture, he did not have exclusive control of all the companies involved. He had yet to obtain the power that would allow him to determine the fate of these enterprises. Gates, the man chosen by Rockefeller to effect the necessary changes, was now setting about that task. Newspapers of the time did not reflect his role in these reorganizations, and it is doubtful that the full scope of his intent was generally known at that time, or for several years thereafter.

Joseph Colby traveled to Everett, and on March 8 he outlined the status of the Monte Cristo mines:

> People do not realize the great problem that we have had to solve here. It has five distinct features, namely, the building of the smelter at Everett, the construction of the railroad from Everett to Monte Cristo, the erection of the concentrator, the building of tramways and the opening of the mines. We have met with considerable delay by the snow, and of course delay in the railroad meant delay to all other features of the proposition. I thought we had handled snow enough in Michigan to know how to get along with it, but I confess the delay has been greater here than I had anticipated. Nevertheless, everything is well done. . . . I was very much pleased with the appearance of the Everett and Monte Cristo railroad. It is a picturesque route but just at this time with the snow banked six or eight feet high on each side of the track and the cold waters of the Stillaguamish plunging down the canyon, the view was not calculated to arouse a desire for any plunge into the stream. [*Everett Herald*, March 8, 1894]

Eugene J. Barney, railroad car manufacturer and stockholder in the

Everett Land Company, made a trip to Monte Cristo on March 26, after which he stated that his party was "greatly surprised and pleased with the wild and picturesque scenery along the Everett and Monte Cristo Railroad, and declared that they had seen nothing to equal it in all their travels over the noted scenic routes through California." Barney was connected with the company which built the passenger cars for the railroad, and the trip gave him a chance to sample his own wares.

As a result of Gates' visit, the railroad was readied to handle the expected steady business created by the Monte Cristo operation. While in Everett, Gates had authorized several improvements on the line: snowshed, additional riprap, side tracks, and a roundhouse to be located at the Everett terminus of the line. The rolling stock was re-shopped and placed in new condition. The four locomotives glistened with polish; the passenger and freight cars had been cleaned, revarnished, and overhauled in the railroad's own shops or those of the smelter. The Granite Falls depot, conceived in politics, was now finished, complete with a telegraph office. Monte Cristo also had a station. The sawmill had been closed soon after the railroad began transporting lumber into the town and the company converted it into a depot to serve the workers and sightseers.

On August 20, 1894, the United Concentration Company started its plant. Since the tramways were already in operation, the firm soon had ore concentrates ready for shipment to the Everett smelter. Thus, five years after the first claims were staked in an uncharted wilderness, Monte Cristo was on the verge of becoming a producing mining camp, and beginning to look like a full-fledged mining town. What had been a quiet alpine valley had become a very active place. The din of the concentrator droned day and night, punctuated by the blasts of explosives from the mines. The odor of burning coal pervaded the valley as smoke poured from the concentrator's tall stack. The distant clangor of steel on steel mingled with the screech of tramway pulleys and brakes. Fish abandoned the Sauk River which now ran white with the tailings from the milling process.

Monte Cristo was a town of contrasts. The dance halls and saloons never closed, their customers coming and going 24 hours a day. The village now had 34 children of school age when the fall term approached, and new buildings sprang up as fast as material could be obtained. Among the more important ones were a post office and schoolhouse.

Herman Siewart Photo
The United Concentration Company's Monte Cristo plant. Seen here during operation, the smoke from the stack and steam from the engine exhaust hint at the din created by the machinery within. '76 Gulch is in the distance at the far right. Also on the right is the "Cliff House" hotel. Notice the covered tramway on the left which allowed mules to haul ore from the aerial tramway collector terminal the year around. This building also marked the farthest distance reached by the railroad, about 1,000 feet beyond the town of Monte Cristo.

LaRoche Photo
By 1894 Monte Cristo was a rough-hewn mining camp. This view is up Dumas Street with its planked surface to combat the mud which was ever present during the rainy season. The images of moving subjects is blurred due to the long shutter time required to expose the picture.

Heavy timbers, pre-cut at Monte Cristo, were transported by surface and aerial tramway to the Mystery and Pride of the Mountains mines to allow completion of the head and bunk houses prior to the onset of winter. A snowshed to cover the tension station on Mystery Hill was also under construction to permit continuous winter operation. The Golden Cord tramway was complete and shipments of ore had begun.

On August 28, the mining companies received a temporary setback when a small forest fire near the town burned down the blacksmith shop and two of the Comet mine tramway's towers, halting operation of that line for a short while.

The overall state of the Monte Cristo operation was summed up by Francis H. Brownell, counsel for the Everett Land Company, when he spoke before an assembly of businessmen who had interests in the venture:

> The Everett Land Company realizes that it is a period of great depression. Real estate is flat throughout the country. Most of you know that the parties originally behind this proposition have sold out to larger stockholders, and it will be treated as a business proposition. Mr. Rockefeller will not put a dollar in until he can see that he will get a dollar back. At the present time no real estate is selling anywhere. It cannot be sold here. Now as [to] the industries here. The Everett Land Company has substantially no longer an interest in their management. Each one will be run for its own business interests on an independent basis. All are subject to changes that cannot be helped. Last November the money was ready and preparations made to operate the Everett smelter in the spring. Then came the strike on the Great Northern, then the floods that blockaded all the railroads, then the railroad tie-up. None of these happenings could have been foreseen. We have an ore contract cut and ore coming in. There are between 150 and 200 men at work at Monte Cristo. Ore is coming down to the concentrator from the Pride of the Mountains at the rate of from 30 to 83 tons per day. Now if the ore is of any value it must be reduced and treated, and as a business proposition the Everett smelter must run and I am glad to say that as a business proposition the smelter for the short time that it did run, ran at a profit. [*Everett Herald*, August 2, 1894]

On August 26, the United Concentration Company made the first recorded shipment of ore from its concentrator to the Everett smelter, thus commencing the production phase of the enterprise. No fanfare accompanied the arrival of the concentrates; the consignment to the

Everett and Monte Cristo Railroad was handled like routine freight business. The original carload was soon dwarfed by subsequent shipments of up to four cars per day.

By the end of August, steam had again been turned on at the Everett smelter to allow the initial stages of a production run to begin. Three weeks later, sixty tons of Dore bars had been shipped to the refinery at San Francisco, and ore was coming into the smelter from British Columbia, Montana, Idaho, and Oregon—even from other continents—to assure continuous operation. On October 8, eleven carloads of ore arrived—seven from British Columbia, four from Monte Cristo. This was typical of the quantity of ore required to run the smelter.

Because only one side of the Monte Cristo concentrator was operating, the amount of ore that could be processed was limited to 150 tons per day, but given the current production rate at the mines, this was adequate. In order that the operation could continue through the winter, the railroad constructed the snowshed authorized by Gates earlier in the year, installing it about a quarter mile below the town. The shed was 180 feet in length, requiring 175,000 board feet of lumber. The rotary snowplow was put in top condition to handle the onslaught of winter, and the Monte Cristo roundhouse did a lively business overhauling the locomotives and other rolling stock. The United Concentration Company had installed an 180-lamp Macher dynamo in the concentrator, and strung wire to light the upper end of the town as well as the mining facilities. On September 24, J. W. Mercer ordered the bulbs that would make the nights brighter in Monte Cristo during the coming winter: "Please send us at once fifty (50)-110 volt-18 candle power lamps to fit socket sent you by this mail. Please return socket with the lamps."

The Wilmans brothers were not faring well financially due to the depression, and during the summer of 1894 Mac went east to raise money. He returned with $10,000 to bolster their failing finances. He was amazed to discover that during his absence both Fred and Steve had terminated their bachelorhood. This was somewhat of a relief to Mac, who had been critical of his brothers' extravagant ways. Fred married Lillian O'Connell, and settled in Seattle, while Steve and his bride, Beatrice Partridge, returned to the family ranch in California. Mac hoped the marriages would stabilize his brothers' activities and retard the flow of money from the family coffers, thus easing their burden until the mines at Monte Cristo became paying propositions. Soon the Wilmanses were shipping sufficient ore from the Comet and Golden Cord mines to allow the running of the second side of the concentrator, which immediately doubled the capacity of the plant to 300 tons per day.

The first returns on the ore shipped from Monte Cristo served to generate new interest in the town's businesses. For years the legend of Monte Cristo had been on everyone's lips, but it became reality when ore was shipped, and money thus brought into the mining companies' treasuries. This spurred a renewed interest in mining locations and property transfers, when Johny-come-latelys attempted to acquire a slice of the pie. The major companies, to protect their interests, sought and were granted patents on their claims; thereby they obtained deeds to the land, not merely the mineral rights. Eighty-nine patents were awarded in mid-October to three mining companies—the Monte Cristo, the Pride of the Woods, and the Pride of the Mountains.

The established mines constructed living facilities, and made plans to operate throughout the winter. Since the boarding houses at the Mystery and Pride mines were complete, the miners would not have to wade through the deep snow each day. They could also obtain provisions by having them sent up to the mines in the empty ore cars of the tramways during their return trip, making frequent hikes to town unnecessary.

In Everett the launching of the first whaleback steamer built at the steel barge works was an indication that the town's businesses were beginning to prosper. The vessel, christened the *City of Everett*, was a sister ship to the *Wetmore*, which had been built at the Lake Superior shipyards. The event was hailed with a parade and picnic held on October 24. Special provisions were made to be certain that all those at Monte Cristo who wished to attend the affair could do so.

Unusual arrangements *had* to be made, because on October 8 a slide had roared down the mountainside at Tunnel No. 4 in the Stillaguamish Canyon, temporarily blocking the road. Three days later, while the section crew worked to clear away the debris, a second slide occurred, taking the life of one man and seriously injuring another. The instability of the rock in the vicinity of the tunnel was to be a recurring curse during the next few years, while the railroad company struggled to keep the line open. Engineer Barlow's words of prophecy were to echo

LaRoche Photo

In the canyon of the Stillaguamish. Tunnel number five is in the foreground. A passenger train is waiting in the distance, near the east portal of tunnel number four. The train was undoubtedly waiting for the photographer to complete his work. Travel was more leisurely in 1894, and unscheduled stops such as this were commonplace.

again and again down the canyon he had advised the company to avoid when it constructed the railroad.

To surmount this obstacle, Conductor Speer and his crew on October 23 carried a "speeder" or pump-car over the slide to the east side of the blockage. The men pumped their way up the track to within three miles of Barlow Pass, then proceeded on foot. After hiking the grade to the pass, they were exhausted but walked the remaining four miles to Monte Cristo in a downpour. They arrived the night before the boat launching in Everett was scheduled to take place. They fired up the locomotive in the roundhouse and coupled it to a boxcar, the only rolling stock on hand, then transported the passengers down the line to Tunnel No. 4. The people climbed across the rock slide to a train waiting on the west side, which carried them the remainder of the way to Everett. They arrived in time to observe the parade and launching, and were back in Monte Cristo that night, returning in the same manner they had come down the line the previous day.

During November the autumn rains turned to snow, and the folly of locating some of the boarding houses in the manner that they had been was made bitterly clear. Shortly after noon on November 23, "a snowslide swept down upon a mining cabin near the Pride of the Mountains mine at Monte Cristo and injured several men." The avalanche occurred just after the night shift had finished its noon meal. Four of the men present were injured; Louis Erickson was struck by a timber and killed.

> Willing hands set to work with might and main, in the face of a terrific gale to rescue their buried comrades. We commenced digging at the mouth of the tunnel, and had worked there about ten minutes when John Felix, one of the night shift, shouted from the bunk house:
>
> "Come over this way and dig, boys; you will find some of the boys here."
>
> Pointing to a plank about 30 feet from where he stood Matt Hangen and big Nelson headed a crew of shovelers for that place while the rest continued to work at the place first started on. After digging about eight feet where Felix had directed us a shoeless foot was uncovered.
>
> "That's Erickson's foot", cried Nelson; "Dig carefully boys, or you'll cut him with your shovels."
>
> The wind blew so hard that we could hardly see to work. Digging around Erickson's foot and leg to locate the position of his body, we

came to the stove. When the stove was raised out, the back of another man came into view, and we soon took Wesley Smith out. He was bruised up some, but not seriously hurt. Then we heard a faint voice that seemed to come from under the snow, seemingly quite a distance away, saying, "For God's sake, boys, hurry and get us out," and you bet we were hurrying for all that we were worth. Digging still further around Erickson's body, which seemed to be wedged in between some timbers and the hard packed snow, we uncovered Charley Stone's head. Charley was in a sitting position, and it was impossible to get him out just then, as his legs were under some of the timbers. It did not take long to make an opening alongside Erickson, and we were pleased to hear the voice of A.M. Creswell. He was lying on his side right by Erickson, and we soon got him out. This made the opening large enough to take Erickson out. Poor fellow, he was limp and lifeless. He had been struck with something on his head, but I don't think that would have hurt him much. His unfortunate position in the snow, hung head downward, together with the great pressure all around him, must have caused his death, his distorted and purple features showing that he must have suffered terribly. After getting Louis out we turned our attention to Stone, and in digging around him came to a pair of hands belonging to someone else. Tommy owned the hands and he was soon taken out, almost chilled to death, somewhat bruised though not seriously hurt. It didn't take long to get Stone out. He seemed to be as unconcerned as if it were an everyday affair. The foreman then called the roll, and we knew that they were all out. Everything possible was done to make the victims comfortable, and all the injured are getting along all right. [*Everett Herald*, November 29, 1894]

Despite the adversities of the oncoming winter, business proceeded as usual, with new patents issued to the Rainy and Monte Cristo companies for additional claims, bringing to almost 100 the total number patented in the area. The various enterprises in the Monte Cristo area discussed the possibility of boring a "union tunnel" into the side of Wilmans Peak, one sufficiently long to pass beneath the operating tunnels of all the mining companies, and raises would then be bored to connect the mines to the union tunnel. The cost was to be shared by everyone, but not all the firms could agree on the division of the costs and some were completely disinterested. The tunnel would eliminate the need for the aerial tramways, which were plagued by mechanical problems and complications due to weather.

One such malfunction almost cost Everett Borden his life on the

Mystery tram in late December. He had been employed as a mechanic to keep the tramway in running condition. While working about 75 feet above the level of the snow, he spotted a runaway ore bucket rocketing toward him, its clutch unhooked from the traction rope. Lacking room to avoid the rapidly approaching car, he had no alternative but to jump. This would have resulted in tragedy had it happened during the summer, but the snow was deep enough to break the impact of his fall and he escaped with only a badly shattered leg.

When 1894 ended, Monte Cristo was an established, producing mining town, and was daily making its mark on the local economy. Although the winter weather did not cause closure of the railroad, it slowed the work at the mines to such an extent that the trains were reduced to one per week, until business picked up in the spring.

One of the Everett and Monte Cristo trains laboring the last few feet to Barlow Pass. The tracks at this point climbed up the Palmer Creek Valley, out of the Stillaguamish watershed. Crossing the pass into the Sauk Valley, only four miles remained until Monte Cristo was reached.

1895

LABOR PROBLEMS

With the advent of 1895 people were cautiously optimistic, although the depression continued unabated. The United Concentration Company was apparently oblivious to the bad financial situation, however, and ordered additional machinery for installation in its building at Monte Cristo. The initial run of the facility during the last four months of 1894 had convinced the operators that too much mineral was washed away in the tailings. The ore slimed badly, thus allowing an excessive amount of metal to escape with the gangue rock. But the Wilmans brothers were confronted by a more serious problem than faced the United Concentration Company. Becaue the ore from their mines was incompatible with the United Concentration Company's process, they decided to build another, independent concentrator, one tailored to the ore from their own mines.

When the new machinery arrived, the United Concentration Company's concentrator shut down to permit its installation. Unable to ship ore, the mine operators performed needed development work on their properties. The Mystery No. 3 tunnel was extended 300 feet farther into the face of Mystery Hill, with a raise bored to connect it with the Mystery No. 2. This raise was dug on the boundary line between the Mystery and the Pride of the Woods claims, and allowed ore from the second level to be lowered to the third and carried down the Mystery tramway to the concentrator. The Mystery No. 2 was also driven 300 additional feet, with a similar raise to connect it with the Pride of the Woods tunnel, thus linking underground all the major workings of these mines. This minimized the necessity for travel on the surface—a boon in winter, when the deep snow made travel difficult and hazardous at best, impossible in extreme cases.

More than 200 men were now employed on development work at the Pride of the Mountains and the Mystery. An immediate result of this activity was the discovery of a new, immensely rich vein—one with the potential to increase the Mystery's output by 100 tons per day, enough in itself to keep the concentrator busy.

In Everett, the Puget Sound Reduction Company announced it had shipped $107,000 worth of bullion during December. This amounted to 3,000 ounces of gold, 60,000 ounces of silver, and 500,000 pounds of lead. Employing 60 men, the smelter was treating upwards of 80 tons of ore per day, much of it coming from the Monte Cristo mines.

Improvements to increase the plant's capacity were completed by February 1, and the smelter restarted for an unlimited production run. The company predicted a steady flow of bullion during the coming months. Everett's economy was additionally boosted by Monte Cristo's prosperity, because the contract for the new crushers and rolls to be installed at the concentrator was awarded to the Sumner Iron Works of Everett.

The railroad began constructing a roundhouse in Everett in early April. When completed, it would ease the burden of work at the one in Monte Cristo, which heretofore had been the only facility of this type on the line. The mechanics could work in the more temperate climate near Puget Sound rather than (during the winter) in the bitter cold of the Cascade Mountains. The railroad company could also supplement its income by taking on outside work during slack periods in its own maintenance schedule. By the end of the year the roundhouse and shops were completed, thus greatly expanding the maintenance capacity of the company and making it less dependent on the facility at Monte Cristo and the capricious weather.

A census taken during January, 1895, indicated Monte Cristo's population was 197 persons—126 men, 31 women, and 40 children. This number included only residents of the town itself, not the several hundred living in the boarding houses of the nearby mines.

A new school building, completed in late March, was welcomed by all. Classes commenced on April 1, 1895, with about 15 students receiving instructions from Mrs. R. R. Howard. Makeshift furniture was used because the new desks, seats, and blackboards already purchased had not yet arrived from Chicago, although they were expected momentarily. The number of school-age children was anticipated to double when business in Monte Cristo returned to its summer schedule. Although most of the miners and workers at Monte Cristo were inclined to spend their time and money on drink and indulgences of the flesh, a few rose to higher callings and created articles of great beauty. One such person was W. O. Welch, a mechanic who fashioned objects from local woods with the skill of an accomplished craftsman. Welch specialized in musical instruments: he built violins, guitars, and viols from spruce and Alaska yellow cedar. He also manufactured inlaid canes and other wooden objects. His work was much in demand, and many company officials returned home from Monte Cristo with one of his instruments.

By the end of February, the small, picturesque village was nearly free of snow, and the old-timers declared winter was over and the "open season" almost at hand. The mine operators predicted a full production summer schedule could be achieved by April 1, if the work at the concentrator was completed.

The promised electrification of the townsite became reality in mid-June, when the Monte Cristo Mercantile Company sported a six-lamp electric chandelier which provided better illumination than the kerosene lamps that had been used. Another improvement was a covered porch running the entire width of the building—an addition appreciated by everyone, given the usual rainy weather in the mountains. With its planked surface and covered porches, Dumas Street gave Monte Cristo the appearance of a typical western mining town, which indeed it was.

Typical, too, were the risks in this community of wooden structures, which as yet had no fire department. In the latter part of July, the Rialto Hotel and Restaurant burned to the ground. The fact that the fire did not incinerate the entire town was somewhat of a miracle, because little space had been provided between buildings. No one was seriously injured, however, and Mr. Barton and his family, who had run the hotel, left Monte Cristo to live elsewhere.

By the middle of April the new equipment for the concentrator had arrived and was quickly installed in the plant. At the same time the old equipment was overhauled. The weather continued mild, and everything was put in order for the approaching "open season." The reorganization of the various companies continued, as Gates proceeded to maneuver and manipulate the corporate structures. He was appointed president of most of the non-mining companies, while C. F.

Rand, of New York, became president of the mining enterprises. Rand had been involved in earlier dealings with the Colby-Hoyt syndicate's mines near the Great Lakes and was highly regarded by Gates.

Overhauling of the tramways to prepare them for the season's tasks was completed in early May. About this time the railroad announced its summer schedule (three trains per week to Monte Cristo), additional miners were put to work in the Mystery and Pride of the Mountains mines, the concentrator was restarted, and business in general returned to its summer level of activity. By early June, Monte Cristo was shipping ore and concentrates to the smelter in Everett. This added to the length of the trains, and provided revenue badly needed by both the railroad and mining companies. The season was to be the first one with the mines in full production, and the owners hoped to realize the potential of their investments. In order to acquire additional funds, and utilize its idle rolling stock, the railroad again ran excursion trains to Monte Cristo on occasional Sundays; consequently, many people visited the mountain hamlet.

Although the nation was still crushed by depression, the year promised to be a turning point for the economy of the Pacific Northwest—at least insofar as Monte Cristo was concerned. The workers and miners, whose interests were often ignored by the companies and syndicates, began to agitate for higher wages and improved working conditions. The laborers felt that if 1895 was to be a banner year for the owners, they too were entitled to a portion of the profits.

The first outward indication of unrest came in early June—a strike at the Mystery mine protesting the abysmal conditions of both room and board. After a meeting between spokesmen for the miners and the company, the parties reached a settlement, and work resumed. This action was the beginning of a new awareness by the miners at Monte Cristo that they were the basis of the whole operation, and that they, collectively, could wield considerable power. More was to be heard from them before the year ended.

Typical schedule of the railroad in its heyday. With four and one half hours required to reach Monte Cristo, the train traveled an average speed of fourteen and a half miles per hour. The return trip, requiring four hours, was covered at the stately pace of sixteen and a quarter miles per hour. This was quite fast when the numerous stops are taken into account. Also, speeds through the canyon of the Stillaguamish seldom exceeded nine miles per hour.

Everett & Monte Cristo Railway

TAKING EFFECT SEPTEMBER 22, 1895.

PASSENGER—MONDAYS, WEDNESDAYS AND FRIDAYS.

No. 1—East Bound.		No. 2—West Bound.
8:00 a m Leave	........Everett.......	Arrive 6:00 p m
8:10 a m "	........Lowell........	Leave 5:50 p m
8:45 a m "	......Snohomish.......	" 5:25 p m
9:15 a m "	. Harford Junction	" 5:00 p m
9:40 a m "	.... Granite Falls......	" 4:15 p m
10:25 a m "	...........Robe..........	" 3:35 p m
10:40 a m "	.... Bogardus	" 3:22 p m
11:05 a m "	...... Gold Basin	" 3:02 p m
11:30 a m "	.........Silverton.........	" 2:43 p m
11:45 a m "	......Perry Creek	" 2:30 p m
12:10 p m "	..... Barlow Pass......	" 2:15 p m
12:30 p m Arrive	.....Monte Cristo.......	" 2:00 p m

MIXED TRAIN—TUESDAYS, THURSDAYS AND SATURDAYS.

No. 7—East Bound.		No. 6—West Bound.
12:45 p m Leave	.... Everett...	Arrive 6:10 p m
1:05 p m "	..... Lowell....	Leave 6:00 p m
1:45 p m "	....Snohomish	" 5:15 p m
2:20 p m "	....Hartford Junction....	" 4:40 p m
3:15 p m Arrive	......Granite Falls..	" 3:25 p m

Train No. 1 connects at Snohohomish with S. L. S. & E. Ry. train for Gilman, Snoqualmie Falls and Seattle; at Hartford Junction with train for Arlington and all points north.

Freight received for all points. For information, rates, etc., call on or address J. O. Whitmarsh, agent.

Freight and Passenger Station at foot of Pacific avenue. General offices, The Wisconsin Building, Everett, Wash.

S. N. BAIRD.
Auditor and General Freight and Ticket Agent.

C. F. Rand visited Monte Cristo in mid-August to look over the various operations and held meetings with the local management. As a consequence, they decided to place compressors in the Pride of the Mountains and Mystery mines, to be run by electricity produced at the concentrator. Manpower would thus be replaced by air drills, which would vastly increase production. They also decided to further revamp the machinery in the concentrator, to increase its capacity and make it more efficient.

Perhaps the most significant, though unexpected, event to occur on this trip was a confrontation between Rand and a select group of miners who showed a flair for timing. They presented him with a petition, signed by most of them, demanding that their wages be increased twenty per cent (from $2.50 to $3.00 per day). This action, needless to say, did not endear the miners to the local company officers, and set the stage for future friction between management and labor. Rand, however, read the petition carefully. The miners reasoned that since their counterparts in California and Colorado received the higher amount, they were entitled to a similar increase. Rand agreed that the men at Monte Cristo were not working less than their fellows in other states, and he decided that they, too, would receive the higher wage.[1]

Before leaving for New York, Rand announced that wages had been increased to $3.00 per day. This action caught Mac Wilmans by surprise. He had just arrived with a few men to resume summer activities at the mines, and had engaged them to work for $2.50 per day. But with the going rate now $3.00 per day, he would have to pay the greater amount. Publicly, Wilmans stated this was a good thing for Monte Cristo because it placed it on an equal footing with other camps in the nation. Privately, however, he felt somewhat differently—the Wilmanses were running short of money and the higher wages would bite deeply into their financial reserves.

With the improvements now installed in the concentrator, the output of Monte Cristo increased weekly. However, the new machinery was not sufficiently effective to treat the ore from the Golden Cord, and the Wilmanses were forced to close the mine in early September. The ore slimed so much when crushed and mixed with water, that a large percentage of the metal content was washed away with the tailings, making the mine a losing proposition. Since the Wilmanses could not afford to build a concentrator, as they had promised earlier, only eight men were retained at the mine to attend to development work. Because they were short of operating capital, the Wilmanses could ill afford an unprofitable mine.

Adding to the complications of mining at Monte Cristo, the tool sharpeners struck in September for an increase in wages to $3.50 per day. Carbide-tipped drills had not yet been developed, and the tool sharpeners were a critical part of the work force. The Monte Cristo Mining Company, however, had elevated wages about as far as it intended to in this depression economy. The local management, still cognizant of the miners' petition, quickly replaced the dissident sharpeners with other men at the old pay scale.

The mining company's woes were magnified when a late summer snowstorm struck Monte Cristo on September 3. The apparent shortness of the "open season" began to worry officials because the onset of bad weather threatened to curtail their operations. The companies proceeded with winter preparations, because they were determined to maintain production throughout the cold months. The Pride of the Mountains mine erected a snowshed over its boarding house to prevent a repetition of the previous year's tragedy when a similar building nearby was crushed by an avalanche, killing one man. The Mystery mine let a contract to extend the No. 1 tunnel, to uncover new ore lodes, and thus increase the output of the mine.

Oliver McLean, one of the original prospectors with the 1890 Packard party, added a new mine to the list of producing companies at Monte Cristo when he announced plans to open the O & B (Oliver and Ben) on the side of Toad Mountain, just above the town. He had bought out Ben James, the co-locator, and was now principal owner of the property. The ore was to be hand sorted, sacked, and carried to the railroad by mules and horses. The project experienced a poor start when James T. Dimpsey, one of the miners, was killed by falling timber shortly after work began. Dimpsey, a pioneer prospector in the Monte Cristo area, had been a partner of James Lillis in 1890. Lillis had been killed by falling rocks at the Summit claim two years earlier. Both had begun their Monte Cristo careers with the Packard party, and had located some of the first claims in the district.

Two days after the summer snowstorm, the *Everett Herald* noted that the vine maple and other mountain plants, nipped by the cool night air, were beginning to take on their autumn hues of red and yellow. At the same time it added another interesting observation:

> Mountain rats are becoming a nuisance in all the mining camps. The Cascade Mountain rat is entirely different from his voracious brother of the Rocky Mountains. Those around Monte Cristo are bobtailed with very large ears and when cornered or alarmed in any way, stamp repeatedly with both hind feet like a rabbit. [*Everett Herald*, September 5, 1895]

The animal referred to was, in all likelihood, the cony or pika, a member of the rabbit family prevalent in the Cascades.

In the 1890s the United States Geological Survey did considerable field work in the Cascades, and in 1895 members of the agency were in the Monte Cristo area gathering data from which to draw maps. A mishap on the trail above Sunday Falls, which involved a member of the party, was reported thus in the *Monte Cristo Mountaineer:*

> A mule belonging to the geological survey pack train and heavily loaded with kitchen utensils, missed his footing and fell 105 feet down the mountain side above Sunday Creek Falls. The fall spilled the hard tack in every direction, sent the jams and jelly tins bowling merrily down into '76 Creek, and knocked sixteen kinds of Skandinavian milk tickets out of the cook stove, but the mule arose as if from a pleasant dream and ambled along with the rest of the train down Sauk Valley apparently uninjured. [*Monte Cristo Mountaineer*, as reprinted in the *Everett Herald*, September 19, 1895]

By the end of September, the O & B Company was packing ore down a steep, precipitous trail from its mine high on the side of Toad Mountain, the path descending 1,500 feet to the railroad. This method of transportation was soon replaced by a windlass system that lowered the hand-selected ore down to the railroad in large buckets, and helped achieve a record shipment of fifteen carloads of concentrates and ore from Monte Cristo during one week in late September. The obstacles created by man and nature appeared to have no effect on the prosperity. A fellow named Massey leased the O & B in early October, and he immediately planned to replace the dangerous pack trains and cumbersome bucket-windlass system with a wire rope tramway to transport the ore. After this was completed, he announced, the mine would be developed on a much more liberal scale.

While the O & B systems took shape, the Mystery tramway had to be shut down due to an unspecified malfunction along the line, and repairs took about two weeks, causing ore to pile up on the mine dump. At the O & B, ten towers about 300 feet apart would support the cable, and the buckets would be fastened permanently to it in the fashion of a modern ski lift. The O & B Company intended to install this tram prior to the onset of winter, bringing to five the number of aerial systems capable of transporting ore to the railroad or concentrator. However, one of these was not operating, since the Wilmanses had closed the Golden Cord due to lack of suitable ore treatment. But they could not afford to let the property remain idle, and plans were under way to lease the Golden Cord properties to other parties. This would assure a stable income for the Wilmans brothers.

All the companies planned to operate during the winter, but most of the families at Monte Cristo left to seek the milder climate of the lowlands. In fact, so many departed, that by the end of October the school at Monte Cristo had closed, due to lack of students. Although pioneers predicted a mild winter, the women and children were taking no chances. However, about 300 persons remained in the town and mines to attend to necessary tasks during the coming months. By the middle of November the mountains had become heavily burdened with snow, and occasional flurries swept across the townsite, a harbinger of more to come.

Although most of the mine dealings at and around Monte Cristo were conducted honestly, almost to a fault, cases of cheating and trickery did occur. One such incident involved a mine in the Stillaguamish Valley that was bought by a man named Keating for the sum of $1,800. The property appeared to be extremely rich in gold—if one could believe the evidence on the tunnel walls. After purchasing the mine, however, Keating discovered it had been "salted" with gold dust. This unethical practice was usually accomplished by loading the gold dust into a shotgun and firing it at the walls, thus imbedding small amounts in the rock surface. Keating sought restitution through the courts, and October 10 he won a judgment to recover the full amount of his investment. While such incidents were rare, the few that did occur gave the mining district a black eye because detractors claimed that *all* the mines had been salted at one time or another.

At the Pride of the Mountains and Mystery, the miners became quite upset when the companies announced an extension of the work day from 9½ to 10 hours, and at the same time raised the rate for room and board from $26 to $30 a month. This all but cancelled the gains the workers had made earlier in the year through their petition to President Rand. The grumbling culminated in a wildcat strike against the company, the surgeon, the cook, and the bunkhouse conditions. Manager William C. Butler had to take the first train from Everett to Monte Cristo, where he listened to a list of grievances read by Patrick Welch, spokesman for the miners. He noted each point, agreed to remedy the problems, and the men returned to work.

The cables were rapidly strung for the O & B aerial system, because the first snows of winter already lay on the ground at Monte Cristo, and the chill air foretold of more on the way. During November the O & B employed 25 men, and transported the hand-selected ore via the newly-completed tramway to the railroad. A dozen or more carloads had been brought down prior to November 14 and were awaiting empty cars to haul the precious rock to the Everett smelter. The success of the O & B awakened more interest in the Monte Cristo area than all the other mines put together, primarily because the owner, with relatively few funds, had established a producing mine in a very short time. Proximity to the railroad and the town played an important role in the O & B story, but it proved that all the major veins were not yet taken at Monte Cristo.

On November 21, the Monte Cristo Mining Company, reflecting the decision made earlier in the year, officially announced that an electric air compressor and drilling machines would be installed in the Mystery third level, and that the company would bore that tunnel beneath Glacier Basin and connect it with the Pride of the Mountains system. This would eliminate the need for the higher aerial cable-way, because ore could be brought underground from the Pride of the Mountains, through the Mystery, to the shorter and lower Mystery tram.

The Wilmans brothers had succeeded in leasing the Golden Cord mine, and by late November the tramway from that facility was running at full capacity. The Golden Cord ore was shipped to the smelter without concentration, due to the incompatibility of the ore with the machinery in the United Concentration Company's plant.

Toward the end of 1895, William F. Stevens, superintendent of the Monte Cristo Mining Company, sent a letter to William C. Butler, general manager, in which he recapped the year's activities. He described the preparations for the air compressor in the Mystery No. 3

tunnel, then listed the veins that had been recently discovered, particularly on the Mystery and Pride claims, and expressed satisfaction with the development of the project. The Mystery No. 1, No. 2, and No. 3 tunnels had all been connected underground and materials could now be carried with ease from one level to another. Two new ore chutes had been built during the year which allowed more rapid movement of the ore between the different elevations. Stevens also implied that new miners would be brought in whenever they could be found. He assumed they would take the jobs of the dissidents—the men who had presented the petition to Rand earlier in the year—whom the local management was intent upon replacing.

A rich body of ore was struck in December in the O & B, which increased the output of that facility. Six thousand feet of heavy electric cable arrived at Monte Cristo, along with the electric Burleigh drills, and the cable was quickly strung along the tramways from the concentrator to the Mystery mine. The snow at Monte Cristo was now three feet deep, and the railroad planned to celebrate Christmas with a special excursion train, charging passengers only a single fare for the round trip.

At Tunnel No. 4, a tragic replay occurred of the landslide which had blocked the railroad a year earlier. Several tons of rock and mud slid from the canyon wall and covered the right-of-way. A section crew was dispatched to clear the debris; but, like the previous year, a second slide came down, killing one man and badly injuring another. This and still another slide delayed traffic on the road for a time in early December, but within a week the trains were running again. As the snow continued to fall in the mountains, two locomotives were required to push the rotary snowplow. Apparently the pioneers' prediction of a mild winter should have been amended; "wild winter" was more appropriate.

Nature celebrated the holidays of 1895 with its own display when a gale roared through the Cascades, dropping a large number of trees across the tracks. On December 23, the regular train to Monte Cristo was forced to return to Everett, having gotten no nearer than ten miles to the village because the crew had become exhausted from removing the trees and the hour had grown late. However, the men cleared the rails in time for the promised Christmas excursion.

The west portal of tunnel number four in an all too common state of disrepair. The unstable rock in this area made this scene a recurring nightmare for the section crews of the railroad, several of whom were killed while attempting to clear slides like this from this location. Notice the lack of machinery: pick and shovel, blasting powder, and the hand car were the tools of the trade. Manpower was cheap, and equipment scarce.

The train which left for Monte Cristo on Christmas morning did not have a merry time. The road had been blockaded since the 18th. For more than a fortnight, a storm had been raging in the mountains, rain, snow, and gales taking turn at the task of making travel difficult. The snow lay about six feet deep on the level, and in many places had drifted to much greater depth.

The train which left Everett on Wednesday of last week (Christmas Day) was a double ender, with the big rotary snow plow in front. It reached Silverton without much difficulty, but beyond that point troubles began. Fallen trees were encountered at many places, over which several feet of snow had drifted, and the plow was therefore helpless to clean the road. The trainmen took their Christmas dinner at Silverton.

Five gangs of section men were secured, and at 4:30 on Thursday morning the train started for Monte Cristo. The fallen trees which had obstructed its passage were laboriously dug out; at one point seven were found bunched across the track. After a day of hard work, the train arrived at Monte Cristo at 7:30, and was welcomed by a general turnout of the population and a hearty hurrah and jubilation. The storm had abated during the afternoon.

After a night and a day of rest, the train started on its return trip on Friday evening, and again had a hard time. The rotary and the caboose were left up the road, the engine and passenger coach coming through, reaching Everett the next morning. They were a sight to see, being snow packed at every point.

The railroad people have since been busy in getting matters in good shape for regular trips. The continuance of the storm makes the task difficult. [*Everett Herald*, January 2, 1896]

Locomotive number three at the town of Robe, headed toward Monte Cristo. The names of the gentlemen on the pilot beam are lost, but Fred Gates enjoyed many such trips into the mountains in this manner. The fireman and engineer are inspecting and lubricating the side rods and preparing the locomotive for its remainder of the journey. Notice the acetylene headlamp. There were no electric generators on the locomotives at this time.

CHAPTER VIII

1896

PROSPERITY

When 1896 made its cold debut in Monte Cristo, the leaden gray clouds continued to deposit vast amounts of snow upon the Cascades. The winter predicted to be mild was, instead, proving to be one of the most severe in memory. However, the operators of the town's enterprises were determined to maintain production regardless of the adverse weather. The railroad's crews were better prepared for the season's vagaries than at any previous time, and two locomotives, in tandem, rammed the rotary plow up the tracks after every major storm. The railroad did not, in fact, adopt its winter schedule, as it had in previous years, but ran three trains every week. The Pride of the Mountains and Mystery mines continued to produce the precious ore and transported it via the tramways to the concentrator, now operating only one side. The Burleigh drills and electric air compressor in the Mystery No. 3 tunnel were in use by January 16 and had established a new standard of efficiency in that mine. The O & B was closed due to heavy snows for about two weeks in early January, but resumed activity when the storms abated, and the company announced plans to operate all winter long.

The upper and lower Monte Cristo townsites were a sorry sight. About twelve buildings, abandoned during the winter, had been crushed by the heavy snow, no one having been present to shovel the roofs clean. This caused concern that a housing shortage would occur in the spring when the families wintering on Puget Sound returned to their damaged homes. The railroad company planned to dismantle the old sawmill building, now serving as a depot, and build a first-class station when the weather ameliorated. Local home owners expressed

hope that the wood from the old building could be used by the returning residents to repair their homes.

Winter turned Monte Cristo into a fantasy land. The storms corniced
and drifted the snow into grotesque shapes that appeared to alter the
contours of the land itself. While work in the mines was hard and long,
the men did have some leisure time. The people at Monte Cristo lacked,
of course, modern means of entertainment such as radio, television, or
stereo sets. Consequently, they did a great amount of reading and
studying in the spare time that was available. During the winter of
1895-96 a debating society was formed at the Mystery mine camp. Card
games were popular pastimes; "peanuckle" a favorite among the residents. Often the railroad was blockaded for weeks at a time, and the
townspeople had to create their own diversions. They could not
"escape" to the lights of the big city.

The national depression continued, and many of the Cornish miners
working at the Colby-Hoyt syndicate mines in northern Michigan lost
their jobs. Work was extremely scarce, particularly for men without
skills. Given the choice of no work or a trip to Washington, a goodly
number chose the latter, because they were a proud people and mining
was their way of life. The first small group arrived in Monte Cristo in
late January, 1896, and began to quietly, gradually displace the dissidents who had been involved in the previous year's labor problems.
The new miners were obedient, slow to anger, and very hard workers.
They were also dedicated family men, and many brought their wives
and children with them. They were accustomed to hard rock mining,
having been brought up in the tin producing region of Cornwall,
England. Most had begun work in the mines while they were still
children. Their presence at Monte Cristo added a dash of color to the
community when their unique Cornish accent was heard in the valley.
They acquired the nickname of "Cousin Jacks," and blended easily into
the Monte Cristo scene.

The concentrator was once again processing ore from the Golden
Cord, and the new machinery appeared to recover more of the metal
content than had been possible the previous year. As a result, sufficient
ore arrived at the concentrator by February 13 to permit starting the
mill's second section and operating the plant at its maximum capacity of
300 tons per day.

On January 20, 1896, while the graveyard shift crew in the Golden

Cord mine attended to its normal tasks, a load of ore, dumped into one of the chutes from the upper stopes, jammed in the narrow, wooden passageway. George Pratt, one of the miners, stepped down to the chute and began jabbing the stubborn clot with an iron bar. Another miner, L.C. Massie, shouted a warning just as the jam broke. The dislodged rock caused Pratt to lose his footing on the narrow beam, and to avoid plunging into the ore head first, he jumped into it and vanished from view, with several tons of rock around him, all rushing down into the Stygian blackness. A third miner, Edward McGavock, climbed down to the lower end of the chute and, aided by the feeble, flickering light of his candle, began to dig. Massie ran to awaken Bass, the mine's operator, and when he arrived at the site, all three began to remove the ore from below. The alarm was spread to the town, and a crowd was soon on hand to aid in the rescue. Before long, Pratt's legs were uncovered. They were kicking vigorously, and this gave new hope to the rescuers. Amazed that he was still alive, much less conscious, they dug with renewed determination, and soon had him extricated. Although short of wind, he was uninjured except for minor bruises.

The O & B was open again after a three-week closure due to snow, but problems of another sort began to threaten the mine's operation. The owner had been so determined to ship ore from the mine before the winter snows arrived, that he had vastly over-extended his financial resources, and the creditors were now clamoring for repayment. The parties negotiated for several weeks, but to no avail, and by early February the O & B was closed because of legal attachments, and debts amounting to about $7,000. The miners had not been paid for several months, and the mine that gave everyone such hope in late 1895 closed.

Winter was hard upon Monte Cristo and making itself felt at every turn. The stationary, or carrying, cable of the Mystery mine tramway had failed and parted, requiring the shutdown of the system. During the previous week, the repair crew working on the tram had watched the snow fall incessantly, piling up with ever increasing depth in drifts and cornices. Thus the men were not too surprised when they heard an ominous rumble high up the side of Wilmans Peak, directly above them, and they fled for their lives. They were lucky that they heeded the first warning, because tons of snow thundered down the mountain. For a moment it appeared that the massive white cloud would demolish the receiving terminal of the Pride-Mystery tram, but the avalanche stopped just short of the building. However, the wall of snow caught the running cable of the Mystery tram and tensioned it so violently that the lower bull wheel, around which it ran, was smashed to pieces.

Slides continued throughout the day, because the temperature moderated and a light rain added to the weight and instability of the snow. One avalanche beginning high on the ridge flanks north of the railway depot ripped down the mountainside almost 4,000 feet and covered the tracks with heavy, wet snow to a depth of 40 feet. The mild spell was followed by a sudden freeze that solidified the soggy mass into ice. The crews operating the rotary plow found the machine virtually useless; the concrete-hard material bent the iron knives and tore them from the plow's rotor as if they were cardboard, and a large crew had to be put to work with dynamite to clear the blockage from the tracks.

About this time, the railroad's locomotives received a needed improvement: compressed air flangers were added to the pilots. These small jackhammers chipped away the ice and snow that was compacted inside the rails, below the plow's reach. The ice which formed there sometimes became hard enough to lift an 80-ton locomotive from the tracks on its wheel flanges, and derail it. The flangers were a welcome accessory, considering the winter climate in which the locomotives were required to operate.

On Thursday, February 27, news of the sudden death of Charles L. Colby stunned Everett. The president of the Everett Land Company was one of the community's founders, and the city had taken his son's name. Colby had been one of the financial forces which had boosted Monte Cristo from a remote, uncharted region into the world mining spotlight, and his death was mourned by many in the Everett and Monte Cristo area.

According to rumors flying in Everett, the Puget Sound Reduction Company's smelter was preparing to build its own gold-silver refinery, thereby saving the costs of having the ultimate refining process handled by another facility. The stories began early in 1896, and persisted throughout the year, without substantiation.

The weather continued to assert its mastery, March making its appearance in the manner of the traditional lion:

> After the genial weather of a fortnight ago, the big storm came as a surprise. The snowfall was heavier in Everett than any other during the winter, about eight inches lying on the level. The Monte Cristo road has

been kept open surprisingly well. A party of young ladies, escorted by Mr. Crooker, on a visit of observation to the mining towns escaped the blockade by good luck and rather enjoyed the novelty of the situation. The train carrying this party started up on Friday, and ran into the snow storm as it climbed the mountains, but got safely through to Monte Cristo, where they remained as guests of Mrs. Miles. The train set out on its return trip on Saturday, but was blockaded by snow four miles this

A typical Sunday outing at Monte Cristo. Hikes and picnics in the splendor of the surrounding mountains were a common activity in the mining town. Notice the alpenstocks (climbing poles) carried by several of the participants. These were popular climbing aids of the day.

side of Monte Cristo, and had to remain there all night. Fortunately some provisions were on board, and more were sent up with the snow-plow that started the next morning to dig the train out. The sight-seers came down on Tuesday, fresh as daisies, and will long remember their experience of mountain life in a blizzard. [*Everett Herald*, March 5, 1896]

Beleaguered by another problem, the railroad embarked in mid-April on an ambitious project to reroute a portion of the Stillaguamish River just downstream from Silverton. The company believed that seepage from the river caused a boggy, unstable portion of land to shift almost continuously. This warped the tracks grotesquely where they crossed the area on a trestle. The constant, expensive realignment of the bridgework prompted the railroad to attempt the bolder plan of changing the river's course to prevent the seepage. However, the company was only partly successful.[1]

About the middle of March, more Cornish miners from northern Michigan arrived in Monte Cristo, as the syndicate continued to replace the previous year's strikers. Due to problems with the weather and the Mystery tram, the concentrator had shut down one side and was again running at reduced capacity. The new efforts at treating the Golden Cord ore proved satisfactory, and the mine operators decided to concentrate all their ore, since enough metal content was now retained to make the operation acceptable. Despite the severity of the winter, 95 men worked in the Pride and Mystery mines, and the Mystery tramway was put back into operation, using a bull wheel cast in Everett. Mining activities were returning to normal after the latest storm.

Except for the portion owned by C. H. Packard, the O & B mine was purchased by eastern parties. They resumed operations immediately while endeavoring to settle the liens against the property which had held up work for a month and a half.

During early 1896, the snow continued to crush houses in both the upper and lower towns of Monte Cristo. When spring drew residents back to the village, the housing shortage turned out to be worse than had been anticipated. The problem came to a focus during the first week in April. Every available space was either bought or rented by people returning to Monte Cristo. Those who arrived at this time found not summer but eight feet of slowly melting snow on the ground. This did not deter them, however, and the settlement gradually came to life following its winter slumber. After all, Monte Cristo was, despite its rough ways, a friendly, close-knit place where people preferred to live—provided the weather did not become too violent. They challenged the housing shortage with varying success—built a new house on Dumas Street, patched several collapsed buildings with lumber salvaged from irreparable ones. Perhaps the most bizarre effort to relieve the problem, however, was the conversion to residences of both the jail and an old shed where explosives had been stored.

During the spring of 1896 another mining area moved into an advanced state of development. This was the Goat Lake district, situated in the valley northeast of Monte Cristo. Pennsylvania capitalists organized the Penn Mining Company and bought many of the mine claims. The developers planned to operate on a large scale in the coming years by exploiting, on their side of the mountains, the natural extensions of the Monte Cristo veins which cleaved two peaks, Cadet and Foggy, from top to bottom. The accessibility of Goat Lake was limited compared to Monte Cristo, because it lacked a railroad and tramway system, but rumors abounded of the owners' plans to open mines in the region. The most visible sign of their effort was the warehouse they built at Barlow Pass to house the company's machinery and supplies. The wagon road from the railroad to Goat Lake began at the pass, and the new building was a transfer station for goods shipped to and from the mines.

On Monday, June 29, the night shift at the Mystery mine ended early in the morning. Most of the exhausted men retired to their bunks after the ten-hour stint, but two young fellows decided to take in the pleasures of the town before relaxing. Sam Strom, 23 years old, had come from Norway, arriving in Monte Cristo in late 1893; Dave LeRoy was a year younger. The two young men became fast friends, working together with five other men in one of the Mystery mine's stopes. They were young enough to have sufficient energy left when the shift ended to visit the town. LeRoy had often called on one of the dance hall girls, and he wanted to impress her with rich gifts, luxuries he could not afford on a miner's wage.

After a few dances and drinks in the saloons, Strom felt tired and decided to return to the mine's boarding house to rest before the next shift started, only a few hours away. LeRoy, on the other hand, was somewhat under the influence of alcohol, and told Strom he was going to remain in town and get a gift for his girl, even if he had to use his six-shooter. Strom didn't take the statement seriously because LeRoy was known to be a gentle person; nevertheless, he begged him to return to the mine, to no avail.

LeRoy had learned that Nathan Phillips, a watch and jewelry peddler, was making one of his periodic visits to Monte Cristo to sell his wares and take watches back to Seattle for repair. After a few more drinks, he was in the mood to obtain what he wanted, by whatever force was required. He sought out Phillips and stalked him through the town while he made his door to door rounds. LeRoy finally built up nerve enough to approach the peddler in the hotel lobby just after 4:00 P.M. He told him that he knew someone who wished to buy a watch, and that if Phillips would accompany him he would take him to the man. The unsuspecting Phillips obliged, locked the satchel containing his wares, and followed LeRoy down the railroad tracks to a point adjacent to the lower townsite.

At this point the miner pulled his weapon and demanded the satchel Phillips wore around his neck. The peddler refused and LeRoy promptly shot him. On Dumas Street several men sitting on the porch of the Pioneer Meat Market heard both the shot and a loud scream that followed. They rushed to the victim's aid, but before they arrived LeRoy shot Phillips twice more. Still clutching his property, the peddler went down, finally releasing his hold on the satchel.

The shock of what he had done then began to seep through LeRoy's stupor as the shouts of the approaching men rang in his ears. Grabbing the satchel, he turned and ran a short distance down the tracks, then headed northward, ascending the high ridge that separated the valley from Goat Lake. The town was aroused to action, and while some of the men assisted the badly wounded peddler, others began the pursuit of LeRoy, who was now far ahead of them. He knew the mountains well, and although a posse combed the hills, he was never apprehended. The rumors were that he had headed for Trail Creek, B.C., and had been seen there, but this was never substantiated.

Nathan Phillips, screaming with pain, was taken to the office of Dr. W.T. Miles, given treatment for his wounds, and transported to Providence Hospital in Seattle, where he gradually recovered. The satchel with about $1,000 worth of jewelry and watches was never recovered.

When Sam Strom awoke for his next shift, he learned he no longer had a partner. He was saddened by the news of what had transpired, sorry he had not taken LeRoy at his word earlier in the day. Had he done so, quite possibly he could have prevented the incident.

Early in July, miners struck ore in an exploratory tunnel at the lower end of the Pride of the Mountains mine. This was welcome news because the mineral in the upper workings of this claim was beginning to pinch out, and the mine's production threatened. The adit, dubbed the "New Discovery," was at the same elevation as the Pride of the Woods mine directly across Glacier Basin. Meanwhile, using the new air drill, the workmen were extending the Mystery No. 3 tunnel at the rate of 100 feet per month, 250 feet beneath the floor of Glacier Basin.

The development work at Goat Lake continued throughout the summer, but the owners and operators said very little about the operation. The wagon road had been completed from Barlow Pass to the lake. Here a barge was employed to float the supplies to the uppermost end of the valley. They were then hauled to the base of the cliff, where a steam engine winched them 2,000 feet up the snowfield on skids to the mine property. The Penn Mining Company had prepared for its first winter operations.

The fall weather brought with it the usual prevalence of sickness, and many of the miners—especially those at Mystery Hill—suffered from severe and protracted colds. A number of men had quit due to poor health, the result of inferior living and working conditions. The mines were cold and dank, and the men labored in them ten hours per day, six days a week. Upon completing his shift, the miner retired to a crowded, one-room bunkhouse that was unheated except for a single wood-burning stove in the center. He had little more than a blanket or two under which to sleep. No mattresses were provided; fir boughs or other makeshifts arrangements had to be used, or one had to try to relax on the rough-sawn boards of the bunk. When a person got wet, which was often, the cramped conditions provided little opportunity for drying one's self. These factors all combined to test the constitutions of even the hardiest individuals.

About this time another group of "Cousin Jacks" from Michigan arrived at Monte Cristo to begin work at the Mystery. They replaced some of the miners who left, also men who had been involved in the labor disputes in 1895.

The O & B was back in operation because tentative settlement of the

The "old camp" of the Penn Mining Company at Goat Lake. The Foggy Mine, operated by this company, was located fifteen hundred feet above the far end of the lake in the eastern spur ridge of Cadet Peak. The headquarters camp of the company was eventually located farther down Elliott Creek about a half mile below the lake.

liens against the property allowed the work to resume, at least temporarily. The Monte Cristo Mining Company, in an attempt to determine whether or not it desired to continue work on the '76 mine, brought in a steam-powered diamond core drill and hauled it into '76 Gulch. The firm intended to bore a 3,000-foot horizontal crosscut hole parallel to the wall of the valley, one that would sample all the major veins in that area. The drilling would be cheaper than tunneling, and the cores obtained would provide a geologic cross-section of the lower slopes of Wilmans Peak. The hole was to be started about 700 feet inside the tunnel, but early snows precluded much progress in 1896.

Down the tracks at Silverton, a discovery other than that of mineral wealth caused considerable excitement, and was poignantly reported in the *Everett Herald*:

> At the foot of a tall cliff of gray sandstone which cleaves the dark slopes of a mountain ridge east of the town of Silverton, from the summit half way down, there were found the whitened bones of a man. From their formation and the fragments of clothing which hung upon them, they evidently were those of a white man. He had apparently climbed the ridge from the Sultan side of the divide, for the Stillaguamish side was found to be inaccessible by the discoverers of the remains. In seeking a way down the face of the great precipice, which stands out bare amid the dense timber, he must have lost his footing and fallen headlong for fully a thousand feet. It may be that death, in mercy, came to him instantly; or he may have only been crippled by the fracture of a leg and have lain for days on that bleak mountain side in helpless agony, far from any other human being, waiting for death to come to his relief.
>
> That man, who must have met his fate years before the finding of his bones made that fate known, was in all probability the first prospector to invade the inhospitable wilds amid which the Stillaguamish River flows. . . . Busy towns have sprung up under the shadow of the crags where this lone wanderer perished, and the great cliff, from which he plunged to death, and at the foot of which his bones are buried, flings back the locomotive's roar and whistle. Hundreds of men are engaged in digging out the mineral he was doomed not to find, the wilds which mockingly answered his despairing cries for help with the roaring of their cataracts and the sighing of the wind in their gloomy forests are now made daily to resound with blasts of dynamite, and the precious rock released by those blasts is borne in trains to the great smelter in Everett. [*Everett Herald*, November 12, 1896]

The operation at Monte Cristo had settled down to routine during the summer of 1896. No fabulously rich new veins were found, and life in the mountain camp had become almost dull to men who remembered the pioneer years. However, the relative calm was deceptive. By November 12 eight inches of snow lay on the ground in the town, with six feet clinging to the mountainsides at higher elevations. That amount of snow at this time of year was not unusual, but the sudden chinook and heavy rain that followed caught the community by surprise.

The warm winds and rain continued without interruption for almost ten days, melting the snow already on the ground, swelling the rivers to and beyond flood stage. The railroad was washed out at many locations, along both the Stillaguamish and the Sauk. The gentle, babbling streams at Monte Cristo became raging torrents, and at least one building—Cleveland and Kline's saloon and lodging house—was demolished and swept down the Sauk River. The establishment's iron safe was found a week later a mile and a half downstream. All work at the mines and concentrator was halted because the men had been pressed into service on the railroad crews.

But as suddenly as it had begun, the rain ceased, the weather cleared, and the air became extremely cold. For the first time in anyone's memory, the Stillaguamish River froze in places, making it possible to skate on its surface. The rivers quickly subsided and returned to their banks.

The freeze proved to be as transitory as the chinook, however, and another warm wind, driving rain before it, roared through the Cascades in early December. This storm washed away the repairs made to the railroad and also did new damage. The shoo-fly curve, built around the collapsed Tunnel No. 7, was eroded away, along with many other sections of track. Little food or other provisions had been stockpiled at Monte Cristo, and without the railroad to replenish the supply, most of the residents were obliged to hike down the tracks to more suitable locations until the railroad was repaired. Only a few persons remained in Monte Cristo. Most of them were simply caretakers and their families, who maintained the mining and other commercial properties in the valley. Almost overnight Monte Cristo became a ghost town. But every able-bodied man was at work attempting to repair the railroad in order to restore production at the mines.

One casualty of the floods, the Skagit River steamer *Monte Cristo*, had delivered some of the first supplies up the river to Sauk City, prior to the construction of the railroad. The vessel struck a snag carried by the swollen Skagit and sank just off shore.

The weather returned to normal by Christmas, and the worst flood on record passed into history. The railroad company predicted that it would have the line in operation by the year's end. However, by that time train service had been restored only to Silverton, and repair work was being rushed above that town to permit reopening at the earliest possible date. The summer season of 1896 had been productive, but when the year ended Monte Cristo was a quiet place with few people on hand. No one was working except the men who remained to clear away the snow falling on the vacant buildings.

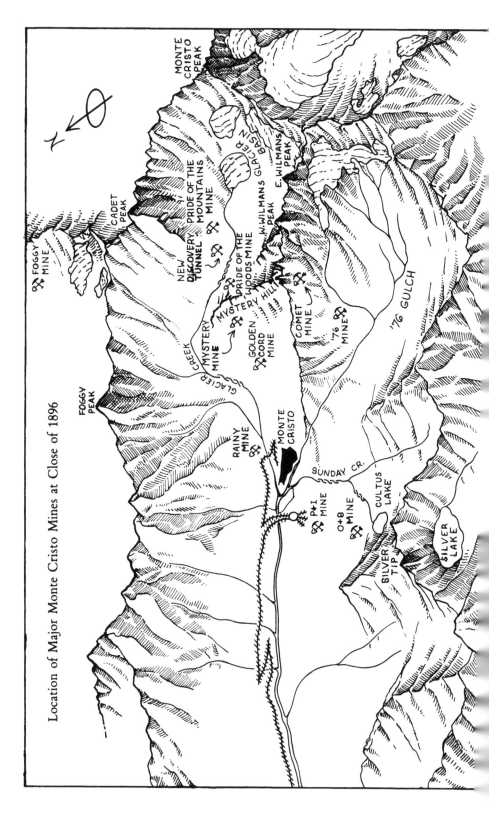

Location of Major Monte Cristo Mines at Close of 1896

MONTE CRISTO PEAK

CADET PEAK

FOGGY MINE

FOGGY PEAK

NEW DISCOVERY TUNNEL

PRIDE OF THE MOUNTAINS MINE

W. WILMANS GLACIER BASIN

W. WILMANS PEAK

E. WILMANS PEAK

PRIDE OF THE WOODS MINE

MYSTERY HILL

MYSTERY MINE

GLACIER CREEK

GOLDEN CORD MINE

COMET MINE

'76 MINE

'76 GULCH

RAINY MINE

MONTE CRISTO

SUNDAY CR.

P+I MINE

O+B MINE

CULTUS LAKE

SILVER TIP

SILVER LAKE

CHAPTER IX

1897

———————◆———————

DISASTER STRIKES

As 1897 began in the quiet, almost deserted town of Monte Cristo, the wife of one of the miners was about to give birth. Too far along in her pregnancy, she had been unable to walk from Monte Cristo to Silverton with the other women after the railroad was washed out. (At the time, trains were running only as far as Silverton.) The doctor had departed several weeks earlier, and the expectant mother was left in the care of the few women who remained in the town, while her husband hiked to Snohomish for medicine. During his absence she began her labor. The women became frightened, placed her on a push car, and headed down the tracks for Silverton and medical aid. Shortly after they left Monte Cristo, the infant was born, and the mother and child were returned to the town.

Despite the railroad washout, and resulting work stoppage, Monte Cristo soon had yet another mining company, the P & I. A development tunnel had been dug 135 feet on the property, which lay immediately below the O & B on the side of Toad Mountain. The mine was only a quarter mile from town, and the new firm made plans for a tramway to deliver the ore, once the ledge had been struck and production begun. The tunnel had exposed a vein of ore assaying $45 per ton, and the company anticipated finding more valuable mineral when the miners reached the main ledge.

Early in February, the company reopened the railroad, and the mines started up again. Near the end of the month, Monte Cristo shipped eleven carloads of concentrates to the smelter. The town was alive and in business again, and people had returned. Winter, however, had not yet relinquished its sovereignty. On Friday, March 19, the train from

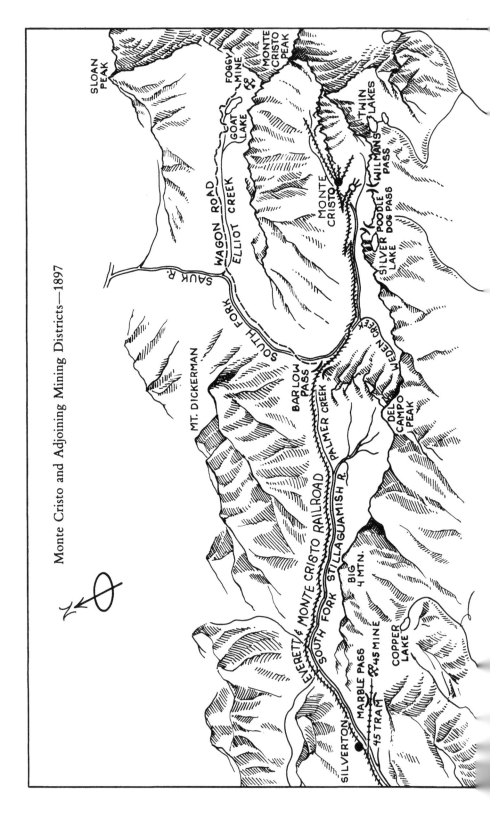

Monte Cristo and Adjoining Mining Districts—1897

SLOAN PEAK

MONTE CRISTO PEAK

FOGGY MINE

GOAT LAKE

TWIN LAKES

WAGON ROAD

ELLIOT CREEK

WILMANS PASS

MONTE CRISTO

SILVER LAKE

POODLE DOG PASS

SAUK R.

SOUTH FORK

WEDEN CREEK

DEL CAMPO PEAK

MT. DICKERMAN

BARLOW PASS

PALMER CREEK

EVERETT & MONTE CRISTO RAILROAD

SOUTH FORK STILLAGUAMISH R.

BIG 4 MTN.

MARBLE PASS

45 MINE

45 TRAM

SILVERTON

COPPER LAKE

N

Everett became snowbound at Barlow Pass and was forced to return to Silverton.

During the spring a new problem began to plague the mine operators when news of gold strikes in Alaska drew men away from Washington to seek their fortunes in the Klondike. Between the sick-list and miners departing for the Far North, the Mystery mine was short of men for the first time.

Ed Graham was one of the men who never made it to Alaska. He was killed by an avalanche on May 31, while descending the side of Wilmans Peak from the Mystery mine. Another man, who accompanied him, was only slightly injured. About the same time, the Mystery mine was the scene of an ore chute accident when Albert Croft, one of the miners, took a 144-foot plunge and badly smashed both legs. He survived, but a month passed before he was up and about again, with the aid of "two good, fast canes." The real tragedy of accidents such as these could have been told by Graham's widow and six chidren, who lived in the East and would now have to fend for themselves.

The P & I Mining Company commenced work on its mine on Monday, April 5, when its crew boarded the train for Monte Cristo. The first order of business was to drive the tunnel, already 135 feet long, another 100 feet to reach the ledge. Then the tramway could be built and production begin.

Higher up the side of Toad Mountain, the O & B, plagued by legal attachments in 1896, was operating with renewed vigor. The lower tunnel had opened a vein of solid ore fully 20 inches in width. But the lower tram terminal, crushed by the winter's snows, would have to be repaired before ore could be brought down.

J. B. Crooker and T. W. Foster, vice president and superintendent, respectively, of the railroad, visited Monte Cristo in April to plan for improvements to the facilities as the winter snows receded. Crooker announced that the company would build a new depot and install additional side tracks to handle the expanded mining activity during the coming summer. Land had already been granted to accommodate the widened right-of-way, and work was to begin immediately. By late April, the mines were shipping 1,000 tons of concentrates per week. Obviously the new facilities would be a welcome addition to the mining community.

Because Monte Cristo had become the center of much activity, a housing shortage more acute than the previous year's was at hand. To help meet the need, Jakie Cohen and Elizabeth Sheedy, long time operators of the Pride Hotel, announced plans to construct a splendid hostelry on Dumas Street. The building would be the glory of the town, with all the finest appointments. Construction would start as soon as the land was purchased. Six weeks later the roof was on the new hotel—which they called Rockefeller House—and the windows and doors were expected momentarily. An impressive structure, the building was three stories tall and stood out from the other establishments.

Tuesday, June 1, was something of a red letter day for Monte Cristo. Although the mining district was the smallest in the state, production had exceeded that of all the others combined. The total output to that date was calculated to be 3,500 carloads of gold and silver ore. Assuming that a carload averaged 25 tons, this amounted to 87,500 short tons or 85,500 long tons. This material had been concentrated to 889 carloads of 25 long tons each, or about 22,500 long tons of concentrates shipped to the Everett smelter. The weekly production of Monte Cristo was exceeding, in some instances, that of the famous Trail Creek, B.C., mines, such as the War Eagle and the Le Roi. This had been accomplished without the contribution of the O & B or the Golden Cord, which were expected to begin shipments shortly, and further increase the output.

Those plans were temporarily stalled, however, when the upper bull wheel on the Toad Mountain tramway of the O & B cracked, thus halting attempts to ship ore from that mine. Not until mid-July did the O & B produce its initial shipment for the year, with "the first load sailing down...about 2 o'clock p.m. and making most pleasant music as it thundered into the ore bins." This was special, hand-sorted, highly argentiferous galena (containing a great amount of silver), and it was sent away for special processing. But the O & B was not the only mine making music pleasing to a miner's ear. At the P & I, the men's "heavy discharges of dynamite" shook up the town "with great regularity" and sounded quite business-like. Superintendent John J. Folstad's miners also produced visual effects; they "had the crest of Toad Mountain looking like a volcano with heavy smoke from a charcoal pit" where they were making "their season's supply of charcoal for sharpening drill, picks and gads."

The Penn Mining Company, operating in the Goat Lake area, reported it

The Penn Mining Company's Foggy Mine above Goat Lake. The tunnel which begary here bored through the ridge, emerging on the other side above the Mayflower Glacier. The upper buildings were set into a notch in the cliff, and the lower buildings were built like ramps to ward off the avalanches which roared down from Osceola Pass, fifteen hundred feet above. This proved to be wise construction practice, for portions of the structures were still standing in 1925. The decay of the wood finally caused the collapse of all the buildings by 1965.

had made considerable progress on the long crosscut tunnel it was driving through the ridge, 1,500 feet above the south end of the lake. On June 15 the company estimated it would reach the main ledge of ore on the east side of Cadet Peak by early fall. All material brought into the Goat Lake region still had to be hauled by wagon teams from the railroad at Barlow Pass up the puncheon road, floated across the lake, then winched up the snowfield to the mine. According to rumors a spur line was to be built from the railroad to Goat Lake, but nothing happened in the way of construction.

About the middle of May, F. A. Bass had been in Monte Cristo, making the necessary preparations to reopen the Golden Cord mine, which he leased from the Wilmans brothers. They did not renew the lease, however, and upon returning to Monte Cristo in late June were dismayed to find their property stripped of everything that hadn't been tied down. Once again in charge of the mine, the Wilmans Mining Company put two shifts of men to work, and production commenced. Apparently the Monte Cristo Mining Company engaged the Sullivan Mining Company to drill the core holes in the '76 mine which had been started the previous year but interrupted by the winter. Sullivan then leased two boilers and hauled them to the mine to supply power to the diamond core drill's engine (taken to the mine the previous year) and began core drilling.

Meanwhile, the Monte Cristo Mining Company had bored the No. 3, or lower, tunnel of the Mystery mine under Glacier Basin, and by July 16 the air drills were at work blasting a raise from the Mystery No. 3 upward to the New Discovery workings of the Pride of the Mountains claim in Glacier Basin. The raise would ascend a vertical distance of over 400 feet, for a total slant distance of 600 feet, and would, for the first time, connect the Pride of the Mountains tunnels to those of the Mystery. When completed, it would allow materials to be brought up from, and ore dropped to, the lower, shorter aerial tram, without having to rely on surface transportation. The Monte Cristo Mining Company predicted that the raise would be completed and in use by the time snow began to fall, thus the miners could avoid traveling above ground during the winter.

The use of air drills in the Pride-Mystery complex increased production to three tons of ore per man each shift, boosting Monte Cristo's production to record rates. However, the ore in the Pride of the

Mountains continued to pinch out when the upper tunnels were drifted deeper into Cadet Peak. Meanwhile, the New Discovery, toward which the raise from the Mystery No. 3 was being bored, had encountered large lens-shaped bodies of ore along the lower portion of the vein. Because of this, the company decided to dismantle the upper terminal of the Pride of the Mountains tram, located on the northeast wall of Glacier Basin, and reassemble it at the New Discovery. The long span, which had presented such a technical challenge during its construction, was removed by a crew of men and pack animals who laboriously hauled the heavy cast iron machinery down the steep slopes to the new site, 400 feet lower than the old.

The railroad was running its popular weekend excursions to Monte

This scene is typical of mining practices with air drills in the 1890s. The drill has been fastened between the walls of the tunnel with a jack screw and is forced into the rock with the crank which the miner on the left is holding in his right hand. Compressed air entering via the hose operated a piston which hammered the drill bit into the rock face of the tunnel.

Cristo once again, and people all along the line, from Granite Falls to Everett, availed themselves of the opportunities to see the country. One person who had a unique way of enjoying the train rides was Frederick T. Gates, the railroad's president. Whenever he was in Washington and the weather permitted, Gates would ride the pilot beam (cow catcher) of the locomotive from Everett to Monte Cristo. He may have been operating the railroad as a business, but he intended to enjoy it while doing so.

Herman Siewart, the railroad's official photographer, spent some time in the Stillaguamish Canyon in late May, taking pictures on behalf of the company. While so doing, he probably saw the first cars of limestone shipped over the new suspension bridge and surface tram from the mine across the river from Tunnel No. 2. The rock was used to produce lime for the paper mill at Lowell and the smelter in Everett. The mine was owned in part by F. M. Headlee, one of the co-discoverers of Barlow Pass, and a resident of Snohomish. The shipments added handsomely to the revenues of the railroad. Local businessmen declared the quality of the lime to be far superior to that produced by quarries in the San Juan Islands at the northern end of Puget Sound, and the shipping was far less costly.

The summer in Monte Cristo had come and gone before anyone realized it, the routine of work seeming to blend each new day into the ones that had gone before. The season's first snowfall "below the regular snow line" occurred on the last day of August, eight days earlier than the previous year. The weather during the week had been "quite raw and cold, with snow falling on all the mountain tops every night."

The last of the popular excursions offered by the railroad took place on September 25, and a large crowd was on hand to see the mountains of Monte Cristo. They also saw, just below Silverton, the long tramway being built by the "45" Consolidated Mining Company (which recently had reorganized the old "45" mine and bought several other companies). The firm's short tram on the other side of Marble Pass had been completed, and the longer one now received the undivided attention of the work crews. Above Silverton, the passengers witnessed a remarkable amount of snow already on the mountains. The intense deep blue of the sky, the dazzling white of the snow-capped peaks, and the reds, golds, browns, and greens of autumn created a backdrop of splendor and beauty as the train negotiated the switchback on its approach to Monte Cristo. In fact, snow already lay on the ground in the village.

The snow made some residents uneasy, especially the ones who clearly recalled the disastrous chinook and warm rains of 1896. Consequently, several families had already left for the lowlands to spend the winter. Most remained, however, and the mines continued to produce at record rates. The P & I tunnel was now 250 feet long, and portions of the main ledge had been reached, revealing a promising amount of ore to be present. The O & B main tunnel was 300 feet in, showed good ore all the way, and negotiations were under way for construction of a concentrator that could process the low-grade ore. Currently, only the high-grade ore was being mined, and it was hand sorted before shipment to the smelter. At the Pride and Mystery, a mere 20 feet remained until the completion of the raise that would connect the mines underground, whereupon a larger force of men would be employed to handle the increased production.

Because the *Monte Cristo Mountaineer* had proved to be unprofitable, the newspaper's publisher, J. H. S. Bartholomew, announced it would be discontinued in early October. This chronicle had championed the cause of Monte Cristo throughout the glory years, and the town's residents were saddened to see it shut its doors. But close they did, and the subscription list passed to the *Silverton Miner* to continue the regional news reporting, while Bartholomew left the region, taking his press with him.[1]

Silverton was one of the principal station stops on the railroad; thus it had become a bustling town by 1897. During the spring months "the sound of the axe and saw" could be heard everywhere in the settlement. The community boasted six hotels, five saloons, and four general stores. In addition, it supported two meat markets, and the same number each of lumber yards, carpenter shops, restaurants, laundries, and barber shops. The village also had one newspaper, a shoe repair shop, an assayer, and one stationery and cigar store. The railroad company decided that the town had become sufficiently prominent to warrant a depot, and within a few weeks the site had been chosen and lumber was on the ground. During the week of May 21, Herman Siewart visited the town and took pictures to be used in a brochure promoting the splendors of the Monte Cristo line.

The mineral deposits surrounding Silverton appeared to have enormous potential—mostly in copper—and some mines were already shipping hand-picked ore to the smelters in Tacoma and Everett. Perhaps symbolic of faith in the community, several companies were considering plans to construct tramways and concentrators to ship and process the ores.

The most ambitious firm was the "45" company, whose mine was in the valley of Williamson Creek, beyond 4,170-foot Marble Pass. The company was erecting a tramway over the pass to the railroad, a distance of more than two miles. Mining was already in progress on the "45," making it imperative that the tram be completed quickly, before the ore bins were full; otherwise the miners would be forced to cease operations. In fact, by early May the "45" mine had amassed an impressive amount of ore in its bins. The owners announced plans to construct a warehouse and ore bunkers at the railroad, just below Silverton, to be connected by the aerial tramway to the mine.

Six months later, the tram was about completed and ready to begin transporting ore to the bunkers. The bins at the mine were filled to capacity with 2,000 tons of ore, and immediate shipment was necessary, or mining would have to stop. The final tensioning of the tramway cable was being accomplished, although the snow continued to pile ever deeper on the mountainsides. Winter was upon the mountains earlier this year than it had been in 1896.

Tuesday, November 16, dawned gray and threatening in the Cascade Mountains, and the temperature climbed above the freezing level at Monte Cristo. The snow, which had been falling steadily for several days, turned to rain, and avalanches thundered into the valleys, the snow having become heavy and unstable. The next day the rain increased and the temperature climbed even higher. A strong chinook now abetted the action of the clouds that were carrying moist marine air into the mountains. The result was a deluge, the water falling in great sheets upon the rocky slopes. As they had the previous year, the rivers rose rapidly toward flood stage. While the storm raged, the daily passenger train made its way up the Stillaguamish Canyon, and the crew and passengers were able to see first-hand the power of nature. They watched the foaming torrent, almost level with the tracks, gnaw on the riprap and log cribbing which tenuously held the road to the canyon walls. The train arrived safely in Monte Cristo that afternoon, but the crew dared not attempt to return to Everett that evening.

Citizens and visitors alike became alarmed. This couldn't happen two years in a row—or could it?

On Thursday, the rain fell harder than before and the temperature rose even higher. The babbling Stillaguamish, described by the syndicate as a "trout stream," became a raging torrent and flowed through Tunnels No. 1 and No. 6 to a depth of several feet. All traffic on the railroad halted, the telegraph line went down, and nothing definite could be learned of the road's condition. Wednesday's train was left trapped at Monte Cristo.

The scene on Friday, November 19, was one of nature on a mad rampage. The rain came down in torrents and the normally placid streams in Monte Cristo rose to levels never before seen or imagined. Glacier Creek flowed through the stables, and the animals had to be cut loose to fend for themselves, else they would have drowned. Water coursed down the mountainsides where streams had never been know to flow before. Monte Cristo, located at the junction of Glacier and '76 Creeks, caught the brunt of the flood. The trestles carrying the railroad across the Sauk River just below the depot were washed away, and the surging water ate so deeply into the bank the depot itself was threatened. The town's terrified residents could only stand by helplessly on the high ground and watch the flood cut its destructive swaths. The accompanying roar was awesome, like a titanic surf driven before hurricane winds. The temperature rose to 61° and the rain, driven relentlessly before the chinook, continued to swell the streams and rivers until they rose far above the levels of the previous year.

The new side tracks at Monte Cristo survived the onslaught, but only because they were held in place by several loaded ore cars parked upon them. The remainder of the railroad fared less favorably, and bridge after bridge was washed away and smashed to flotsam. All through the Stillaguamish Canyon the log and timber cribbing crumpled like jackstraws and was swept downstream by the torrent. The tunnels in the canyon became packed with debris, part of it fragments of the bridges that had been destroyed farther upstream. One span of the Howe through-truss bridge was ripped from its support pier by another bridge carried down against it. This caused the larger span to drop into the foaming eddies, and it too was demolished. All communications were knocked out, and no one dared move into the mountains, all paths of travel having been cut by the flood.[2]

The rain abated on Saturday and the temperature dropped 24 degrees in as many hours to a more seasonable level. The next day the full extent of the damage caused by the storm began to be appreciated, when people, bewildered and dazed by the weather's violence, emerged from their shelters to observe what nature, running amok, had accomplished. T. W. Foster, the railroad's superintendent, walked from Robe, at the head of the canyon, to Granite Falls, and reported that the entire five miles of roadbed in the canyon was gone. Not damaged, but gone. Only the tunnels, some packed with debris and huge boulders, remained to remind one that a railroad had, at one time, run through the canyon. The passenger train which had gone up to Monte Cristo on Wednesday was now stranded.

Surprisingly, the mines at Monte Cristo sustained relatively minor damage. But, without the ability to ship ore, they were closed until the railroad could be rebuilt. The tramways had sustained only slight damage, but they were now useless unless the mines were operating, and they too were shut down. A few people left Monte Cristo for the low country, because food shortages were a real possibility. However, a small herd of beef cattle was driven into the town over the old wagon road in an attempt to prevent starvation. Although this was a noble effort, the snows were beginning to fall again, and soon no traffic would be able to move over the old road. Moreover, the railroad company announced that it could not possibly restore the line to operating condition before spring. This caused panic among those remaining in Monte Cristo, and many began the long walk out.

Leaving the town was not an easy task. The refugees were forced to walk more than 30 miles—14 to Silverton the first day and 17 to Tunnel No. 1 the next. Beyond that point, regular passenger trains ran to Everett, leaving Tunnel No. 1 late in the afternoon in order that people could make the trek from Silverton. A daily pack train operated on the old wagon road between Tunnel No. 1 and Silverton to prevent the valley from becoming completely isolated.

The "45" Consolidated mine at Silverton was forced, along with the rest of the mines, to discontinue operations because, with the bins full, no place remained to store additional ore. Ironically, the railroad was destroyed the very week that the "45" Consolidated completed its tramway and was on the brink of success. All mining activity in the Stillaguamish and Monte Cristo districts had come to a halt.

Parker McKenzie, a well known real estate man and contractor, walked from Silverton to Snohomish in December. His story, told to the *Snohomish County Tribune*, was perhaps typical of those who fled Monte Cristo:

> He says the trip along the road is well worth taking, owing to the wonderful manifestations of the power of the flood. In one place a heavy steel rail is coiled like a spiral spring and stands straight up in the air. Another place a steel rail sticks out over the bank sixty feet or more and right at the end, within ten inches of the fish plate is broken square off. Again the ties will all be loosed from the rails and all be carried along for hundreds of yards under the rails and all piled up like cordwood, the rails still being in place. Some places the force of the water was lengthwise the track and forced the rails in the position of letter N's making the road appear like bridge spans. Still another freak of the flood was the winding of a steel rail around a big spruce tree like a huge anaconda and then by some means tree and all is lifted ten feet in the air....Bridge 27 was washed down the river and landed squarely upon the piers of bridge 25 so that a few spikes are all that is needed to make bridge 25 good. These are only a few of the wonders of the flood which Mr. McKenzie reported. It is too bad he did not have a camera with him so that those unacquainted with him could be convinced of the strange powers of that fateful flood. [*Snohomish County Tribune*, December 17, 1897]

According to the rumors, the company planned to avoid the Stillaguamish Canyon when it rebuilt the railroad. Two disastrous floods had convinced its officials that the local people knew what they were talking about in 1892 when they had advised against building along the river. Engineer Barlow was finally vindicated in his view that it was not a safe place for a railway.

On December 11, Frederick Gates made an announcement in New York which shocked and stunned everyone connected with the mines at Silverton and Monte Cristo: the railroad would not be rebuilt. He stated that the road had "never paid dividends and the mines in which the owners were interested had not panned out." The line had been, he continued, a losing proposition, with the profits eaten up by the enormous maintenance costs, especially during the winters. Not enough freight was carried to make it pay; therefore it would remain closed.

The mine operators were not alone in decrying the closure of the railroad. The line had catered to a considerable tourist business during the summer months, and the excursionists also lamented the new state

Wallace & Callaway Photo
Tunnel number five can be seen through tunnel number four. The cross bracing was
required at the nearer tunnel due to the instability and constant shifting of the rock
through which it was bored. You are looking up the tracks toward Monte Cristo.

of affairs. The comments of one writer on the subject were printed in the *Snohomish County Tribune*:

> Now that it is announced that the Everett & Monte Cristo railroad will not be built, regret will be occasioned that the beautiful scenic route through the Stillaguamish canyon will be closed to tourists, and nothing will be more missed than the famous kissing tunnel which marked the entrance of the railroad into the canyon. This tunnel is 900 feet long, and from its cool depths flows mineral waters and across its echoing caverns stretches a belt of magnetic iron. This iron is the cause of the wonderful properties of the tunnel. Together with the ozone which the mineral waters of the tunnel produce, and the magnetic current which is occasioned by the passing of the train, passengers are seized with a remarkable osculatory desire. Men have even been known to kiss their wives under the influence of the magnetic current, while callow youths never stopped kissing from the time the train entered the tunnel to the time it emerged from the other side. The lamps were never lighted while going through the tunnel, and the echoes of the puffs of the engine and the noise of the train drowned the loud resounding smacks which would otherwise have shocked elderly ladies and newspaper men. When the tunnel was passed, the train again came out in the sunlight, girls would be seen arranging their hair, wives would be blushing pleasantly and old maids sitting in seats with gentlemen would be noticed to be wearing a joyous smile. The things had long attracted the attention of a naturally observant reporter, but as he was of a timid and retiring nature, and never presumed to sit next to a lady while passing through the tunnel, the true state of affairs remained a mystery. . . . The snap was first given away when an elderly milliner from Seattle overcome by the magnetic current threw herself upon Conductor Speer and overwhelmed him with caresses. The road promptly sent her a bill for twenty kisses at 5 cents each. But the final exposé came when an excursion train packed with rosy-cheeked girls and their lovers stopped square in the middle of the tunnel, giving them full shock of the subtle sweet fluid. The unfortunate men who were alone in this car unfeelingly yelled "break away", "rats", "here comes the light", "I'll tell ma", but the force of the current could not be overcome, and since then the tunnel has been known as the kissing tunnel. [*Snohomish County Tribune*, December 17, 1897]

While some people could take the closing of the line lightheartedly, as witnessed by the foregoing, men with jobs or fortunes invested along the line could not. Monte Cristo was suddenly almost back where it had been in 1892—without transportation or communication of any kind.

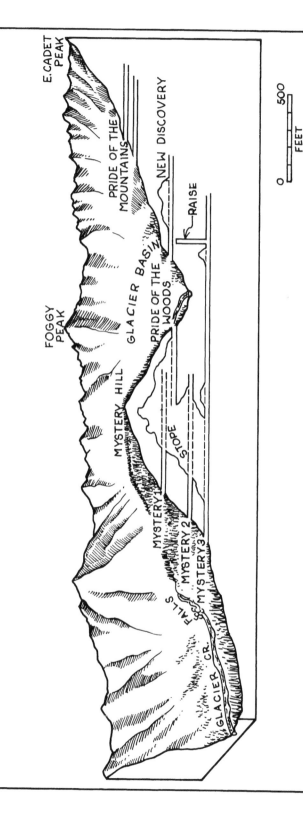

Cross Section of Pride-Mystery Mine Complex, Looking North, as the Tunnels and Stopes were Situated in Late 1897

CHAPTER X

1897-1901

ROCKEFELLER'S POWER PLAY

The unthinkable had happened: the pair of slender steel ribbons which had been Monte Cristo's lifeline was gone. News that the Everett and Monte Cristo Railway had closed was met with disbelief and anger by Stillaguamish and Sauk businessmen. While some development work could continue at the mines, shipping ore was now impossible. Consequently, the mines could not produce even when sufficiently developed. Rumors flew thick and fast that the refusal by the Rockefeller interests to rebuild the line was a bluff to gain control of the mining properties or to force higher freight rates for mineral shipments. Residents along the abandoned route declared that it was only a matter of time before the local miners built a new railroad themselves.

But the fact remained that Frederick T. Gates, acting on Rockefeller's behalf, had decided in 1894 that the individual companies were to be business ventures which would rise or fall on their own merits, and the railway had fallen. If a giant like Rockefeller had failed, could local men succeed?

On December 13, 1897, the *Seattle Post-Intelligencer* placed the blame for the situation squarely where it belonged:

> As to the question whether the railroad has paid, there are some facts which Mr. Crooker has overlooked. The preliminary survey was made by M. Q. Barlow, an engineer who was thoroughly familiar with the peculiarities of the Puget sound country and its climate. He found two routes, one down the Sauk and the north fork of the Stillaguamish to a connection with the Seattle & International [formerly the Seattle, Lake Shore and Eastern] at Arlington; the other down the south fork of the Stillaguamish to a connection at Hartford Junction. The former was pre-

ferable, on the ground of cost and good grades, but the latter was chosen on account of the good indication of minerals then found at Silverton, and because it was a more direct route to Everett, the objective point, thus reducing the mileage on which trackage must be paid to the Seattle & International. This decision was reached in face of the declaration of Mr. Barlow that it was a "hell of a rough country to get through." Knowing the country and having seen the river at a freshet, Mr. Barlow ran a line high above its ordinary stage of water. This necessitated long high trestles and deep side-hill cuts, which were very expensive. His work was reviewed by another engineer whose experience had been chiefly in the prairie states and who was expected to find a less expensive line. He found it by coming down into the canyon, in spite of warnings as to the wickedness of the river when on a rampage, and by making a series of tunnels and cribs on sharp curves. It was washed out in 1892, when half finished, and has had the same experience every November. It is true that it has never paid interest on its cost, but last year that was not the fault of the traffic, but of its location. In 1896 it earned $50,000 over operating expenses and this was to have been used in paying interest, but the annual washout compelled its expenditure in repairs. There was a large increase in the net earnings this year, but the whole road has been swept out of the canyon. [*Seattle Post-Intelligencer*, December 13, 1897]

Contrary to the news releases, the railroad was not entirely out of business. Regularly scheduled trains operated daily to Tunnel No. 1 to meet the wagon train from Silverton, which used the old puncheon road. Shipments from the shingle mills between Granite Falls and Hartford also provided a brisk business. Shortly after the washout, the railroad company approached two major enterprises and inquired whether they would favor greatly increased freight rates if the line were rebuilt. The "45" Consolidated Mining Company politely rejected the offer, but the Penn Mining told the railroad to "go to hell"—it would build its own line rather than submit to rate blackmail. Immediately thereafter Gates announced that the route would remain dormant. The "45" Consolidated then made tentative plans to construct a road—either wagon or rail—from its property down the Sultan River basin. During the winter, the company did the survey work for a rail line, and indicated that construction would begin when the weather permitted.

Despite the earlier announcements, the Everett and Monte Cristo Railway quietly began rebuilding the line from Tunnel No. 1 through

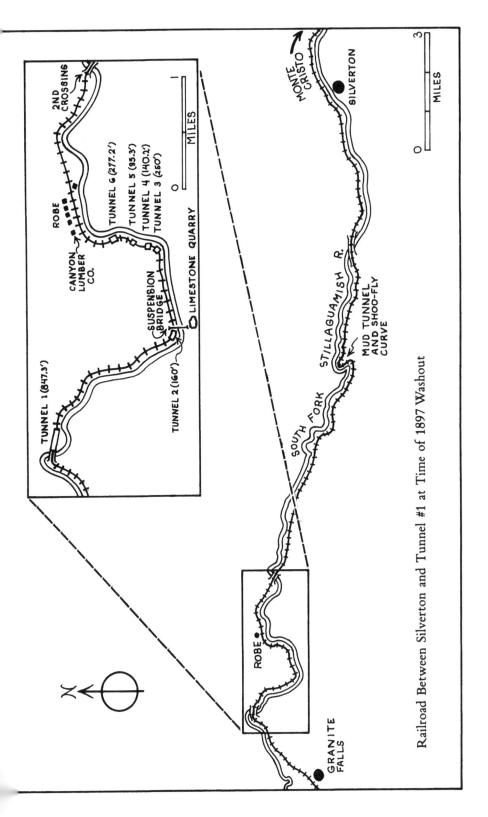

Railroad Between Silverton and Tunnel #1 at Time of 1897 Washout

No. 2 in order that limestone could be shipped from the quarry. Because the rock from this area was of high quality and in great demand, the railroad felt it was economically feasible to rebuild the line through Tunnel No. 2. This spurred rumors that the tracks would be restored as far as the Robe shingle mill, at the canyon's head, to allow shipment of shingles from that establishment. The next step would then be extension to Silverton and the "45" mine. But talk of rebuilding beyond Tunnel No. 2 remained a rumor during the winter of 1897-98.

The major mines and concentrator at Monte Cristo were closed and had been reported to be "abandoned to the owls and avalanches." This was not entirely accurate because a few men had been employed to maintain and secure the properties. All other personnel, however, had left the town by the end of 1897, and with the advent of the new year Monte Cristo was virtually deserted. But the miners were not totally dismayed by the washout. On January 7, John J. Folstad arrived in Monte Cristo to start work on the P & I mine. C. H. Packard and C. F. Jackson formed a new company, the Philo, with properties located adjacent to the Mystery and Pride of the Woods on Mystery Hill.

Although Monte Cristo refused to die, it had become a quiet place. The concentrator was looked after, as were the supplies in the mercantile company's store. No goods were sold from the latter, but a man was in charge of the place. This led to rumors that the items were to be used during the coming season to aid in reopening the mines.

The railroad company had not entirely vetoed rebuilding, and survey teams cruised both north and south of the Stillaguamish Canyon, seeking a new, safer route for the line. Meanwhile, reconstruction of the railroad through Tunnel No. 2 continued into March, in order that the valuable lime quarried at that point could be shipped to market.

At Goat Lake, the Penn Mining Company employed a force of 15 men throughout the winter. The workers continued to bore the big crosscut tunnel beneath Osceola Pass, south of the lake, and had penetrated more than 1,300 feet into the ridge by late February.

Meanwhile, an action occurred in Everett that was to have far-reaching and long-range impact in western Washington. The Puget Sound Reduction Company decided to install an arsenic extraction plant at its smelter. The demand for arsenic trioxide as an insecticide and industrial reagent had made such a facility feasible, and since much of the ore in the area contained up to 27% arsenic, locating it in Everett was logical. The new addition would make the concern the largest arsenic extractor in the world, with the possible exception of one in Wales. As a consequence, the company could pay higher rates for ores brought from the Cascades, and this in turn meant that some of the marginal mines could be opened. The costs could be reduced even more by the addition of still another improvement—a refining plant (long in the rumor stage) able to manufacture gold 24 karats fine from the Doré bars produced by the smelter.[1]

On May 6, 1898, General Manager J. B. Crooker of the Everett and Monte Cristo Railway announced the company's intention to rebuild the line as far as the shingle mill in order to retrieve several boxcars loaded with shingles, and to obtain a stockpile of steel rails to be used on spurs and repairs elsewhere along the right-of-way. The work would be of a temporary nature, because survey crews were still seeking a permanent route which would avoid the canyon. This news rekindled hopes among the miners, since most of the roadbed was intact between the canyon's head and Silverton; to reach the town all that would have to be replaced was the Howe truss bridge at the second crossing of the Stillaguamish.

While awaiting completion of the tracks up the canyon, an enterprising Silverton resident named Dan Sutherland established his own railroad on the deserted right-of-way between the town and the second crossing washout. The rolling stock consisted of one push car powered by gravity when going down the line, by elbow grease when coming up. Sutherland whimsically named the makeshift company the Silverton, Mud Tunnel, and Great Western Railway. He made a daily round trip to pick up and deliver mail and supplies sent across the Stillaguamish via a temporary cable tram at the site of the missing bridge. In keeping with the name, a trip along the right-of-way was described as "exciting and novel in the extreme," the management guaranteeing "more scenery, short curves and hair breadth escapes to the rod than on any other railroad in the United States."

The Rockefeller interests, represented by J. B. Crooker, filed suit against two mining companies—the Pride of the Mountains and the Mystery—on April 18, 1898. The suit was accompanied by a petition requesting that William C. Butler, superintendent of the companies, be appointed receiver. The court granted the petition, and the mortgages on the mines, held by a New York trust company, were foreclosed.

This action forced many of the smaller co-owners of the companies out of business. Since Rockefeller controlled the trust company which held the mortgages, he had now gained exclusive control of the major properties at Monte Cristo. The *Engineering and Mining Journal*, along with several local newspapers, predicted that with the final consolidation of his interests in the mines, Rockefeller would quickly rebuild the railroad.

But predictions and rumors did not transport goods, and late in April the Penn Mining Company, still operating at Goat Lake, was forced to cut its crew to eight men due to lack of food and other supplies. Then, in June, the "45" Consolidated Mining Company asked for bids to haul 3,000 tons of ore from its mine near Silverton. The bids were expected to be quite high, because they would have to include the costs of construction and maintenance of a road to the property. The "45" company had discovered that surveying for a railroad and constructing one were two quite different matters. The company's railroad never materialized. But rumors persisted that the Everett and Monte Cristo had submitted a bid to ship the ore, which would have necessitated immediate reconstruction of its line to Silverton. Nothing happened, however, and in September the "45" Consolidated Mining Company announced it would build a wagon road up the Sultan Valley to transport its ore from the mine. Then, having concluded that the Monte Cristo line would not be rebuilt, the "45" company packed out the few tons of ore which had been transported over its aerial tramway to the Silverton bunkers just prior to the washout, and put 50 men to work on the route along the Sultan.

Conjecture on the fate of the railroad came from every quarter, while survey crews charted routes on the flanks of Green Mountain and Mount Pilchuck, north and south of the canyon. Another proposal—to rebuild through the canyon at a higher elevation—meant that the tunnel roofs would have to be raised, and the cribbing anchored to the rock walls to prevent washout. But, while the rumors flew, the railroad quietly began removing the temporary trackage from the canyon in late September, 1898, to avoid losing the precious rails to another November flood. During the summer, access had been provided to the shingle mill at Robe, and the boxcars recovered. Much to the consternation of the mining men up the line, however, two miles of rails were torn up just below the second crossing bridge washout to be used elsewhere.

The company made no attempt to replace the bridge, estimated to cost $16,000, which would have permitted extension of the line to Silverton.

When 1898 ended, nothing had been resolved concerning the railroad's reconstruction. No major shipment or development work had been possible at the mines during the year, and hope was fading for many small companies and businessmen as mortgages were foreclosed on their properties.

On January 7, 1899, William C. Butler, receiver of the Mystery and Pride of the Mountains, deeded the assets of the two mining companies to J. B. Crooker, thus making official the control of the properties by the Rockefeller interests. The amount Rockefeller paid was $328,071.94, which represented the total debts of the two companies. The stockholders in the old companies were allowed to retain shares in the new company by paying an assessment of about $101.50 on each 1,000 shares of old stock held by them. The men who had thought the refusal to rebuild the railroad was a ploy to gain full control of the mining properties were now certain of it, as the evidence at hand demonstrated. In March the two companies were combined, together with the assets of the United Concentration Company, into one large concern, the Monte Cristo Company. This action gave Rockefeller ownership of both the mining and shipping aspects of the business. Since he already possessed the railroad and smelter, his consolidation was now complete. Anyone who harbored doubts about Frederick Gates' effectiveness as a corporate manipulator and administrator had to be simply unaware of what had happened. With all aspects of the business in his control, and acting on Rockefeller's behalf, Gates could now either operate the properties or dispose of them as he saw fit. Many mining men "hailed with delight" the consolidation and saw in it the seeds of renewed prosperity for the Monte Cristo district.

The situation at Monte Cristo in January, 1899, could perhaps be summed up best by a bit of "mountain wisdom" that appeared in a Montana newspaper, the *Helena Independent*, in 1895:

> Drink, and the gang drinks with you;
> Swear off, and you go it alone;
> For the barroom bum who drinks your rum
> Has a quenchless thirst of his own.
> Feast, and your friends are many;

Fast, and they cut you dead;
They'll not get mad if you treat them bad,
So long as their stomach is fed.
Steal, if you get a million,
For then you can furnish bail;
It's the great big thief that gets out on leave,
While the little one goes to jail.

[*Helena Independent,* reprinted in the *Everett Herald,* December 19, 1895]

By March, the railroad was again laying tracks up the old right-of-way in the Stillaguamish Canyon toward Robe. Officially, the road was to be rebuilt only to the shingle mill at Robe, but—as an article in the *Snohomish County Tribune* noted—work was, in fact, performed above that location. However, during an interview with J. B. Crooker, the reporter could learn nothing concerning the rebuilding except that Tunnel No. 1 was being strengthened.

Rockefeller visited Everett in June. By appointment, both he and James J. Hill—builder of the Great Northern—arrived in their private railway coaches to discuss Everett's future. Rockefeller had long desired to sell his shares in the Everett Land Company, as well as the wharves, waterworks, street railway, and other properties connected with the city. The question had always been who would purchase them. Having chosen Everett as a main stop on his railroad, Hill felt that he could not allow the city to fail because that would prove detrimental to the railroad. Besides, Hill had other plans for Everett.

During their brief meeting—it lasted one afternoon—Hill purchased all of Rockefeller's interests in Everett. The newspapers speculated that Hill had also bought the Monte Cristo railroad, but that proved to be unfounded. The *Snohomish County Tribune* decried the sale, stating: "The City of Chimneys, Snohomish County's pride, the Gem of Port Gardner and the Whaleback's home, is doomed. . . . No more will the boomer boom, or the land shark prosper." Although Rockefeller retained control of the railroad and the mining and smelting companies, he did not consider Monte Cristo worth visiting during his only trip to the region.

Mining did not interest Hill, but timber did. Frederick Weyerhaeuser, a close friend and associate, had become a lumber baron in the Midwest before Hill's railroad reached the coast. Weyerhaeuser had had a long discussion with Hill concerning the industry's decline in the central states and its potential on the Pacific coast. He visited Everett and decided to relocate there. With this in mind, Hill bought the Rockefeller interests in Everett. The city was destined to become a timber town, and Hill's associate was to be its driving force. This would guarantee Hill's railroad a large share of the lumber shipping business, because the major markets for the product were in the East and the Midwest.

Mining activity at Monte Cristo was now at a virtual standstill, as supplies coming into the area slowed to a trickle. Only minor development work was being done. On the other hand, at Goat Lake the Penn Mining Company was driving its long tunnel with dogged determination. By early July it had been bored 2,700 feet into the mountain and had tapped no less than ten ore bodies within the ridge. The company planned to work throughout the winter despite the difficulty it faced in obtaining supplies. The "45" Consolidated Mining Company, which was running short of money, had been mortgaged for $50,000 to Charles D. Pinkham, son of Lydia Pinkham of patent medicine fame, while "the big '45' tram swayed idly in the wind in silent protest." The extra funds were required because the construction of the wagon road down the Sultan Valley had badly drained the company's treasury.

When the year 1900 arrived, it was accompanied by rumors that the Everett and Monte Cristo Railway was soon to be sold to the Northern Pacific. As proof, the newspapers pointed out that H. H. Warner, master mechanic for the Northern Pacific at Edison, Washington, had been observed examining the Everett and Monte Cristo's properties. But no official announcement was made until February 3. The Northern Pacific, which had sought access to Everett, did not purchase the entire railroad, but only that portion between Snohomish and Everett, together with all shops and yards in the latter. The Monte Cristo line retained trackage rights into Everett, as well as its rolling stock and tools, plus the 42 miles of its right-of-way from Hartford Junction to Monte Cristo.

The Everett and Monte Cristo Railway quickly announced that contracts had been let to rebuild the right-of-way into Monte Cristo. An arrangement had been made between the railroad and the "45" Consolidated company which guaranteed a minimum shipment of

3,000 tons of ore per month in return for reopening the road. In order to transport the ore to the Silverton bunkers the "45" Consolidated immediately began getting its long tramway ready. With this, a flurry of activity began up and down the line, as miners rushed back to their claims to prepare for the return of prosperity.

During April, Crooker announced that repair of the railroad's Bridge No. 16 at the second crossing of the Stillaguamish would begin at once. No chances were taken where the line passed through the canyon, although it followed the old right-of-way that had been plagued with so many problems. The tracks were set in concrete where they passed through Tunnel No. 6; beyond the tunnel, all the way to Robe, they were not only set in concrete but also supported by concrete retaining walls. Concrete was also used in the canyon at several other locations which had been vulnerable to washouts in the past.

The design of Bridge No. 16 at the second crossing was modified from that of its predecessor. Where a couple of through-span Howe truss bridges had been used previously, the company now employed a single span, located at a higher elevation, and the river bed was altered so that it passed straight beneath, making no turns. The engineers hoped this would preclude future washouts of the structure.

On Saturday, May 19, the first train in nearly two and a half years pulled into Silverton, and once again "the snort of the iron horse was heard in the streets."

> The train got in at 7 o'clock and the whole population was at the depot to greet it. The roar of giant powder filled the air. Capt. Price made a speech, Billy Lord recited an original poem, Wm. Bouck read the Omaha Platform, Dan Sutherland fell into the Stillaguamish, Superintendent Foster responded by giving three sole cheers for Queen Victoria and the E. & M.C., and Engineer Sutton donned his best clothes. [*Snohomish County Tribune*, May 25, 1900]

After all, it was an occasion to celebrate!

The telegraph office was quickly placed in working order, and communication with civilization established. By August trains made daily scheduled runs to Monte Cristo, and the work at the mines commenced. Monte Cristo, a ghost town for more than two years, had come back to life.

Josiah E. Spurr, a noted geologist employed by the United States Geological Survey, arrived at Monte Cristo in July, and remained for several months. His task was to establish, for the first time, a complete, comprehensive survey of the mineral deposits of the Monte Cristo Mining District. With all the experts and mining activity which had been concentrated at Monte Cristo during the past decade, no one could or would take the time to gather the enormous amount of data required to compile a comprehensive, in-depth study of the area's mineral resources. Spurr and his assistants would be the first to accomplish this task.

The geologists established an office in a small cabin near the concentrator at Monte Cristo. Spurr carried a portable barometer and compass with him on his daily treks to the various mines and mineral locations in order to accurately establish the elevation and position of the different places he visited. He gathered specimens, took photographs, and wrote copious notes of his observations. His assistants drew maps of the various mines and made drawings of the vein outcrops.

So great was the amount of data gathered, that it wasn't until 1902 that the monumental work was finally published, as part of the twenty-second annual report of the United States Geological Survey. In fact, Part II of the report was taken up entirely by *Ore Deposits of Monte Cristo, Washington*. This gave mining men their first opportunity to study—prior to making large-scale commitments for development work on a claim—the history, mineral content, and geologic processes which created the mineral deposits. The agency's teams had completed their map survey work several years earlier, and the quadrangles of Monte Cristo were also available. They provided details of the surface features, while Spurr's work supplied information on the subsurface structures.

The Everett and Monte Cristo Railway underwent reorganization on August 25, elected new officers, and dropped "Everett" from its name, becoming the Monte Cristo Railway Company. This action formally acknowledged the fact that the company's right-of-way no longer stretched to the "city of smokestacks," as Everett liked to be called. Work continued in earnest all along the line, and the railroad was put in condition to withstand the fury of another winter.

With the railroad operating again, the atmosphere in Monte Cristo was charged with excitement: the passenger trains were packed with former residents returning to pick up where they had left off almost three years earlier. Much had happened to everyone during their absence, and many were the tales related as old friends brought each other up to date. But, while the people had undergone change during the quiet years at Monte Cristo, the town had also been altered. The winter snows and spring storms had taken their toll. Houses had to be rebuilt or repaired, roads and trails leveled and graded, and, with winter approaching once again, wood had to be cut for fuel, food preserved for the long, cold months ahead.

At the mines, 60 men were put to work immediately by the Monte Cristo Company, which now controlled the Mystery and Pride mines, along with tramways and the concentrator. The mill was quickly put into operation and within three weeks was handling 70 tons of ore per day. The dynamo had suffered severe damage during the years of idleness, and required more than a month of repairs before it could be used. When it was finally operating, and again supplying power to the air compressor at the Mystery mine, the Burleigh drills were employed to finish the 600-foot raise to the New Discovery tunnel of the Pride of the Mountains in Glacier Basin. The raise, which was crucial to the underground connection of the mines, had been only about 20 feet short of completion when the railroad washout in 1897 halted its construction. The Monte Cristo Company estimated that at least ten years' supply of ore was at hand in the mines, and more would surely be found when the tunnels were bored to greater depths.

So great was the population explosion along the railway after its reopening, that Dick Terwilliger, a Republican Party organizer, considered it worthwhile to charter a passenger train and make a whistle-stop speaking tour just before the November elections. "The big fat man," as the rotund Terwilliger was known, held audiences spellbound when he spoke from the rear platform at stop after stop along the line. He claimed to have held one group's attention for "two hours and sixty-four minutes"; it must have been a long day. But the Democrats never attempted to gain equal time.

CHAPTER XI

1901-03

REBIRTH OF MINING

J. B. Crooker resigned as general manager of the Monte Cristo Railway
Company in early January, 1901, and local people voiced their desire
that he be replaced by a more liberal individual. Crooker's staunch Bap-
tist faith had prevented the railroad from running Sunday excursions to
Monte Cristo, for he had not been receptive to operating the line on the
Sabbath. J. O. Whitmarsh, a congenial fellow well known in the area,
took over as general superintendent. He re-established the Sunday ad-
ventures, and the railway quickly became the most popular tourist route
in western Washington.

During an excursion, the first impressions gained by those riding in
the open-top observation cars were usually sensations of awe and
splendor. An eye witness account printed in the *Everett Daily Herald*
illustrated the emotions involved:

> If you knew just what you are missing you wouldn't wait. Nobody
> asked me to write this, and it's not an advertisement, but I'm possessed
> of an impulse to talk of the place just as when you've been to see some
> famous painting and it has left its impress upon your mind in such a way
> that you feel you must tell your friends about it. . . . It's a most delightful
> ride of about three hours—which hardly seems one; and on your return
> trip you see more than when you go up, as you may comprehend. . . .
>
> Perhaps you've seen the mountains before. So had I, as we see
> them across a stretch of miles, as one travels back and forth across the
> continent, which is not by any means to be despised; but when you are
> taken right up a long, deep canyon till you come to a place where you
> can go no farther, and it's the end of the canyon, railroad and all—almost
> litterally bumping up against a gigantic mountain and stopping unex-

169

pectedly, and are set down in a great basin completely surrounded by
monster pyramids of solid rock walling you in from the outside world,
from which huge prison there is no escape save by the one gap through
which you came; with even the train's noise and commotion suddenly
hushed into a great stillness, and apparently nothing to be heard but the
distant splash and rush of the waters down the mountain sides; and you
stand in a sort of trance and look up speechless and bewildered at the
array before you. Then you may believe that you are actually in the presence of mountains and feel them vastly more. [*Everett Daily Herald*, July
6, 1901]

With descriptions like this, it is little wonder that the trip became immensely popular with tourists.

At Silverton, the "45" Consolidated Mining Company completed
restoration of its long aerial tramway, which had been delayed by the
winter snows, and expected to start transporting ore to the railroad by
July 1. At Monte Cristo, on the other hand, ore had been shipped
regularly throughout the winter. The raise from the Mystery to the
New Discovery tunnel of the Pride of the Mountains had been completed, and new drifts were being driven into Cadet Peak and under
Glacier Basin from this new shaft. They opened new ore bodies which
greatly increased the mine's output. Monte Cristo had returned to the
routine that had been abruptly disrupted in 1897, and it was difficult to
detect that any interruption had occurred.

The routine was not to be Monte Cristo's fate, however, for disaster
struck the Pride of the Mountains mine on Friday, June 15, when the
headhouse was consumed by fire. No one was injured, but forty boxes
of dynamite were destroyed and many tools were lost. Production at the
mine came to a halt while the men were put to work repairing the damage. Three weeks elapsed before the mine was again capable of deliver-
ing ore to the concentrator.

With no way to extinguish them, fires were a constant menace to remote settlements in this age of wooden structures. On July 8, Lee's
store in Silverton was reduced to ashes, just as the proprietors, after
weathering the hard times, were beginning to benefit from the new
wave of prosperity. On July 17, three dry kilns of the Canyon Lumber
Company in Robe were destroyed; but, through hard work, and luck,
the mill was saved.

On Sunday, July 14, the railroad ran an excursion to Monte Cristo with some new equipment. In addition to the usual passenger coaches, the train pulled four observation cars attached at the rear. They were open-topped and equipped with bench seats, thus giving the riders an unobstructed view of the scenery. Whenever the weather cooperated, they were the most sought-after seats on the train. So popular, in fact, were these Sunday excursions, that on July 28 the train consisted of six coaches and four observation cars hauled by two locomotives, and accommodated 500 passengers. Superintendent Whitmarsh had had a pavilion erected on Sunday Flats near the base of Sunday Falls, above Monte Cristo, where the tourists could, when the journey ended, have a leisurely lunch and enjoy the sparkling water and surrounding attractions. Or, if they were so inclined, they could take a guided tour through the concentrator to learn about the ore concentration process.

The first run of the "45" Consolidated's tramway near Silverton was made on July 4, and a month later ore was arriving at the railway at the rate of 40 tons per day. This amounted to 1,200 tons per month, and with 20,000 tons in the mine's bunkers it would require almost a year and a half to transport it, even if additional tunneling was not done. But mining continued without letup, and the future looked sanguine for the company.

Fire was again a major news item when the business district of Hartford—the lower terminus of the railway—burned on September 2. The hotel, saloon, general store, post office, and several other businesses and private homes were destroyed. A week later, the Canyon Lumber Company at Robe, damaged by fire earlier in the year, was again its victim when another dry kiln and 60,000 feet of lumber were lost. As earlier, the mill itself was saved from destruction.

The last excursion for the year was run in mid-September, when the weather began to foretell winter's approach. Snow was already half way down the mountainsides by September 26. The rotary plow was placed in readiness to maintain regular daily schedules throughout the long winter months, and a shed was constructed over the turntable at Monte Cristo to prevent the pit from filling with snow and thus stopping the table from turning. On prior occasions, the snow had been shoveled by hand to enable the engine or rotary plow to be turned, a long and laborious task. The new building would greatly facilitate the handling of equipment at the Monte Cristo end of the line during the winter.

However, Whitmarsh put to rest the fears of flooding during the coming season:

> We have put new riprapping in along the canyon, and the road's apparently secure against floods should they come. But the present indications are that there will be but little high water. Practically all the old snow is gone from the mountains, and none has fallen during this month. It is the October snows we fear most, and ordinarily the fall during this month is heavy. In November usually follow warm chinook winds, melting the snow and causing the floods from which we have suffered most in the past. But October this year has been a remarkable month, and I look for no devastating floods along our line. [*Everett Daily Herald*, October 29, 1901]

At Monte Cristo, 150 men were at work in the Mystery and Pride mines, and operations continued throughout the winter. The concentrator was remodelled to bring it up to current standards, since most of the machinery was almost ten years old, and much the worse for wear. The possibility of operating it with water power rather than steam was explored because Glacier Falls would easily provide an adequate water head and the company would not have to pay the cost of hauling coal up the railroad. But, while hydropower was considered and available, it was never used at the concentrator.

The Everett smelter was expanded to handle the new activity. Roasters were added to treat the ores containing arsenic and sulphur, and two boilers, stripped from the defunct nail works, were installed to provide additional and standby power for the operation. The steady production of ore from the Monte Cristo and Silverton mines, in addition to that bought elsewhere, kept the facility operating continuously.

On December 23, the last nail was driven on the turntable shed at Monte Cristo, just as the season's first heavy snowfall began. By Christmas eve, 18 inches had accumulated on the ground, and the town took on its customary winter mantle. Few people left to spend the winter elsewhere, because renewed confidence in the railroad convinced most of the residents that it was now safe to remain. The roadbed had been reconstructed along a much more solid plan than originally and little chance was seen for a repeat of 1897. When 1901 was ushered out and 1902 began, Monte Cristo was the same bustling community that it had been during the summer months.

Silverton was also a beehive of activity, and new residences and business buildings were constructed at a feverish pace. The snow did not diminish the excitement in the town or in the surrounding hills. The Independent began production, sending its first load of ore to the smelter on January 10. Many mines approached their production phase, spurred on by the success of the "45" Consolidated, whose long tramway system had been transporting ore to the railroad for six months. The Bonanza Queen installed a 12-drill air compressor, and planned to add a concentrator. Visitors to Silverton stated that they had never seen the area in such a state of agitation. Development work continued to uncover new veins of copper-rich ore, and additional Eastern capital poured into the district.

By the middle of February, the Monte Cristo Company's mines were producing an average of 150 tons of ore per day. This output was concentrated to 35 to 50 tons for shipment to the smelter.

John Ramdio, a tunnelman in one of the mines, met with a serious accident in May when he was caught in a premature powder explosion while boring a new crosscut tunnel. He was taken to the Everett City Hospital, where he was reported to be "receiving repairs to various portions of his anatomy." He suffered from severe lacerations on his legs, a badly mangled left hand, and a left eye so terribly injured the doctors expressed doubt he would regain his sight in it. Such were often the prices paid in this dangerous occupation.

On Monday, May 19, railway company officials announced a summer schedule that provided Monte Cristo with daily passenger service. The train would leave Everett at 9:30 A.M. and return at 5:00 P.M. The company also commenced excursions, to be operated on the same basis as they had been during the prior year, including the use of the popular open-top observation cars at the rear. Connections were arranged with trains from Seattle so that passengers traveling from that city to Monte Cristo would be able to make the round trip in a single day with minimum delay.

One of the Monte Cristo trains, running westbound just below Granite Falls, rounded a curve and came upon a crew of Japanese section hands who were frantically attempting to lift their hand car from the track. They were too late—the locomotive, unable to stop, struck and demolished the car, sending M. Kusumi and G. Shimooka to the hospital. Fortunately, their injuries were not too serious, and they were soon back on the job servicing the tracks for the railroad.

MONTE CRISTO RY.

Scenic Line of the Northwest

The only line to the Silverton, Goat Lake and Monte Cristo Mining Districts

MONTE CRISTO RAILWAY
Station foot of Pacific Ave.

Commencing May 19, 1902

Trains will run through to Monte Cristo Cristo and return daily except Sundays.

PASSENGER

LEAVE	ARRIVE
Everett.....9:30 a.m.	M. Cristo....1:00 p.m
M. Cristo...2:20 p.m.	Everett......5:20 p.m.

For rates and other information call
on or address

C. F. M. TINLING,
Agent.

Freight and Passenger Station foot
of Pacific Avenue, Everett, or

J. O. WHITMARSH
Gen'l Supt

On May 21, in order to assist in handling the increased passenger traffic on the railway, the company placed a completely refurbished train in service on "this one road in the Northwest which Seattle newspapers have not yet attempted to annex."[1] Drawn by an American-type locomotive (a 4-4-0 or eight-wheeler) which had been polished to a mirror finish, this train was the first one to bear the new logo of the railway company on its tender. The emblem was an interlocked M and C surrounded by the legend "Monte Cristo Railroad Company; the scenic line of the northwest." The letters were gold against the black

In June, 1902, locomotive number 99 first carried the new Monte Cristo Railway logo seen here on the tender. The "Everett" had been dropped from the name because the line's tracks no longer connected to that city. The train is pictured on the 150 foot deck span Howe truss bridge at the lower end of the canyon of the Stillaguamish. It has just emerged from tunnel number one headed toward Granite Falls.

Advertisement for the railroad which appeared in the Everett Daily Herald in May, 1902. Daily passenger service was resumed following a reduced winter schedule.

background of the tender. The passenger coaches were resplendent in their rich, deep brown color, with "Monte Cristo Railway" emblazoned on their sides in gold.

The train included a new combination mail-baggage car immediately behind the tender, and on July 1, the first day of the new fiscal year, a postal clerk was on board. This made it possible to provide intermediate service to points along the line for the first time. Previously, all mail was sent to Everett in sealed pouches, sorted, then sent back to its destination the same way on the next available train. But now a letter written in Monte Cristo to someone in Silverton no longer traveled via Everett; the mail was sorted en route before the train reached the next stop. Letters were left at the proper station, thus greatly speeding the mail service.

Colgate Hoyt, one of the partners of the syndicate which founded Everett, paid a visit to Monte Cristo on May 28. He had provided much of the initial capital for Monte Cristo's construction, and was the first to interest John D. Rockefeller in its enterprises. Hoyt made the trip escorted by J. O. Whitmarsh and went up on the morning train to look over mining property of which he was part owner. He also had investments in the Everett Improvement Company and the paper mill, an indication that he had come through the depression of the 1890s without too much difficulty.

While he was in Monte Cristo, Hoyt may have spoken with Lionel Bilodeau, assayer and superintendent of the concentrator. Bilodeau had just decided to install a system to recover many of the tailings that were being washed down Glacier Creek during the concentrating process. He had watched the waste material color the creek milky white for many months and wished to devise a method whereby some of the lost mineral could be recovered. He hit upon a flotation/settling idea, and the tanks were to be installed upon obtaining clearance from the company's offices in New York. The equipment consisted of large vats through which air bubbled from below, while water with the tailings was admitted from the side. The tiny bubbles of air attached themselves to the individual grains of the tailings and those containing metallic mineral were heavy enough to sink to the bottom, dragging their bubbles with them. On the other hand, the little spheres of air caused the lighter grains of gangue to float to the water's surface, where they were skimmed off and flushed into the creek.

While Bilodeau looked after the interests of the concentrator, one of his blacksmiths, Mike McNulty, completed a project which was to spread the fame of Monte Cristo far beyond the mountain valley in which it lay. McNulty had once worked underground in the Mystery mine, and he was thoroughly familiar with its many tunnels and stopes. Using his blacksmithing skill, he fashioned an elaborate working model of the mine, which he called the "Little Mystery." Everything was detailed—the mules that hauled the ore cars, the tramways, forge, tools, anvils, et cetera. He had worked on the project for a year, hand forging and filing all parts of the exhibit. The air drills operated on compressed air, and, through a system of mirrors, observers could look into the various shafts and tunnels, which were illuminated by electric lights. Mining men who observed the model marveled at the skill and accuracy with which it had been constructed; the excursionists called it the next best thing to seeing the mine itself. The model was displayed in what had formerly been the Monte Cristo Hotel, where it could be viewed upon payment of an admission charge of ten cents. Later it was shown around the country in Washington exhibits at several fairs and expositions.

Monte Cristo's scenic fame had also spread considerably, and, in June, J. J. Engelhardt, a San Francisco artist, arrived in Everett to paint the wonders of the Cascade Mountains. He immediately traveled to Monte Cristo, making sketches of the more picturesque spots along the way. At this time of year he was able to capture the "kaleidoscopic panorama of bold, rocky mountains covered by snow at their summits and traced down through the green timber...by the white finger of lingering winter." He said that paintings of the area—particularly of Monte Cristo—had attracted the attention of art stores in San Francisco and had created quite a demand. Engelhardt promised to display his canvasses in San Francisco, and he thought this would assist in heading tourists in the direction of Monte Cristo.

Snohomish County was, however, getting more than its share of visitors during the summer of 1902. Among other groups, the Grand Army of the Republic's Washington-Alaska Encampment announced plans to hold its annual gathering in Everett. The program included a one-day excursion to Monte Cristo on Thursday, June 26, which was to be the highlight of the affair. A special train, personally attended to by Superintendent Whitmarsh, left Everett an hour before the regular pas-

senger train and took the men and their ladies into the mountains. At
Monte Cristo the group gathered for a photograph in front of the mercantile store, now run by James Kyes, formerly a motorman for the
Everett Street Railway Company. But unexpected guests arrived with
the other visitors that day. Kyes had joined the townspeople in greeting
the throng at the depot, only to discover that his wife and two young
children had also made the trip.

*Members of the Washington-Alaska Encampment of the G.A.R. pose for their pic-
tures in front of the Monte Cristo Merchantile Company's store on Dumas Street at
Monte Cristo. They made the excursion on June 26, 1902, and spent the day enjoying
the scenery of the Monte Cristo mountains.*

Elizabeth Kyes had never been to the mountains before and she was deeply impressed by the setting. Because her son had not been in good health, and the family doctor suggested the mountain air would be good for him, she returned in July with the children to spend the entire summer at Monte Cristo. During this time she took her first hike into Glacier Basin, where she saw an old mining camp high up the mountainside, a cookhouse in the valley, and tramway cables strung like cobwebs among the hills. Returning to town exhausted, she was convinced that her move to Monte Cristo had been a good one.

Newcomers to Monte Cristo in 1902. Joe Cook, center, spent his youth at Monte Cristo, eventually becoming a miner for one of the companies there. In 1977 he still lived in Everett in semi-retirement as an auto mechanic.

The Sunday excursions to Monte Cristo were now regularly carrying 500 people on each trip, and they were usually accompanied by a brass band. On July 13, the first train to employ a band consisted of two engines, eight coaches, and three observation cars. On the trip through the Stillaguamish Canyon, one locomotive pulled while the other pushed, to avoid derailing cars on the tight turns. One can only speculate what this ensemble must have sounded like—a cacophony of chugging locomotives, screeching wheels, and band music reverberating up an down the canyon. Excursions were held throughout the summer, with tourists arriving from Seattle by steamer, or via the Northern Pacific, to meet the Monte Cristo trains, and up to 600 people were taken to the village on a single day, brass band and all.

While the masses were enjoying the euphoria created by these trips, behind the scenes the corporate workings of the Rockefeller interests were quite active. On September 16, Rockefeller—already divested of his Everett interests and the lower portion of the railroad—sold the remainder of the line to the Northern Pacific. This left him holding only the mining company at Monte Cristo and the Everett smelter—the last vestiges of his once extensive interests in the area. Although it took ownership of the line between Hartford and Monte Cristo, the Northern Pacific planned no immediate changes—it would operate the railroad as an independent subsidiary for the time being. The company's first offical act was to close the Monte Cristo depot at Snohomish, which meant that all subsequent business had to be handled at the Northern Pacific station.

The mines at Monte Cristo were steadily producing about 1,000 tons per week, having never quite regained the 1,500 tons output of the glory years, 1896-97. Down the line at Silverton, the Copper-Independent Consolidated Mining Company cleared ground south of the town for a new 250-ton concentrator, to allow more economical operation of its mine. The "45" Consolidated mine, also in the Silverton area, was still transporting 1,200 tons of ore per month down its long tramway to the railroad.

When the summer of 1902 ended, the residents of Monte Cristo decided that the dozen children present in the town warranted the opening of the school. This was exciting news for the Kyes family, they all had grown fond of the community and desired to remain through the winter. Consequently, Elizabeth Kyes closed their Everett residence.

The interior of the Monte Cristo Merchantile Company's store at Monte Cristo during the summer of 1902. Fresh produce and meat were brought up on each train to supply the needs of the town. Hard goods of every type were also sold. Kerosene lamps, spare chimneys, and fuel cans line the top shelf behind the counter.

The usual snows fell in December, only to be followed by warm rain driven before a chinook. This caused the rivers to rise to dangerously high levels by the year's end; but the railway was in no immediate danger, due to the heavy construction of the roadbed after the 1897 flood. Production in Monte Cristo continued at a steady pace as 1902 closed and 1903 made its debut.

Western Washington was badly flooded in January because the December rains had become heavy downpours and the rivers spilled over their banks. Although it was not washed out, the railroad had its share of problems. On December 31, a mud slide blocked the line between Tunnels No. 2 and No. 3, trapping the passenger train on the Monte

Cristo side. The debris was quickly cleared, and the train reached Everett the following day, arriving 24 hours late. By January 5 the trains were unable to operate between Everett and Snohomish because the area was one immense lake and the tracks were under water. Local residents hailed the situation as the worst since the 1897 floods had disrupted all rail traffic in the area. Since no outgoing trains were available on which to send the mail, most of it stacked up in Everett, but a portion was sent to Snohomish and Monte Cristo via steamboats on the Snohomish River. A part of the trestle work on the Monte Cristo Railway was damaged by the flood, but the Northern Pacific brought in section crews to make repairs. Consequently, service on the line was not seriously impaired.

The flood subsided in late January, snow fell in the mountains, and the temperature plunged. Winter had finally settled in to stay. Toward the end of the month a blizzard raged in Monte Cristo and the rotary plow was required to keep the line open for service. Nevertheless, mining continued as if summer had arrived, although the railroad operated on a reduced schedule. The snows did not let up, however, and on February 11 the passenger train was marooned when the pilot beam plow mounted on the locomotive proved inadequate to clear the way. The train had been halted between Barlow Pass and Monte Cristo; but, since the Northern Pacific had recently moved the rotary plow to its Pacific Division, the Monte Cristo train crew had to dig itself out. At noon on February 15, the train finally returned to Everett, having been gone four days, spending three of them as a captive of the deep snow in the Cascades.

The parents of Monte Cristo's children received a rude shock about this time when officials determined that not enough funds were available to continue operating the school. This meant that parents with school-age children would have to leave town immediately in order to seek schooling elsewhere. The problem was compounded by the unruly weather which plagued the area; passenger service was desultory at best. The parents had to wait three days until a locomotive and caboose pushed its way into the town. After a cramped trip to Silverton in the caboose, they transferred to a waiting passenger train to complete the trip to Everett. The move proved to be a panic situation, however, because the school at Monte Cristo continued its program, although at times it had only three students.

Work on the Copper-Independent's concentrator in Silverton progressed well, and the company decided to install a cyanide plant on the
property. If built, it would be the first in the Monte Cristo area, and
would make feasible the chemical reduction of gold ores on the
premises, thus eliminating the costly shipments to a distant smelter.
The gold was to be sold directly to the United States Assay Office. But
the plans went awry and the facility was never completed. On the other
hand, copper ores were processed through the mill and shipped as usual.
By late February, 1903, most of the machinery was on the ground and
being installed, despite heavy snow and cold, driving winds. The more
Silverton developed, the more the community showed promise of becoming a real producer.

On Saturday, April 30, a bad accident occurred on the railroad. A
freight train carrying a load of concentrates from Monte Cristo had left
Robe and entered the Stillaguamish Canyon at its normal speed, eight
to ten miles per hour. But as the train approached Tunnel No. 3, the
engineer saw a large boulder drop down the rocky face and land between the rails. The collision could not be avoided, and the
locomotive's pilot climbed over the rock, causing considerable damage
to the undercarriage before the train could be stopped. This was bad
enough, but no sooner had the train halted than a rock slide followed
the boulder down the canyon wall. The debris struck the train just behind the tender, derailed the first two freight cars, and left them hanging precariously, 40 feet above the foaming Stillaguamish. The men
could do nothing but walk back to Robe and send to Granite Falls for
help. The next day a section crew arrived at the scene to clear the slide
and get the train moving again.

During March, winter still reigned in the Cascades. The major
through trains on the transcontinental lines were "due when they
arrived," because the companies had no way of predicting track conditions in the mountains from day to day. On the Monte Cristo Railway,
the passenger train which left Everett on March 10 was stalled by heavy
snow at Silverton (where the elevation was only 1,500 feet) and unable
to return down the line. The train had dug its way up the line, preceded
by a rotary plow, but the machine had sustained damage and failed
shortly after the crew attempted to leave Silverton. Consequently, the
trip to Monte Cristo had to be canceled. Two days later the train arrived
back in Everett with the damaged plow. Monte Cristo was momen-

tarily isolated, but the plow was immediately placed in the shops and repaired. Several days later, the train again attempted to reach Monte Cristo. This time the plow worked flawlessly and service was restored to the town.

Yet a month later avalanches continued to delay traffic on the railway when heavy winter snows, made still heavier by spring thaws and rains, rumbled down the mountainsides and buried the tracks. On April 16, one such slide near Barlow Pass blocked the track and imprisoned the passenger train in Monte Cristo for two days. When June brought warmer weather and melting snows, the Northern Pacific made improvements to the road—bridges were filled in, culverts placed, curves straightened, and tracks graded. This activity renewed the old rumor that the Monte Cristo line was to become part of a new cross-country route, and created considerable excitement in Granite Falls.

With the improvement work under way, the Northern Pacific published its summer schedule which called for the trains to remain at Monte Cristo overnight. They would leave Everett every day at 1:10 P.M., bound for Monte Cristo, and depart the town the following morning at 7:00 A.M., arriving in Everett at 10:10 A.M. In addition, a few special excursions were run, but not on a regular basis as in the years past.

Meanwhile, production at the Monte Cristo mines continued to average 1,000 tons of ore per week. But the Rockefeller interests, under the direction of Frederick Gates, moved to divest Rockefeller of his last holdings in the Pacific Northwest—the Everett smelter and the mining company at Monte Cristo. During the summer, rumors were afoot that Charles Sweeney—a Spokane man with investments in the Coeur d'Alene district of northern Idaho—intended to buy the plant in Everett and let the miners themselves control the smelter. On August 15 the smelter and mining company were sold to the Federal Mining & Smelting Company, a Coeur d'Alene combine backed by Rockefeller and Gould. However, this action did not completely divest Rockefeller of the smelter and mines, and more was to come.

The New Discovery tunnel of the Pride of the Mountains mine became one of Monte Cristo's leading producers. In accordance with the normal routine, the miners spent the first half of the shift drilling. When the men broke for lunch, the "powder monkeys" placed and fired the charges. Then, during the second half of the shift, the workmen once again engaged in drilling, with the final charge of the day placed and detonated between shifts.

On September 6, 1903, at 4:20 P.M., the last half of the day shift was almost over at the New Discovery when a powerful explosion ripped through the headhouse. Frank Kouchon, Joseph Vallentine, and Maurice Vanuti were so badly mangled that officials could not be certain of their identity until the evening roll call provided the missing names. The men had been in the headhouse thawing the powder prior to taking it into the mine to be used for the last shot of the day. Thawing was required because the "giant powder"—which consisted of sticks composed of nitroglycerine combined with a chemical similar to black powder—was so volatile that, if it got too cold, it could easily crack and detonate at the slightest jolt, or else not detonate properly when desired. The explosion had occurred while the thawing process was under way.

Orvill Kimball, the eight-year-old son of J. I. Kimball, the mine's shift boss, was assisting his father. He was opening the door to the blacksmith shop when the blast occurred on the opposite side, violently slamming the door shut and propelling him back into the room. The unconscious boy landed in the middle of the shop, and his father, who had been standing at the rear of the building, ran through the swirling dust kicked up by the blast, picked up his son and carried him home. Ironically, the boy's mother, who had been a nurse and had cared for many injured miners through the years, was now obliged to administer to her own son. The lad was taken to the hospital in Everett on the first train. He was soon up and about, and back home in Monte Cristo, but his hearing had been permanently impaired.

Shortly after the blast, Kimball investigated the accident and discovered that A. Nyman and Joseph Polish had also been injured by the explosion, although not seriously. He first suspected that the powder in the thawer had detonated, but upon inspection it was found to be intact.

This type of disaster was fairly commonplace in the mines, perhaps because many powder men handled the explosives in a nonchalant manner. Kimball theorized that the men had been carrying the thawed powder, together with the caps used to detonate it, in their pockets. Although the powder was sensitive material to handle, the caps were hair trigger, and one of the men could have accidentally bumped the ones he carried, thus setting off a chain reaction that exploded the powder. Only the explosives still clamped in the cast iron thawer had not detonated.

The Rockefeller interests now moved rapidly. In September, the Federal Mining & Smelting Company sold the Everett smelter and the Monte Cristo Mining Company to the American Smelting and Refining Company for a sum exceeding $1,000,000. The smelter trust—or ASARCO as it was called—was not interested in the mining company, but Rockefeller, who was intent on divesting himself of his mining enterprises in the Cascades, had made it an inseparable part of the deal. But ASARCO wanted control of the smelter badly enough, that it agreed to buy the entire package, leaving Rockefeller, after 13 years, free of his Pacific Northwest investments.

He was not entirely free, however, because Frederick T. Gates was not only shrewd enough to minimize Rockefeller's losses but also cognizant of the enormous potential presented by the lumber industry in western Washington. All the funds obtained through sales of the various mining and smelting companies were immediately plowed into the Everett Timber & Investment Company. Gates purchased the stock of the owners and placed Brownell in charge of timber purchases and sales. He acquired about 50,000 acres of timbered land in Washington and 40,000 acres on Vancouver Island, British Columbia. When prices rose, the lands were sold for handsome profits, some for nine times more than had been paid for them. Before he was through, Gates had turned the losses into gains, with over 1,000,000,000 board feet yet unsold on which had already accrued two or three million dollars more profit.

Through Gates' efforts and wise judgment, Rockefeller had come out ahead. But what of Monte Cristo, now in the hands of the smelter trust, controlled by the Guggenheims, who were not interested in the mines? No action was immediately forthcoming, and no one would say what was to be done. The people in Monte Cristo became apprehensive while the days wore on, and the work at the mines continued at an uneasy pace.

Events happened fast, however, in the final months of 1903. On October 5, a deed was filed with the county auditor which finalized the ownership of the remaining portion of the Monte Cristo Railway Company by the Northern Pacific. The line was no longer considered a separate company but a branch line of the Northern Pacific. The name

Monte Cristo Railway was dropped and the line became the Monte Cristo branch of the Northern Pacific.

During the same week, the mortgage on the "45" Consolidated mine was foreclosed. Originally purchased by Charles H. Pinkham, it had been held by the Pinkham estate after his death. Despite the enterprise's admirable shipping record, it did not earn enough to pay its way, and an outstanding debt of $77,000 was filed against the company.

The mountains were covered with five feet of snow by mid-November, but the railroads remained open and trains ran more or less on schedule. Mining continued at Monte Cristo with no word yet from the new proprietors. Although they brought in experts to inspect the property, they had released no public statements. Meanwhile, a property discovered the year before above Weden Creek, two miles below Monte Cristo, was found to have a good showing of nickel and copper ore. The owners formed a new company and made plans to develop the property as the Mackinaw mine.

The second shoe dropped on December 3, when ASARCO announced that the Monte Cristo mines had been closed. The company had already begun removing the machinery and other salvable items, but it decided to continue operation of the concentrator until all the remaining ore had been processed and sent to the smelter. Since the supply of ore in the bins would last only about two weeks, the concentrator's life was measured in days. Actually, the mines had been closed on November 30, but the news was not released to the public until three days later.

Although the Rainy and Golden Cord mines continued to operate, the closure of the other mines, both at Monte Cristo and at Silverton, meant a vastly reduced railroad schedule, and traffic over the road was much reduced. The local newspapers complained that Rockefeller had deliberately unloaded the railroad first, with the implication that mining would continue; only then were the mines sold and closed, greatly diminishing the need for the railroad's services. A few men went so far as to claim that the Monte Cristo Mining Company had been run at a loss between the transactions simply to facilitate its sale. Whatever the maneuvering, the mines were now closed, with no hope of reopening them in the foreseeable future.

Monte Cristo was subjected to an exodus in late 1903. But lack of employment, not the weather or the railroad, caused the migration. The

Northern Pacific did not run a Christmas excursion train, and the
people who remained enjoyed little merriment in the silent and somber
mining camp. As 1903 faded into history, the men still working left to
visit their families during the holidays. Behind them, the snows of
Christmas and the New Year fell upon a deserted Monte Cristo.

Josiah E. Spurr Photo
Standing just below the Mystery number three tunnel, looking down the long aerial
tramway where it left Mystery Hill and leaped to the single 102 foot high tower on its
way to the collector terminal whose roof can be seen to the right of the tower. The town
of Monte Cristo is in the distance.

CHAPTER XII

1904-06

THE DECLINE BEGINS

As the new year began, the recent mine closures and bankruptcies along the Monte Cristo branch of the Northern Pacific created a gloomy outlook for all enterprises in the district. Tempering this mood, however, was the discovery of the new prospect on Weden Creek, about two miles down the Sauk River from Monte Cristo. The Mackinaw Mining and Milling Company had driven a 100-foot tunnel on its property and discovered ore rich in copper, gold, silver, and nickel. The latter element made the claim a curiosity in the region because the metal had never before been discovered in any quantity on the western slope of the Cascades. By June, 150 feet of tunneling had been dug on the property, and in July over $50,000 was invested in the mine by eastern capitalists. The chance to open the only nickel mine in western Washington seemed irresistible, and attracted the necessary money. Development was accelerated, with ore shipments promised by fall.

But on January 15, a large mud slide near the collapsed Tunnel No. 7 ripped out 300 feet of track, putting the railway out of commission for several days and trapping a train above the slide. In early March, Monte Cristo was blockaded by snow, since no rotary plow was available to clear the tracks, and service ended at Silverton. However, on April 1 a rotary plow opened the way into the hamlet. The weather had been severe during the isolation, the heavy snow collapsing the roofs of the railroad roundhouse and the vanner building at the concentrator. A portion of Dumas Street built of trestle work had also succumbed to the weight of the snow. Subsequent to the closure of the mines, maintenance crews had not been employed at the Monte Cristo properties, and without snow removal winter damage was inevitable. Although

189

the tracks were open, a reduced schedule was still in force, only one train per week running to the mountain terminus.

Business matters were not helped when, on April 12, a petition was filed in superior court asking that a receiver be appointed for the Rainy Mining Company because the firm's indebtedness exceeded its ability to pay. The Rainy was one of the two mining companies that had been operating at Monte Cristo, and the news of its failure did not bode well for the future of the mining district. The court action left the Golden Cord the only going concern, and not much ore was being shipped from that property. The Rainy Mining Company was sold at a receiver's auction in June, and a reorganization effected to put the company in a position to again operate the mine.

On June 30, 1904, Louis Nobles, a mining expert from Denver, Colorado, acting on behalf of the American Smelting and Refining Company, arrived in Monte Cristo to evaluate the mines; his investigation lasted two weeks. Nobles would only say that he was impressed by the area; he released nothing for publication concerning his findings. The answer came in mid-October when ASARCO asked that a receiver be appointed for the Monte Cristo Mining and Concentrating Company. ASARCO alleged that it had advanced payroll money to the mining enterprise during its last months of operation, but repayment had not been made. In a related action, Snohomish County brought suit against the mining company for collection of back taxes amounting to $9,641,01. Although the county's suit was quickly settled, the properties were placed in the hands of a receiver to determine what could be salvaged from the now idle company.

During 1904, ASARCO reconditioned the Everett smelter and started it up again. As a result, by mid-year bullion was once more being shipped from the wharves on Port Gardner Bay. The city of smokestacks was not yet totally a lumber town. The refusal of ASARCO to open and operate the Monte Cristo mines, combined with its desire to make the smelter profitable, had created a contradiction: early in 1905, E. B. Braden, the smelter's manager, issued a demand to local miners to produce more ore—and, of course, they were expected to ship it to his facility.

Much to the dismay of the area's residents, no excursion trains ran to Monte Cristo during 1904. The world's fair in St. Louis had siphoned off most unused passenger cars to handle its traffic. Moreover, a memorandum to the Northern Pacific agents established an official company policy that Sunday excursions were to be scheduled only for special occasions where the public demand was great. The memorandum cited the fact that such trips required the crews to work overtime, and seldom repaid the costs of running the trains.

James Kyes and K. L. Forbes, an Everett resident, bought the store at Monte Cristo during the summer and went into business for themselves. Later, when the town was blockaded by winter snow, the hotel ran short of food supplies and purchased the store's entire stock of meat.

During the winter, when the rotary plow cleared the tracks into the town, people could watch it, as Elizabeth Kyes described, "coming up from the switchback with electric sparks flying in every direction." The flashes were probably caused when the iron rotor knives struck pebbles in the snow. The mining company operated a small plow that was used to keep Dumas Street clear, but everywhere else the snow was 12 feet deep.

The year also marked the closure of the old Monte Cristo Hotel in Everett; it was sold to the Sisters of Providence for use as a sanitarium. Shortly afterward, a new hospital building was built nearby.

Although the Monte Cristo railroad traversed rough terrain and was subjected to violent winter weather, surprisingly few fatal accidents had occurred during its operation. But on February 5, 1905, at 5:30 P.M., a special train—consisting of an engine, tender, and caboose—was transporting bridge and rail inspectors along the right-of-way for a routine check of the roadbed. The train was backing up the line near Robe, traveling 18 miles per hour along a straight, level stretch. Without warning the tender's wheels left the track, sliced into the roadbed, and caused the tender to veer sharply to one side. The coupling linking it with the caboose shattered, and the tender overturned, separating from its trucks. This, in turn, caused the locomotive to tip. When the engine hit the ground, the cab broke loose and shifted forward, trapping the men and breaking the pipe leading to the whistle. This released clouds of scalding steam which enveloped the cab and the men who were inside.

Robert E. Love, the engineer, suffered 10 hours of agony before he died early the next morning; C. Carstensen, the fireman, was killed almost instantly. William Hester, engine watchman, and three bridgemen—John Carlson, John Potts, and Guy Bartlett—were terribly burned, but lived through the accident. Conductor McMurray and the other inspectors were in the caboose and escaped injury due to the coupling's failure.

The wife of a railroad man who lived in a nearby house rendered invaluable aid to the wounded men while they waited the interminable hours for help to arrive. The Northern Pacific dispatched a special relief train the moment it received news of the disaster, and the dead and injured men were taken to Seattle as quickly as possible. Hester died on February 7; three days later Bartlett became the fourth victim of the mishap when he passed away in a Seattle hospital.

The wreck was quickly cleared, the inspection continued, and a few weeks later a crew was at work repairing the roadbed and bridges on the line.

One of the tasks undertaken by the railroad company was an attempt to stabilize Tunnel No. 4 in the Stillaguamish Canyon. Although the support timbers were 15 inches square, they were beginning to shift because the rock in this area was unstable. The site had been the scene of severe rock slides and at least two fatalities. The solution, at least for the moment, was to double-shore: put new bracing inside the old. This would reduce the clearance between the rolling stock and the sides and roof, but appeared to be the only way to hold back the crush of the canyon wall.

On July 6, Tunnel No. 4 almost claimed another victim when the scaffolding used to emplace the new timbers collapsed, causing the workmen to fall about eight feet to the roadbed below. Most escaped with only minor injuries, but Ed Stewart landed flat on his back, damaging his spine. The men were taken to Granite Falls, about five miles down the track. Stewart was paralyzed, but the injury proved to be temporary, and he was soon back on the job. The double-shoring staved off the advancing canyon wall and prompted this note to be added to the railroad schedules: "Bracing in Tunnel No. 4 will not clear man on top of box car."

The mines in both the Monte Cristo and Silverton areas did not ship much ore during 1905, but a great amount of development work was accomplished. Minerals from the Sunrise properties near Barlow Pass had won an award at the St. Louis fair, and the mine showed promise of becoming quite productive in the near future. At Monte Cristo,

Re-timbering tunnel number four in the canyon of the Stillaguamish. New timbering was added inside that already installed to attempt to prevent further collapse of the structure by the relentless crush of the shifting canyon wall. The scaffolding collapsed on July 7, 1905 injuring several of the men who fell to the tracks below. The timbers were cut outside, carried in on the hand car and hoisted by block and tackle to the platform, then trimmed and fitted into place by hand.

however, only small crews were working in the Golden Cord and Rainy (still the only mines operating in the area); shipments were minimal and of low grade for lack of a concentrator.

Despite the reduced activity, the hazards of the job managed to make themselves felt. On June 9, Fred Peterson was the victim of one such incident in the Rainy mine. The winch was lifting him up the shaft, but the rope broke when he was 50 feet above the bottom, and man and bucket plummeted down into inky darkness. They struck Charles Anderson, who was waiting his turn to be raised. Miraculously, both men escaped with only cuts and bruises.

Not so lucky was John William, a cook at one of the mines. The few children who still lived in Monte Cristo would occasionally visit the various mining camps around the town and fraternize with the cook and miners. On June 23, a group of youths visited the building where William was employed. He was talking and joking with the boys, several of whom had brought their rifles. During a playful tussle, one of the guns was accidentally fired, and the bullet struck the cook in the abdomen. He was rushed to Monte Cristo, placed on an engine, and hurried toward medical aid. About 12 miles from Granite Falls, William died of his wound. The death was ruled accidental during an investigation conducted by Deputy Coroner Bakeman; but, accidental or not, it pointed up the danger of handling weapons or explosives in a careless manner.

On August 11, 1905, the Wilmans brothers returned to Monte Cristo to attend to their mining companies. Of greater importance to the village watchers, however, was the fact that the Wilmanses made an extensive investigation of the Pride of the Mountains, Pride of the Woods, and Mystery mines all abandoned nearly two years earlier when the Rockefeller interests sold them to ASARCO. Miners speculated on the significance of the investigation, and by early November a persistent rumor was afoot that the Wilmanses were going to purchase and reopen the mines. Fred Wilmans refused to confirm or deny the story's validity, thereby adding fuel to its fire. But the rumor was confirmed when the Wilmans brothers formally announced that negotiations were under way with ASARCO "for the purchase of all its holdings in the Monte Cristo district." As soon as the deal was completed, the Wilmanses would "commence active operations in the mines."

The transaction included the concentrator, tramways, and all mines held by the smelter trust. Concurrently, the brothers obtained a controlling interest in the floundering Rainy Mining Company. This gave them control over all the larger mines in the area. The Wilmanses had been the first financiers to pour funds into Monte Cristo, and everyone now concerned watched and waited as they showed, once again, their faith in Monte Cristo. The Wilmanses also reincorporated the old Golden Cord Mining Company, renamed it the Justice Mining Company, and planned new tunnels to strike the ore at lower levels than ever before on that property.

During the summer of 1905, James Kyes was appointed postmaster of Monte Cristo. He also went to work in the Golden Cord mine, and for about two months operated the air compressor during the day, while his brother Dan did the same job on the night shift. Kyes' son and father-in-law were left to run the mercantile store in town. The Kyes family had moved into one of the better company houses, located between '76 Creek and Sunday Falls on an area known as Sunday Flats.

The Wilmans brothers were not the only Monte Cristo pioneers to show an interest in the area in 1905. Frank Peabody, who with Joseph Pearsall had staked the first claims, employed a crew of men to perform development work on his Sidney mine in '76 Gulch. This tunnel, on the old Rob Roy claim, was drifted into one of the district's first known veins, at the base of Wilmans Peak, in an attempt to strike the ledge of ore at a greater depth than in the past.

Winter began its annual encroachment on Monte Cristo. The leaves turned red and yellow, and a chill could be felt in the air. The Northern Pacific reported the line was in better shape to withstand bad weather than it had been for many years, with new riprapping and retaining walls in place to prevent washouts and rock slides. The Mackinaw Mining Company had completed its headhouse in the Weden Creek basin in time to conduct winter operations, bolstered by new capital provided by its eastern investors.

On October 1, a storm second only to the devastating one of 1897 slammed into the Cascades and unleashed its fury upon Monte Cristo. The downpour lasted for three days, swelling the mountain streams to foaming torrents which lashed and tore at their banks. Telephone and telegraph lines between Monte Cristo and Silverton were broken, and residents feared that the railroad would be washed out. The Northern Pacific's preparations proved adequate, however, and the trains continued to run to Monte Cristo. The temperature then dropped, turning the rain to snow, and the mountains were once again whitened.

When Christmas arrived at Monte Cristo, mining activities in the Justice were on schedule, and a 12-foot vein of ore had been struck in the lower tunnel. The operations at the Rainy were suspended, pending action by the new owners (the Wilmans brothers), and the Pride and Mystery remained idle. Development work was done on the Rantoul and Philo in Glacier Basin on property which paralleled the Pride. Although this winter did not appear to hinder the progress of the mining companies, little more than development work was done.

But, as observers learned on February 24, 1906, more was happening in the courts than at Monte Cristo. The Wilmans brothers and Edward Blewett had filed suit against Colgate Hoyt and Leigh Hunt, the former owners of the Pride and Mystery, to recover $186,000 which they alleged was owed them from their sale to the Colby-Hoyt syndicate in 1891. The original transaction consisted of a $175,000 cash payment and a bond for another $175,000 to be guaranteed by the mine's production. But the bond had never been paid, and the Wilmanses and Blewett were now suing to collect.

The plaintiffs claimed that insufficient records had been kept of the production, while the defendants insisted that the mines had been a losing proposition and payment of the bond was not warranted. The case was fought for almost six months in New York before the court granted judgment in favor of the plaintiffs. This news was greeted favorably in the area, because it meant new capital and renewed production from the major Monte Cristo mines.

James Kyes continued as postmaster at Monte Cristo, in addition to attending to his duties as a merchant. He was a "jack of all trades," and his skills were increasingly in demand in the camps due to the renewed interest in mining. Once again his son and father-in-law were left to run the store. Among his other skills, Kyes was handy with hammer and saw, and many of the mine structures around Monte Cristo were either built or modified by him.

On May 6 the Northern Pacific returned to its summer schedule on the Monte Cristo branch, prompted by the increase in tourist and sportsman traffic, as well as the renewed mining activity. The Bonanza Queen at Silverton now shipped one car of ore per day, and new development work was evident all along the line. Ore cargoes trans-

ported by the Monte Cristo branch, together with those from out of
state, kept the Everett smelter busy.

The railroad locomotives burned coal for fuel. As it was consumed,
the ashes dropped into the ash pan for later disposal. The embers were
red hot, and not all fell into the ash pan. Early in August, one such way-
ward spark from a passing locomotive started a forest fire on the side of
Long Mountain, about two miles below Silverton.

> For a time it looked as though the entire place would be surrounded by
> the flames. The trees crashing down the mountain side sounded like
> cannon all night Friday and Saturday morning. Ten or twelve large trees
> had fallen across the railroad track so that the trains were unable to pass.
> Some of the trees were six feet in diameter and had to be blasted from the
> tracks before the road was clear. Fifteen new rails were set. The wind
> shifted Saturday and carried the most dangerous portion of the fire in
> another direction. [*Everett Daily Herald*, August 13, 1906]

The cannonading referred to was probably the trees exploding as their
internal moisture was rapidly vaporized by the intense heat. Fires of this
nature were common along steam railways, and sometimes were ignited
by sparks from the brakes as well as by the locomotive. This blaze had
caused only an uneasy night in Silverton, but had the wind not changed
the town most likely would have been destroyed.

Late in 1906 the Wilmans brothers announced their long-awaited
plans to resume production from the Pride and Mystery properties. The
news was greeted with jubilation by local businessmen. However, no
sooner were the Wilmanses' intentions known than a noted mining
"plunger," wielding a great deal of money, purchased almost all their
Monte Cristo properties. Samuel Silverman, who made the handsome
offer to the brothers, had interests in mines in Idaho, eastern
Washington, British Columbia, and Alaska. Four mining companies—
the Pride, Mystery, Justice, and Wilmans—were consolidated into the
Monte Cristo Mines and Metals Company.

Silverman made plans to reopen the properties at the earliest possible
date, but the task proved formidable because in the spring a snowslide
had damaged the Pride tramway, rendering it inoperable. Moreover,
the structures had received little or no maintenance for several years.
Thus, the heavy winter snows had caused part of the concentrator's
roof to collapse, with subsequent damage to the machinery inside.
Much of the equipment had been stripped from the Pride and Mystery

when they were purchased by ASARCO, and it would have to be replaced before operations could begin. This, however, did not seem to bother Silverman, and he proceeded with his plans.

Late in October the rivers of western Washington were once again flooding. Winter had come a bit early, with warm rain driven before the usual chinook. The local newspapers noted that nine years had passed since the big flood of 1897 had washed out the Monte Cristo railroad. Fortunately, a recurrence of that event was not at hand, and little damage was sustained, although passengers on the trains described the "mad rush of the water through the gorge" as a "sight to make one shudder, though something sublime." The tracks were only a foot or two above the water line. In late December, flood water loosened the rock near Tunnel No. 2, temporarily blocking the road, but no direct damage occurred.

CHAPTER XIII

1907-13

THE DECLINE CONTINUES

On New Year's Day, 1907, the railroad remained blocked at Tunnel No. 2, while more mud and rocks oozed onto the tracks. After two weeks of futile effort by the crews to open the line, a sudden drop in temperature stabilized the mud. The debris was then removed, and service restored. Traffic returned to normal, with the rotary plow making regular trips to clear away the snow, which was constantly replenished by the winter storms.

Only two weeks following restoration of traffic beyond the mud slide, the service was interrupted again when a locomotive and rotary plow set fire to the timbering in Tunnel No. 1 at the lower entrance to the canyon. Fully half of this 833-foot "long tunnel" had been bored through unconsolidated rock and mud, with reliance placed upon the shoring for its support. When the timbers burned and weakened, the bore gradually filled with tons of debris, which blocked the tracks and stranded the locomotive and plow up the line. The railroad investigators who arrived predicted the collapse could not be repaired in less than two months.

Meanwhile, the isolated engine made the run back and forth from Tunnel No. 1 to Monte Cristo, meeting the train from Everett each scheduled day. Passengers and freight had to be laboriously hauled over the headland through which the tunnel passed in order to complete the journey. On February 2, the locomotive made its last trip to Monte Cristo; the fuel had run out. The company planned no further service above the tunnel until it could be rebuilt.

This closure marked the first of several setbacks for Samuel Silverman's efforts to restore production of the Monte Cristo mines. He had just announced plans to increase his work force from 60 to 300 men, but with the railroad inoperative and supplies scarce, the crew would, instead, have to be reduced. Other companies along the line were compelled to take similar action.

The Northern Pacific imported a large gang of men to handle the work at Tunnel No. 1. Hydraulic equipment was used to sluice away the mud and loose rock, and a major effort was thus launched to clear the line. But two months' time for repairs turned out to be too optimistic an estimate. Service was finally restored to Monte Cristo on May 27, when the first through train since the collapse made the trip to the town. His way now open, Silverman proceeded with his plans for the mines. He enlarged the work force, put a crew to work repairing the concentrator building, and ordered new machinery for both the mill and mines.

Silverman had some new ideas in mind to make Monte Cristo a paying proposition. One was to market the arsenic in the ore as a saleable commodity instead of considering it a liability as it had been in the past. Since the Everett smelter had an arsenic extraction plant, he entered into negotiations with the management in an attempt to receive compensation, rather than be penalized by the presence of arsenic in the ores. When no agreement could be reached, he ordered machinery for a roaster and extractor to be installed at Monte Cristo. This would insure that the ores which arrived at the smelter would be practically free of the substance, and the Monte Cristo Metals and Mining Company would have a marketable product in the form of arsenic trioxide. Silverman then offered bonds for sale against the company to finance his plan.

On May 31, 1907, the first full carload of ore shipped from Monte Cristo since the fall of 1903 reached the Everett smelter. This cargo still contained its arsenic because the extractor at Monte Cristo was not yet completed. But the concentrator had been rebuilt and generally put in top-notch condition, with new machinery installed where necessary, plus an addition to house the roaster.

Under the aegis of this new capital, the community had quickly resumed its old atmosphere. According to one visitor, the resumption of mining was "already having its good effect on the hustling little mountain town"; in fact, the community had "taken on a lively appearance by giving occupants to many houses for a long time deserted." With the trains running on their summer schedule, tourists flocked to the hills to revel in the scenic grandeur. Among those who made the pilgrimage were four young ladies from Everett and Seattle, together with their escorts. Anna Cuthbertson, Harmah Kingston, Edith Stead, and Florence Otto climbed Cadet Peak from Glacier Basin in late July, and claimed the honor of being the first party of women to have done so. They were typical of an increasing number of people who came to Monte Cristo merely to enjoy the scenic splendor and leave their personal imprint.

Silverman had poured an enormous amount of money into his Monte Cristo properties, as witnessed by the total renovation of the concentrator with its new machinery. The miners built new houses to replace the ones crushed by snow during the previous years of neglect; they also brought their families to Monte Cristo to live, and a population explosion reminiscent of the old days was at hand. The company shipped several carloads of concentrates per week to the Everett smelter, and prosperity seemed assured.

But, by September, 1907, it had become evident that everything was not going well. Not only had Silverman been unable to obtain an agreement with the smelter regarding the sale of arsenic from his Monte Cristo ores, but also a recession in 1907 had prevented his disposing of most of the bonds he had issued. Silverman's failure to sell the bonds had created a shortage of operating capital within the Monte Cristo Metals and Mining Company. The first casualty, the arsenic extraction plant, was never completed, although more than half its machinery was on the site. The winter's snows slowed the mining operations, which in turn curtailed ore shipment, and this fact, coupled with the lack of new money, forced the company into receivership. Consequently another promising Monte Cristo enterprise was nipped before it could flower into a viable proposition.

Only a handful of families elected to stay in the village through the winter of 1907-08. The mines were closed, maintenance work the only employment to be found. The railroad schedule was reduced to two trains per month during the winter, and a number of those had trouble getting to their destination due to rock and mud slides and the deep snow. The first to reach Monte Cristo in three months arrived on April 18, 1908, and was greeted with a sigh of relief by those living in the nearly deserted town.

On June 11, the Northern Pacific announced the summer timetable for the railroad, and it was, for the first time, unchanged from the previous winter's schedule. During the summer of 1908 only two trains per month traveled the full distance to Monte Cristo. Because the mines had been closed, additional traffic was unwarranted on the line.

One bright star in the gloomy outlook was the Philo mine, next to the Pride property, in lower Glacier Basin, which employed three shifts of men. The management had announced plans to begin shipments of ore later in the summer. In order to transport it, a mile-long tram would have to be completed to replace the Pride tram damaged by a snowslide in 1906. While the operation looked good on paper, no ore was produced in 1908.

The Robe Lumber Mill lost another dry kiln to fire during the summer, but once again the mill was saved. The plant was now owned by the Johnson-Dean Lumber Company, one of the few enterprises providing a steady business to the railroad above Granite Falls. The firm was logging extensively in the nearby hills, and by the end of 1908 plans were under way to remove the mill from its old site. This action was precipitated by Johnson-Dean's desire to compete with other lumber mills in the sale of large poles and timbers. But, due to the serpentine nature of the railway through the Stillaguamish Canyon, the Northern Pacific had refused to ship anything that could not be packed into boxcars, because the danger of derailment on the tight curves was too great. This prompted Johnson-Dean to look for a site below the canyon. Although a new shingle mill at Gold Basin, just below Silverton, supplied some business to the railroad, loss of the mill at Robe would be a major setback to continued operation of the branch line.

The last train into Monte Cristo during 1908 left Everett on October 31, and was delayed several hours by a snowslide at Barlow Pass. The railroad then announced the termination of train service into the town until, sometime in the spring of 1909, business would warrant its resumption. However, the biweekly service would be continued to Silverton throughout the winter.

Monte Cristo was about to be isolated due to lack of business, but not totally so. Otto Norman, who planned to spend the winter in the village with his family, obtained the contract to carry the mail between Silverton and Monte Cristo. Walking on snowshoes, he made the 28-mile round trip twice weekly throughout the winter. He left Monte Cristo on Mondays and Fridays; Silverton on Tuesdays and Saturdays.

This service, along with the telegraph between Silverton and Everett, maintained a tenuous line of communication with the outside world.[1]

Another deluge of rain driven before chinook winds caused extensive damage and flooding throughout western Washington in January, 1909. The Monte Cristo branch line did not escape unscathed: a large mud slide near Tunnel No. 4 buried 200 feet of track to a depth of 25 feet. For a month the crews attempted to clear the debris, but daily slides created hazardous conditions and rendered their efforts futile. Then a sudden drop in temperature solidified the unstable, soggy soil and the work was completed. On February 19, the first train in 30 days arrived in Robe.

J. C. Morton, manager of the Northwest Consolidated Mining Company on Weden Creek, reported in late May that during a walk from his property to Silverton the track was bare except for a snowdrift in the cut at Barlow Pass. He expressed the hope that rail service into Monte Cristo, however sparse, could be resumed at an early date. But on June 8 the Northern Pacific publicly announced that operation of the line beyond Silverton would not be profitable, and that the company would restore service only if the major mines at Monte Cristo were reopened. The schedule called for just one weekly train, to leave Everett every Saturday and go as far as Silverton.

Nevertheless, on October 1, a special, unscheduled train arrived in Monte Cristo, carrying officials of the Northern Pacific on an inspection tour. The men saw a nearly abandoned town of silvered buildings standing defiant against the elements, which were slowly taking their toll. If the railroad people were checking whether or not enough business existed to resume rail service, they had their answer.

So briefly were they at Monte Cristo, that only a watchman ever knew of their presence. When he saw the locomotive approach, he thought he was dreaming because no train had reached the village in a year.

In order to maintain a legal right to a mining claim, $100 worth of improvements had to be made to the property each year. In 1909 James and Dan Kyes were hired by the American Mining Company to perform the required assessment work on the O & B mine on Toad Mountain. The Kyes family was now well known and respected in the Monte Cristo area. James Kyes was still the postmaster and co-owner of the mercantile store. The brothers had labored for three weeks on the

Constructed in part by James Kyes while he was employed at the Del Campo Mining Company operation in Gothic Basin, these buildings served the upper tunnel located above Weden Lake. This tunnel bored serpentine fashion along several fracture zones but struck no ore. The tunnel is only about 600 feet long. Silver Tip Peak is in the distance.

mine when they were challenged by Ben James, one of the claim's original locators. Thinking they were being attacked, the men armed themselves and, following a brief confrontation, James left. Not wishing to engage in a shootout, he sold his supplies and returned to Everett where he told the O & B Mining Company, which had hired him to do its assessment work on the mine, that he wasn't about to place his life in danger and they could hire someone else to do the job.

The O & B company did just that by engaging Irvine and Clayton Packard, sons of the original owner, to assume the responsibility. The company also took legal action, and when the Packards journeyed to Monte Cristo, they had a court order which forced the Kyes brothers, working on behalf of American Mining, to relinquish that company's claim on the property.

This fight between the two companies had been brewing since January, 1906, when the claim had been jumped by Alex Kozmovski, who alleged that the O & B had not made yearly improvements to the property, and thus had forfeited its rights. Kozmovski had transferred his claim to H. D. Cowden, who sold it to the American Mining Company, of which he was the principal stockholder. During the 1907-08 season, claimants from both companies attempted to do assessment work on the mine, but they thwarted each other by brandishing guns and making threats. Thus, for several years no development had been accomplished by either side. The matter finally reached the courts in 1909 and it was resolved, to some extent, with ownership placed back in the hands of the O & B Mining Company. Although the yearly work could now proceed, the O & B did not produce any ore. Nor did the other mines in the area.

Early in 1909, ASARCO, the Guggenheim trust, once again showed interest in the Monte Cristo mines. Josiah E. Spurr, who had written the definitive geologic treatise on the area in 1901, was now employed by the Guggenheims as a consulting engineer. The local press expressed the hope in February that ASARCO would repurchase the mines and operate them on an expanded scale. The newspapers reasoned that, with Spurr and E. L. Newhouse, ASARCO's traveling general manager, at the helm, success would finally be assured.[2]

When he controlled the mines, Samuel Silverman had blasted one tunnel of the Justice mine from the Thomas claim, under the No. 3 Mystery tunnel on Mystery Hill, a distance of 6,800 feet. The tunnel struck the vein through which the Mystery tunnels passed at a point 400 feet beneath the No. 3 Mystery adit. The plan had been to bore a raise to the No. 3 tunnel, thereby connecting underground the Pride of the Mountains, Pride of the Woods, Mystery, and Justice mines. Silverman had run out of money, however, before the project was completed. This lower tunnel, 400 feet below the lowest Mystery tunnel, tapped that vein at a depth never before achieved in Monte Cristo.

Spurr ventured into this tunnel in 1909 during his extensive investigation and reappraisal of the mining properties on behalf of ASARCO. He checked the possibilities of reopening the mines, and submitted his findings later that year. The report was not made public, but the newspapers knew of its existence. His conclusions, arrived at through precise geologic and accounting procedures, indicated that the mines would, in the final analysis, lose the operator $0.28 on each ton of ore mined. As had been the case in all the Monte Cristo mines, the amount of mineral present in the long Justice tunnel was much less than the apparent richness of the surface outcrop. Spurr concluded that the value decreased with depth, and that a loss would be incurred because the richer deposits had previously been removed. His report resulted in the mines remaining idle.

Monte Cristo had no rail service in 1909, and, except for the one special, none of the trains ventured beyond Silverton. However, in early November an excursion train ran to Silverton, the first in almost six years. But it was not intended to be a trip to show the passengers the scenic wonders. The Imperial Mining Company, which had purchased the old Bonanza Queen and a few other properties, ran the excursion to give prospective investors a first-hand look at its property. Although many who made the trip that day were probably looking for mining property investments, undoubtedly some went along merely to enjoy the scenery and perhaps had memories of earlier excursions when they rode in open observation cars and marvelled at the mountain grandeur.

The annual fall flood came on November 30, and the rivers attained their highest marks since the 1897 disaster. A massive slide at Tunnel No. 2 completely blocked the road for a time, requiring a large crew of men to remove it. Only small washouts occurred on the line and, except for the stretch of track from Snohomish to Lowell—which was completely submerged—service along the road was uninterrupted through and above the Stillaguamish Canyon.

The beginning of 1910 was accompanied by an unusually severe winter in the Cascades, with heavy, wet snows that piled deep on the deserted structures in Monte Cristo. One by one they succumbed to the enormous weight. With no one present to remove the snow, the roofs collapsed and the buildings were flattened. Spring arrived late that year, and when the snow melted, visitors were horrified by what the winter had done to the village. Monte Cristo now presented a pathetic scene to those who had known the town in its heyday. Most of the buildings on Dumas Street were gone; even some of the ones constructed during the 1907 rush had collapsed, leaving a picture of devastation. Wags joked that the town was in hibernation, but an advanced stage of decay would have been a more apt description. A notable survivor was the hotel constructed by Cohen and Sheedy at the turn of the century. Originally called Rockefeller House, and more currently referred to as the Royal Hotel, it now stood virtually alone.

The weather halted the trains going to Silverton, and by springtime rail traffic was able to reach only the shingle mill at Gold Basin, about nine miles below the town. Rock and mud slides had done extensive damage along the road, and only the fact that a mill existed at Gold Basin prompted the railroad to keep the line open to that point. The snow melted slowly and men were put to work repairing the line between Gold Basin and Silverton. The optimists predicted renewed service into Monte Cristo during the coming summer, but that was not to be. Just when the crews appeared to be making progress, another rock and mud slide roared onto the track from the unstable canyon wall near Tunnel No. 4, blocking the line completely. According to the *Everett Daily Herald*, some of the boulders which rolled upon the track were "half the size of a box car." The slide occurred on May 28, and by June 7 the line had been reopened through Tunnel No. 4, but trains still could travel only to Gold Basin.

Minor development work continued at some of the Monte Cristo mines during the summer of 1910, but the cost of packing supplies into the now isolated area was too great to permit any serious operation. The only interest shown in the mines was a visit by two members of a group of New York bankers touring the west coast, investigating mining, oil, and timber prospects. Local newspapers speculated that the financiers had taken options on the Pride and Mystery, would assemble the arsenic extraction plants (some of the machinery was still on the property), and open the mines for production. But, like many rumors, this one was without substance, and nothing happened.

Another slide at Tunnel No. 4 temporarily blocked the road on October 5, halting train travel at Granite Falls. Four days later, however, the slide had been cleared and traffic reopened to Robe, at the head of the canyon. Trains were not traveling to Gold Basin, and the tracks beyond Robe had fallen into disrepair. On October 13, a new disaster occurred—the shoring in Tunnel No. 2 gave way and tons of loose rock and mud filled part of the passage. Merchants in Robe and beyond, who had just ordered their winter supplies, were caught unprepared and had to find other means of transporting goods past the obstruction. The railroad company elected to abandon service beyond Granite Falls for the duration of the winter, an action that created considerable anguish among businessmen in the Stillaguamish Valley.

Snow began falling in the mountains in early October, and the little work that was under way at Monte Cristo quickly terminated when the few residents left the town. With no train service beyond Granite Falls, not many persons remained in the hills that winter.

On February 28, 1911, a special train, carrying several officials of the Northern Pacific, made an inspection tour to the collapsed Tunnel No. 2. The company did not announce the purpose of the trip, but it may have had some bearing on action it was to take about four months later. Because of the continuing, expensive maintenance work required, the railroad had to decide whether to close the line or to make improvements in the Stillaguamish Canyon. The company chose the latter solution, closed the line beyond Tunnel No. 1 and put a crew to work in the canyon. Tunnels No. 2 and 4 were singled out for special solutions. They had been bored through extremely unstable rock and mud, and both had been the scene of most of the slides which had blocked the road intermittently over the years. The Northern Pacific decided to destroy the tunnels and run the tracks through deep open cuts where they had formerly been.

Unstable rock higher up the cliff was also to be blasted into the canyon to preclude its sliding onto the tracks in the future. Work began in early August to clear the tunnels, and continued into October. The crews used large charges of powder to tear away the roofs of the tunnels and reduce the size of the boulders. The men could then excavate the debris and make the open cuts.

J.A. Juleen Photo
An explosion of blasting powder assists in clearing the debris of tunnel number four from the right of way. The tunnel which plagued maintenance crews for many years was finally removed and converted into an open cut.

J.A. Juleen Photo

Plagued by collapses and land slides at tunnels number four and two, the Northern Pacific decided in the summer of 1911 to close the line for several months and eliminate the bores altogether. Seen here is all that remains of tunnel four after the powder monkeys finished with it. All that remained was to clear the tracks of the debris, a formidable task with the tools available.

The open cut that was once tunnel number two. The deck of the suspension bridge used to carry limestone from the quarry across the Stillaguamish River is seen just beyond the cut.

Meanwhile, in Everett ASARCO was dismantling the smelter which had been so closely tied to the railroad's initial construction and the opening of the Monte Cristo mines. The smelter had not been operated for more than a year, the one in Tacoma having processed all the local ore. In fact, some of the machinery in Everett was shipped to Tacoma and the rest scrapped. Although the main plant had not been operated for some time, the arsenic extraction facility at Everett had continued to handle ores rich in that element for the Tacoma smelter. The ore was shipped first to Everett where the arsenic was extracted by roasting, then to Tacoma for smelting. But in February, 1912, the roasting plant at Everett closed its doors and ASARCO announced that handling of arsenic in the future would be accomplished in Denver. The last vestige of the mining industry in Everett, the city once predicted to become the "Pittsburgh of the West Coast," had faded into history.

Despite its isolation, the Monte Cristo Mining District was the scene of considerable development activity during the summer of 1911. The new Del Campo Metals Company led the way with its prospect in the Weden Creek area, just three miles below Monte Cristo. Peabody continued his work on the Sidney mine in '76 Gulch, and an English concern, the Eclipse Mining Company in Silverton, was busy on its new prospects. But by the end of the year the Bonanza Queen Mining Company went bankrupt and was sold at a receiver's sale. One of the company's bond holders then filed suit to recover his losses in the venture, spawning more litigation before active operation of the property could resume.

On October 13, the Northern Pacific announced it would accept freight and passenger traffic to Robe for the first time in a year. Work continued along the line, and within two weeks it had been opened to Gold Basin, and the mill at that place resumed operations.

The railroad was again serving Silverton by the end of 1911, although a few minor slides temporarily blocked the line in the Stillaguamish Canyon during the wet winter months. Speculators were optimistic that the line would be open to Monte Cristo by the summer of 1912. Rumors hinted that the Northern Pacific was studying the feasibility of using gasoline cars—they were then becoming popular on interurban routes throughout the state—on the Monte Cristo branch, but the company neither confirmed nor denied the stories. However, in April one of the railroad's local officials stated that the Monte Cristo line was "not in a very bad condition between Silverton and Monte" and could easily be put into shape for regular operations.

During the summer of 1912 the usual band of prospectors and developers arrived at Monte Cristo. A few brought their families to the town, but living in the isolated community was difficult at best. With the trains running only to Silverton, essential supplies had to be packed 14 miles to Monte Cristo, a slow, expensive process. Not enough people lived in the town to support a post office, and the facility was discontinued during the summer. This left James Kyes without his job, and the mail was subsequently sent only to Silverton.

No production work was in progress, and the larger mining companies no longer bothered to employ watchmen on their properties, leaving them open to intruders. Vandalism became common as people learned about the unprotected mines in the mountains. Considerable damage was done that summer to the Pride and Mystery as well as to the old Bartholomew house in Monte Cristo. The townsite was in a general state of decay, the winter snows having crushed the roofs of more buildings, exposing them to the elements, and the ones which survived the weather were doomed to a fate at the hands of vandals. Most of the houses on Dumas Street were gone, smashed flat by the weight of winter snow. Many of the mine structures had been swept away by avalanches or severely damaged by tourists. Much of the mining, tramway, and concentrator machinery had been hauled away by salvagers to be sold for scrap metal or used on other claims.

Monte Cristo rapidly took on the air of a ghost town, relieved only by the few prospectors who doggedly returned each year to find that lucky streak which would bring them fame and fortune. In late November, 1912, Cohen and Sheedy, long the proprietors of the Royal Hotel on Dumas Street, purchased the New Wilson Hotel in Anacortes. They left Monte Cristo, and with their departure the town's last hotel closed its doors.

The railroad received a considerable amount of attention toward the close of 1912. More than 100 men worked in the Stillaguamish Canyon, relaying ties, straightening the roadbed, and placing new ballast and riprap along the right-of-way. Rumors abounded that the railroad would reopen to Monte Cristo in time for the 1913 summer. One of the workmen stated that the line would, in fact, be operated to Monte Cristo during the coming year, but this was not officially confirmed.

However, the Del Campo Mining Company, which for three years had
hauled all its supplies to Weden Creek on flat cars pulled by mules,
announced that production was about to begin and that the firm would
require rail service to the Weden Creek Station. Because of this,
observers reasoned, the Northern Pacific was obligated to repair the line
between Silverton and Monte Cristo, and re-establish service by the
summer of 1913.

If plans did exist for opening the line to Monte Cristo in 1913, the
winter weather was not cooperating. By late January the snow was
seven feet deep in Silverton, with an unmeasured depth at Monte
Cristo. Rail traffic stopped at Robe, and the company made no attempt
to operate trains above that point. Small slides in the Stillaguamish
Canyon kept the section crews busy maintaining the service to Robe,
much less Silverton. One man, who battled his way on foot through the
deep drifts, was two days traveling from Silverton to Robe. He reported
that supplies in Silverton and other points along the line were running
low. The severe weather and heavy snow had made it difficult to pack
food and other necessities into the isolated area. So critical did the
problem become, that most persons limited their intake to one ration
per day, and the settlers along the railroad appealed to the Public Service
Commission. The agency, whose job was to assure that private and
government organizations operated in the public interest, ordered the
Northern Pacific to reopen the railroad from Robe to Silverton in order
to relieve the snowbound populace. Consequently, for the first time in
many years the Monte Cristo line witnessed a rotary plow in action.
One of the company's rotaries had to be brought down from near the
Stampede Pass tunnel to clear the line into Silverton. The snowplow
made short work of the job, and supplies once again flowed into the
town.

Although the settlers along the railroad had been holding their own
while they battled the elements, the miners at the "45" Consolidated
mine had given up and left. Too much snow lay upon the mountains to
allow operation of the mine. The men's leaving turned out to be a
fortuitous decision, however, because during the winter a massive
avalanche came down the south side of Marble Pass and destroyed most
of the buildings—the sawmill, bunkhouse, powerhouse, and
headquarters. The company attempted in March to recover some of the
machinery from the wreckage, but made no immediate plans regarding

the mine's future. However, in late April, Nate Jones, manager of the "45" Consolidated Mining Company, prepared to go to the mine when conditions permitted in order to begin the reconstruction of the facilities.

As winter gave way to spring, people who used the railroad began to inquire when the line was going to be opened to Monte Cristo. The Del Campo Mining Company had a crew at work, and the Mackinaw and Peabody, now idle, were reported ready to resume operations the moment rail service was restored. Pressure brought by the many business and mining men along the right-of-way prompted the county commissioners to petition the Public Service Commission to order the line reopened. The county officials also desired access to the town so they could repair a portion of Dumas Street built on log cribbing which had collapsed. In the midst of this, an arrangement had been made whereby John F. Birney, long-time county engineer and one of the designers of the railroad, had contracted to buy the major Monte Cristo mines. Birney immediately met with members of the Public Service Commission to voice his desire that service be restored.

The commissioners held a hearing to consider the matter of rebuilding the line. After much discussion and testimony, the Northern Pacific agreed to the plans put forth by Birney to reopen the railroad if the costs of doing so were kept below $10,000. Birney indicated he would undertake the project for that amount, but as the tracks were then buried beneath three to six feet of snow, further action was postponed until the spring thaw.

Prior to the beginning of summer, engineers toured the tracks between Silverton and Monte Cristo to estimate the cost and effort required to reopen the railway. With their report in hand, they appeared before the Public Service Commission, but shortly before it met to discuss and decide the case the parties reached a compromise settlement. The railroad company agreed to rebuild the line on a temporary basis, to allow light weight and occasional operation. The light weight service would be rendered by a gas car, or "galloping goose," as it was popularly called, to be purchased by Birney's Ben Lomond Mining Company. The gas car would haul personnel and light equipment over the line. The miners had sought and received trackage rights over the Northern Pacific between Hartford and Monte Cristo to allow the "galloping goose" to operate.

Hope was rekindled in mid-summer that the Monte Cristo mines would soon be reopened. Rail service, albeit light duty, was restored to the town, and Birney enthusiastically prepared his properties for production. People returned, some to homes they had left years earlier. Many were disappointed, because the Monte Cristo they remembered was gone, replaced by a scattered collection of ramshackle buildings, most of which were uninhabitable. Clearly, it would be an uphill battle for Birney to reopen the mines and put them on a paying basis.

J.A. Juleen Photo
One of the Hartford-Eastern gas cars with trailer on the turntable at Monte Cristo.
The main beam of the turntable, which once headed the eighty ton steam locomotives
toward home, is still in place in 1977, and can still be rotated.

CHAPTER XIV

1913-20

REQUIEM TO MINING

On April 19, 1913, John F. Birney predicted that within two months he would ship ore to the Tacoma smelter, which had contracted to handle all that he could supply. By the time summer arrived, that facility was owned by ASARCO, which had recently dismantled its Everett plant and consolidated its Pacific Northwest operations at Ruston, near Tacoma. ASARCO had restarted the idle arsenic plant in Everett, where the ores received treatment prior to the smelting at Tacoma. All was in readiness for Monte Cristo to again become a producer.

Five years had passed since a regularly scheduled train had come into Monte Cristo. In fact, four years had gone by since *any* train had visited the town. Thus the prospect of reopening the line stirred the community into a frenzy of activity. Birney had 30 men working for his Ben Lomond Mining Company in the old Rainy shaft, with ore ready to be shipped upon completion of the road. As forecast, the other properties began development work—the American, Peabody, and Mackinaw mines started anew after several years of inactivity.

The reorganization of the American Mining Company in 1913 was to have far-reaching consequences for Monte Cristo. The company was one of the concerns which had feuded for years over the ownership of the O & B property. The reorganization involved a change in officers, with the name of the new company's treasurer, F. W. Boston, added to create the Boston-American Mining Company. Since the 1909 litigation had awarded ownership of the O & B mine to the O & B Mining Company, H. D. Cowden, president of the American Mining Company, had begun prospecting farther down Toad Mountain. He reasoned that an adit bored from a point 75 feet above the railroad turntable

217

would strike the ledge of O & B ore 1,500 feet below the surface out-crop. If the ledge was unbroken to this unprecedented depth, the lower tunnel would "block out" an immense amount of ore and assure mining during the foreseeable future at Monte Cristo. This was an enormous gamble, because all previous attempts to find mineral deep in the earth at Monte Cristo had ended in failure. Nevertheless, while Birney attempted to drain the Rainy shaft, ten men were at work for the Boston-American Mining Company at the base of Toad Mountain, driving a tunnel toward the O & B ledge.

On July 21 the first train on the reopened line rumbled across the trestle over the Sauk River and into the yards at Monte Cristo. The run was only for track building and maintenance purposes, but its signi-ficance was felt from Everett to Monte Cristo. Within a few days the railroad scheduled one regular train per week to the town, but Birney's gas car had not yet arrived. Seventy-five men were working the five re-opened mines at Monte Cristo, and many of them lived in the old Royal Hotel on Dumas Street, one of the few structures sound enough to withstand years of heavy snows and neglect. The hotel had, in fact, been reopened by Birney in connection with his claims, and it was now equipped with electric lights and other conveniences. Business was brisk, and Monte Cristo began to take on a semblance of its former activity.

However, by late August, complaints were voiced up and down the line regarding the one train per week, which now ran only to Silverton. Evidence that the service was inadequate was demonstrated on August 13, when the train was delayed at Hartford due to extreme over-crowding, and an extra car had to be obtained and added to the "consist" to handle the 176 passengers wishing to make the trip. The train, which also carried 26,000 pounds of cargo, went only as far as Sil-verton. Thus the people and equipment bound for Monte Cristo had to travel beyond Silverton on makeshift cars, both motorized and horse-drawn. Birney's efforts to obtain a "galloping goose" failed when he discovered that the company from which he had ordered the gas car had none in its inventory. He then arranged to have one built at Granite Falls.

By mid-August the water level in the Rainy shaft of the Ben Lomond mine had been lowered by a compressed air bailer to the second level, and Birney predicted that in about two weeks the mine would be dry and producing. The operation obtained its air from a water-powered compressor located about a half-mile above the mine near the base of Glacier Falls, the source of the water. On August 28, just as Birney was within sight of his goal, the compressor house caught fire and burned, destroying all the machinery in the process. So rapidly did the fire consume the structure, that operator Davis did not have time to save his coat. Birney supposed that some form of spontaneous combustion was responsible for the blaze; but, whatever the cause, the mine would have to remain idle until new equipment could be obtained and another building constructed.

In concert with the activity at Monte Cristo, the Pacific Telephone Company constructed a new line up the railroad right-of-way, and near the end of August, Monte Cristo was accessible by telephone from the cities bordering Puget Sound.

Birney arranged for extension of the old concentrator spur to the Rainy shaft of his Ben Lomond mine in order to eliminate the extra handling of the ore required when hauling it to the railroad. He also planned to construct a small smelter at the mine to reduce the ore to "pigs" for shipment down the rails, significantly lowering the shipping costs as well as retaining more of the metal content.

Except for a minor slide in the Stillaguamish Canyon, the railroad remained open into 1914, and development work at Monte Cristo proceeded without major incident. Late in January, however, snow delayed traffic above Silverton and halted the extensive repairs the company was making in that area. Then, on January 28, a slide near Tunnel No. 4 severed the line, closing traffic to Silverton. The mining companies at Monte Cristo had only skeleton crews to accomplish work during the winter, but adequate supplies had been stockpiled to sustain them through the period of isolation, therefore no hardships were anticipated.

As the sun moved northward, heralding the spring of 1914, activity increased at Monte Cristo and other points along the railroad. The Boston-American Mining Company announced the discovery of an eight-foot vein of mixed low- and high-grade ore in its Toad Mountain tunnel. The Ben Lomond Mining Company's Rainy shaft had produced over 400 tons of ore which could be shipped when rail transportation became available. The Northern Pacific had many crews making repairs to the line while the snow melted from the roadbed between Silverton and Monte Cristo. One crew was "riprapping 'the pot hole,' where the stream had dug out a cavern near the roadbed." Another, "fortified by a piledriver," was replacing trestling near Monte Cristo.

Weekly service was re-established during the summer between Everett and Monte Cristo. Once again the trains were of mixed freight-passenger configuration and picked up loaded ore cars on the return trip. Although the frequency of service did not excite residents up the line, they were getting more than had been available for some time; the first passenger train in six years arrived at Monte Cristo on June 24.

The company sent a steam shovel up the line to assist the workmen who were improving the roadbed between Silverton and Monte Cristo. According to rumors, the Northern Pacific intended, when the roadbed had been stabilized, to establish biweekly service to Monte Cristo. But, like many rumors in the past, this one never materialized. When the Snohomish Moose Lodge attempted to organize an excursion to Monte Cristo in late July, the railroad refused on the grounds that the roadbed between Silverton and Monte Cristo was too unstable for such a large train to negotiate safely. Birney, however, was now running his converted motor car up and down the almost deserted line, supplementing the Northern Pacific's once a week schedule. The last train in 1914 made the trip to Monte Cristo on December 16. The service was then suspended for the balance of the winter; although "not a great quantity of snow" covered the right-of-way, it was "enough to stop traffic" on a railroad that was "not guarded against the white visitation by a rotary plow."

Most of the mining companies planned to maintain skeleton crews to handle development work during the winter. By the spring of 1915, however, Birney, who had been largely responsible for the resurgence of activity in Monte Cristo, was in financial trouble, and the courts placed the Ben Lomond mine in receivership. The now familiar boom and bust pattern at Monte Cristo had again repeated itself. The problem was not that the mine was not producing, but that the returns could not match the expenditures. In fact, a great amount of ore lay in the Ben Lomond bins, but it could not be shipped due to the snow blocking the railroad tracks. The receiver, W. A. Simmons, filed a petition on April 1, 1915, asking the court's permission to sell the ore to defray the costs of selling the property. He anticipated that shipment could not be made before May 15, when the tracks were expected to be free of snow, even if the petition was granted. The value of the property was placed at $62,466.

Meanwhile, the Boston-American Mining Company bored steadily deeper into Toad Mountain.

Because increasing pressure from government agencies forced it to maintain operation in the public interest, regardless of whether or not the service was profitable, the Northern Pacific in early 1915 sought a way to unburden itself of the Monte Cristo branch line. While the railroad company was looking for a way out, the Rucker brothers, who had been instrumental in the founding of Everett, and who now operated a large lumber mill at Lake Stevens, were attempting to renew an annual contract with the railroad which gave them trackage rights on the Monte Cristo branch. The contract was necessary because they owned or leased large tracts of timbered land along the right-of-way, and the railroad was their lifeline to these properties. But when negotiations were undertaken to renew the agreement for 1915, the Northern Pacific refused. This meant strangulation of the Ruckers' source of logs for their mill. However, the railway company offered them an alternative—a ten-year lease giving them control over the line between Hartford and Monte Cristo. Although the Ruckers were lumbermen and not railroaders by trade, the Northern Pacific had them backed against a wall. On May 11, 1915, the Ruckers signed an agreement that made them the operators of a general common carrier in both freight and passenger traffic. However, they approached the task with their usual gusto, created a new firm to operate the line, and named it the Hartford Eastern Railway Company. They immediately announced that gasoline cars would replace steam power for most of the passenger and light freight work on the line.

This turn of events had caught the Ruckers unprepared, and they had to make plans hurriedly. They ordered new equipment, and on August 28 the first of several gasoline-powered vehicles arrived in Everett. The bus, built by the White Company, was driven to Everett on conventional solid rubber truck tires. They were then removed and flanged railway wheels installed in their place. This "galloping goose" looked like a motor bus on railway wheels, which in fact it was.

Quite different from the White machine was another gasoline car ordered by the Hartford Eastern and built to special order in Seattle. This vehicle resembled a standard interurban "combination" car, with space for baggage and freight as well as passengers, but it was somewhat smaller, measuring 30 feet in length. Power was supplied by a 50-horsepower engine mounted on the forward truck and connected to the single-drive axle by two chains. In addition to 30 passengers, it could carry two tons of baggage. The arrival of these machines generated keen interest in Everett, the residents foreseeing the time when they could make trips to Monte Cristo to enjoy the scenic splendor as they once had.

The Ruckers soon received a taste of railroad operation in the Cascade Mountains. By February, 1916, seven feet of snow lay on the ground at Monte Cristo, and massive avalanches blocked the rails all along the line under tons of snow. During the winter the heaviest snowfall since 1893 was recorded in the Puget Sound basin. So much snow fell that the Great Northern had to use rotary plows to clear its sea level line along Puget Sound between Seattle and Everett, and the route over Stevens Pass was inoperative for several months. Barns and houses in the river valleys were crushed by the weight on their roofs. Most buildings in Monte Cristo sustained similar damage. With the exception of the Royal Hotel and a few smaller structures, everything at Monte Cristo, including the old concentrator, was flattened. Service on the Hartford Eastern was at a standstill for a time, because the company did not have a rotary plow to clear the rails. Mining operations in the mountains came to a sudden halt when the miners fled to the lowlands.

The few residents left at Silverton filed a complaint with the Public Service Commission, seeking restoration of service. However, the commission, noting the unusually severe weather conditions, left the matter in the hands of the Hartford Eastern management to resolve whenever snow conditions permitted. By March, service had been restored to Silverton, with one freight train per week, and daily passenger service provided. No attempt was made to open the way into Monte Cristo because heavy snow clung to the mountains and huge avalanches covered the tracks in many places.

The summer schedule of the Hartford Eastern Railway Company appeared in the *Everett Daily Herald* in late May, and Monte Cristo was reconnected with the lowlands. Mining activities resumed with haste when the companies sought to make up the time lost during the idle winter months. The Northwest Consolidated's mine at Weden Creek installed a new tramway to transport its ore to the railroad; the Boston-

American at Monte Cristo put a force of men to work on its crosscut tunnel, just above the railroad turntable, to drive farther toward the ledge.

The Ruckers revived a long-forgotten tradition in mid-June by running an excursion for 200 visiting bankers to Monte Cristo. The train, pulled by a standard locomotive, consisted of flat cars equipped with railings and seats, reminiscent of the observation coaches of past years. The caboose carried the refreshments. Only one mishap marred the trip: a flatcar derailed at Barlow Pass. The accident was timely, however, occurring at the lunch hour, and the contents of the caboose were served while the crew put the car back on the tracks. On the return trip that evening the train made an unscheduled stop when John J. Juleen, noted Everett photographer, lost his new panama hat and insisted that he be allowed to retrieve it. Such were the risks of riding in open observation cars, not to mention cinders in the eyes or the threat of a sudden downpour.

A week later another excursion train ran to Monte Cristo. This one was open to the general public, and 154 people visited, or in some cases revisited, the mining town. Several days before the trip a customer approached H. K. Akles, the passenger agent, with an unusual request. He stated he was F. F. Cassiday, a Portland physician, and he wished to transport a motor car to Monte Cristo. The passenger agent was certain the doctor was mad. Ordinarily such a request would not be unusual, but no roads existed in Monte Cristo, so what possible use could a person make of a motor car in the community? The answer was quickly forthcoming when the doctor explained that he operated the Cass-Crest mine (which he owned) on Mystery Hill and the Philo (which he leased), and he needed an engine to run his air compressor. The motor car was in poor condition but had a good engine. Therefore, in an early version of piggy-back service, the crew attached an extra flatcar to the train just ahead of the caboose, and gawking observers along the right-of-way saw the first motor car to travel to Monte Cristo. When the train left Everett, rain was falling, but the skies were clear in the Cascades, and "the sun shone and shot dazzling diamond rays from snow-capped peaks and vast snow fields."

A slide in August cut the road at Tunnel No. 3 below Robe. A week's time was required to remove the obstacle. The canyon proved that it played no favorites and it made trouble for the new operators just as it had for the railway companies that preceded them. But nature was not the only element of concern to the Ruckers. The mail carrier, Grover McDowell, had for years used a gasoline-powered speeder to make his appointed rounds along the line. This practice had been acceptable under the Northern Pacific's limited service, but the Hartford Eastern ran one or two gas cars every day and the potential for a collision along the winding right-of-way was too great. The Rucker brothers repeatedly asked McDowell to refrain from using the speeder, but he refused. Consequently, they were compelled to bring legal action, and after a brief appearance in court, McDowell began riding the daily gas cars when he delivered the mail.

During the autumn of 1916, the Northwest Consolidated Mining Company on Weden Creek shipped its first carload of hand-selected high-grade copper ore to the Tacoma smelter, the first such shipment from the area outside Monte Cristo since the reopening of the railroad. On October 19, the Boston-American Mining Company made a startling announcement: the long crosscut it had been driving into the base of Toad Mountain since 1913 had struck the main "ledge" of O & B ore 1,500 feet below its outcrop, exactly where the company had predicted.

The statement hailed the strike as disproving Josiah Spurr's theory that the ore chutes in the Monte Cristo district lost value with depth. The tunnel had been driven 2,850 feet into the mountain before the ledge had been struck, and if the reports of an average value of $5 per ton in gold were correct, this discovery would, indeed, signal prosperity that Monte Cristo had never before realized. The Boston-American claimed to have 120,000 tons of ore blocked out, assuming that the ore was continuous to the surface outcrop. The discovery represented the deepest encounter with ore of significant value in Monte Cristo's brief history, and the news created a genuine stir in the area.

However, the glowing terms that were used to express the value of the strike had to be tempered by what knowledgeable mining men said about the Boston-American operations. The *Mines Handbook* for 1916 concluded its appraisal of the company's activities thus:

> The statements made by the management in the literature put out are grossly misleading. Provided the "ledge", when found does contain shipping ore, and can be profitably worked, it is certain that the costs and net profits promised by company's literature, will never be realized.

Oblivious to these barbs, the Boston-American reiterated its intentions to increase the work force at Monte Cristo and to build bunkers to handle the large quantity of ore it expected to remove from the mine. But winter settled over the Cascades once again, putting the company's plans on the "back burner" until after the spring thaw. However, the fury of the winter weather did not prevent the firm from purchasing other properties in the Monte Cristo district. During the winter of 1916-17, the Boston-American bought or had quitclaimed to it many claims, both old and new. Nor did the adverse comment in the *Mines Handbook* dampen the enthusiasm of the officers and stockholders. This was demonstrated by H. D. Cowden, who was both the president and an owner, when he moved his family from Illinois to Washington in the summer of 1916.

Less than two weeks after the announcement that the ledge had been struck, a massive rock slide blocked the Hartford Eastern tracks at Tunnel No. 3. Although freight could not be hauled past the obstruction, the Ruckers arranged to detour passenger traffic via motor car on the old Johnson-Dean logging road. But by late December the issue of access through the canyon was academic since the entire line beyond Granite Falls was blocked by snow. The subsequent melting at the lower elevations in early 1917 did not alleviate the problems in the canyon. Repeated slides near Tunnel No. 3 kept the railroad more often closed than open. In desperation, residents up the line once more complained to the Public Service Commission in an attempt to force the company to provide more steady, reliable service into their area. This resulted in the Hartford Eastern placing a "rock shed" outside the eastern portal of Tunnel No. 3 to deflect the slides over the tracks and into the river.

With Monte Cristo snowed in, mining activities were reduced to development and maintenance work. The Boston-American Company kept a small force preparing the crosscut tunnel for production the following summer. Tragedy struck the company president's family when Cowden's son was killed in an avalanche near Monte Cristo in the spring of 1917 when he was aiding in the development work. A large group of men hiked over the snow from Silverton to haul the bodies of Harry Cowden and "Mackintosh" Johnson down the snowy grade on sleds. The two boys, who had been the best of friends, had died together while on a mission of mercy. They had been looking for another miner who they thought was lost in the snow. Ironically, he was all right, but had failed to keep his promise to telephone the Monte Cristo camp.

During April the railway plowed its line to Silverton, while warm spring weather slowly melted the accumulated snow. But, as Frank Fleenor discovered, the thaw was late in the mountains in 1917. The deputy game warden had hiked into Monte Cristo on May 6 to seek violators of the fishing laws, but instead of fishermen he found four feet of snow. In fact, the ground was white all the way from Gold Basin to Monte Cristo. This situation did not coincide with the Boston-American's plans to establish a producing mining camp at Monte Cristo.

On July 10, the conditions were finally favorable enough in the town that a group of the company's stockholders, all from Illinois, took the journey to Monte Cristo to decide what provisions should be made for their future mining effort. They elected to construct a bunkhouse and a headquarters/cookhouse on the flat just below the Toad Mountain adit. Upon completion of these structures, a 200-ton concentrator was to be built above the bunkhouse near the base of Sunday Falls. It was to be constructed in two sections, the first capable of handling 100 tons of ore per day. If production warranted, the company would build the second section to expand the mill's capacity to 200 tons.

By late September the bunk and cook houses were almost completed, but the concentrator was just beginning to take shape, with the first timbers set in place. Construction of an aerial tramway 4,600 feet long had also been started to carry ore from the old Justice mine to the new concentrator. As a result of all this activity, the future appeared to hold promise of renewed prosperity. But at this time an event took place which altered forever the future of Monte Cristo.

The nations of Europe had been deadlocked for almost three years in a devastating war, while the United States maintained a position of neutrality. During the early months of 1917, it became increasingly evident that the conflict could not be avoided, and late in 1917 the country entered the war. Even with three years to observe the war's progress and to arm itself, the nation was caught unprepared, and the cry went out for the mobilization of men, money, and industry to meet the challenge. Lives were changed overnight when men were called to arms to face the threat in Europe. Because industry was mobilized to support the war effort, marginal ventures like the Boston-American

Mining Company were "retired" for the duration. Except for development and maintenance work, mining at Monte Cristo came to a halt; the men and money were needed elsewhere. In addition, nature, as though in concert with man, caused the most severe flooding ever recorded in the area, and isolated the town. Never since the flood of 1897 had Monte Cristo's prospects looked so bleak.

The old smelter in Everett was gone, its stacks having been toppled in 1915 to recover the brick, the buildings dismantled two years later. They were moved to the Norwegian-Pacific shipyards to house machinery for the construction of ferro-cement ships to aid in the war effort. Serious questions were raised as to whether mining, on any scale, would ever again be attempted at Monte Cristo. Even the railroad, that vital lifeline to the outside world, was threatened, but not by the war. A new form of personal transportation was becoming popular and usurping its share of the railroad's business, with roads being built farther and farther into the mountains. Thus, by 1918 one could travel in a motor car to the base of Mount Pilchuck. Although the automobile road was poor, the railroad began to feel the loss of business.

As the nation became more deeply embroiled in the European conflict, more manpower and money were siphoned from local enterprises and directed toward the national commitment. The Boston-American Mining Company could muster only enough manpower and funds to handle assessment and maintenance work at Monte Cristo. The concentrator and tramway, just begun in 1917, were left untouched throughout 1918.

That is not to say that the mountains surrounding Monte Cristo were inaccessible or unvisited in 1918. Quite the contrary, because the Hartford Eastern had re-established its summer schedule to the town. But the people who rode the cars that year were more interested in the scenery than they were in tapping the mineral wealth. Perhaps the largest and best organized group to use the railroad in the summer of 1918 was The Mountaineers, an alpinists' club headquartered in Seattle. Led by H. B. Hinman, C. G. Morrison, and M. M. Diewart, this party spent a month touring the mountains bordering the Stillaguamish and Sauk Rivers. They began the trip by riding the gas car from Hartford to Granite Falls, then hiking to the falls on the Stillaguamish. Disdaining transportation, they walked eight miles up the railroad's tracks, through the canyon, to a camp at the base of Mount Pilchuck. They

Walker Photo
Edmond S. Meany, president of the Seattle Mountaineers on the 1918 summer outing at Monte Cristo.

climbed the mountain in soggy weather and returned the next day, thoroughly convinced that the winter rains had set in.

Aboard the gas car once again, they moved on to Silverton, where a second base camp was established. Here the hikers made side trips to many local sites, but the group soon split, with one party remaining at the Silverton camp while the other climbed over Marble Pass to Copper Lake to spend the night. The following day, the members of this second group ascended the glacier above the lake and crossed the pass between Vesper and Sperry Peaks. Then, taking the Sunrise mine trail, they descended over Headlee Pass to the Hartford Eastern tracks at Buck Creek. Because the exhausted group had been scheduled to return to Silverton the previous night, Dr. Hinman hiked eight miles down the tracks to Silverton to report, lest the waiting party should become anxious about the group's safety. He arrived in the town about midnight, and the other members reached Silverton the next day. They immediately raided the commissary, as they had run out of food on their extended trip.

The alpinists pitched their next camp at Buck Creek, along the railroad, and climbed Vesper Peak. The climbers then left the tracks at Barlow Pass and hiked eight miles down the Sauk River and up Elliot Creek to Goat Lake. They camped near the outlet, and took several short hikes in the vicinity, among them a visit to the Penn Mining Company's abandoned Foggy mine. They noted that the miners had bored completely through the ridge; but, as was the case with many other mines in the area, they had failed to tap "the ledge."

While part of the group remained at the lake, the more ambitious ones climbed over the southwest ridge, via Ida Pass, and descended into Monte Cristo. They hiked down the railroad tracks to the Weden Creek station, then followed the Del Campo Mining Company's trail and ascended toward Gothic Basin. Along the way they passed two mute reminders of early mining efforts—mines that had been abandoned by Northwest Consolidated and the Del Campo Mining Company. Upon reaching Gothic Basin, they turned their steps northward and ascended Del Campo Peak. The following day they trekked back to Monte Cristo in a pouring rain and camped in several vacant buildings. They were fortunate that a few were still standing, because the oft-threatening rain appeared to have come to stay. The Goat Lake group then rejoined them.

The weather improved and the mountain climbers hiked to Blanca Lake via Twin Lakes, then returned via Wilmans Pass through '76 Basin.

The final climb of the outing was an ascent to the south summit of Cadet Peak. Leaving Monte Cristo early in the morning, the climbers began to appreciate, as never before, the extent of the mining effort that had once been made in the area. They passed, in succession, the ruins of the old concentrator, the rotting tramway towers with their cables now on the ground, and numerous mines—the Wilmanses' old Justice, the Mystery, and, finally, in Glacier Basin, the Colby-Hoyt syndicate's defunct Pride of the Mountains and Pride of the Woods. Near the top of Cadet Peak, where a splendid view awaited, the remainders of mining days were ubiquitous; small surface workings and prospect holes were encountered almost to the summit.

During the course of the outing, the climbers placed register cylinders on Vesper, Del Campo, and Cadet. The day following the ascent of the latter, the group boarded the railroad's gas car for the return trip to the lowlands.

Although this party was the largest to visit the area in 1918, it was by no means the only one to do so. The Ruckers ran excursions to several points along the line, and a veritable army of organizations and individuals roamed the countryside. The Monte Cristo scene was changing: the clangor of steel on steel and the blasts of the miners and "powder monkeys" were giving way to the nailed boot, the rope, and the alpenstock.

After the war ended, the American economy gradually returned to normal. The soldiers came home; money relegated to the war effort was released into consumer channels. Under the aegis of this economic rebirth, the Boston-American Mining Company set about to re-establish its disrupted development at Monte Cristo. The firm announced in early 1919 that operations would resume as soon as the snow melted in the abandoned town.

But on March 2, 1919, a large slide—composed of mud and rocks rather than snow—buried the line just above Tunnel No. 1. Because the steam-powered fire pump at the Ruckers' lumber mill at Lake Stevens could not be used while its foundation was rebuilt, the railway company loaded it onto a flat car, carried it to the canyon, and, operating it with steam from a locomotive boiler, pumped water to sluice the

Monte Cristo circa 1919. The Boston American Mining Company was the only commercial mining operation in the area at this time. The new concentrator, built by the company, is the large structure just right of center. Below and to the right is the headquarters/cookhouse which remains standing in 1977 serving as a lodge for visitors. '76 Gulch is in the distance.

slide away. Upon removal of the débris, however, the Ruckers discovered that 200 feet of track had been swept into the river and would have to be replaced.

Nature was not the only force impeding the efforts of the Boston-American Mining Company. Although the company claimed the primary value of its ore was gold, the fact was that much of the worth lay in copper. The government had stockpiled great quantities of copper during the war and was now releasing it into the commercial market. As a consequence, the price of the metal dropped rapidly. The Boston-

American had an enormous task ahead in this post-war economy if it was to live up to the promises of its brochures.

While the mining company encountered an uphill struggle, those engaged in the tourist trade did not. With the advent of the automobile, Americans experienced mobility they had never known before, and the businesses along the Hartford Eastern received their share of this new prosperity. The Ruckers had opened a hotel in Silverton to cater to visitors who rode the railroad's gas cars with increasing frequency. The Boy Scouts had established Camp Buchanan, as a base for summer activities, on an old homestead at Tyree. And, in Monte Cristo, Dr. Cassiday, who had been operating the Cass-Crest and Philo mines on Mystery Hill, had also turned to the hotel business. He purchased and reopened the old Royal Hotel on Dumas Street, but renamed it the Casscrest Inn.

By the summer of 1919 the Hartford Eastern had a tourist Mecca on its hands, and scheduled daily gas car service up the line, with two cars a day required to handle the business on Fridays, Saturdays, and Sundays. The Casscrest Inn held dances on Tuesday and Thursday evenings, and served chicken dinners on Sundays. The hotel's daily rate for room and board (applied on a weekly basis) was $3.00 per person.

Meanwhile, the Boston-American Mining Company moved ahead with its plans. By mid-August Monte Cristo had begun, once again, as it had many times in the past, to rise up like Banquo's ghost and assume a semblance of its former activity. The erection of the new concentrator progressed well, and the 4,600-foot tramway from the old Justice mine neared completion. Charles A. Riddle, the company's vice president, was so impressed with the operation and the area that he had a splendid house built in 1919 just below the Casscrest Inn. "Doc" Welch, who lived at Barlow Pass, provided much of the labor for constructing the house. He was assisted by James Kyes, who was now general superintendent of the Boston-American Mining Company.

John Andrews was one of several stockholders of the Boston-American Mining Company who were becoming concerned about their investment. He arrived in Monte Cristo in the fall of 1919 to oversee his company's progress. Andrews hailed from Washington, Illinois, a small town near Peoria, as did many of the company's stockholders. When he stepped from the gas car that beautiful autumn day, Andrews must have been aware that the primary activity at Monte Cristo was not

J.A. Juleen Photo
Built by James Kyes and Doc Welch, the Riddle house was considered the finest private dwelling ever constructed at Monte Cristo. Built c.a. 1918, the home survived until the summer of 1944 when a spark from the fireplace ignited and reduced it to ashes.

mining but tourism. And, considering the panorama of the surrounding mountains and snowfields, the reason had to be apparent. After satisfying himself that the mining company was not realizing profitable returns from its rich ores, Andrews returned to Illinois, although during his visit he was charmed by Monte Cristo and resolved to come back. He had stayed at the Casscrest Inn, and, as fate would have it, he returned two years later and took over the operation of the establishment.

J.A. Juleen Photo
A one-horse excursion on the Hartford-Eastern. Mrs. Juleen, the photographer's wife, is the lady standing at the left of the back row sporting a folding Kodak at her side.

With the arrival of winter, the Hartford Eastern again battled the snow and rock slides. Chinook winds and floods caused some damage and tied up traffic from time to time. The Everett Mountaineers held a winter outing at the Ruckers' hotel in Silverton in February, 1920, and ascended Halls Peak and Long Mountain, in addition to hiking to Lake Kelcema. The climbing was fairly easy because comparatively little snow had fallen in the mountains.

As winter blended into spring, the tourists began their journeys into the hills. As a result, voices were raised in favor of building a road to

Silverton, thence to Barlow Pass, and, finally, down the Sauk River to Darrington. The ever-increasing popularity of the motor car created new demands for highways, and the Good Roads Association led the effort to obtain them. One already ran into Gold Basin, and the proposed road would merely be an extension of this.

Although the road was still just a suggestion, Monte Cristo and all points along the Hartford Eastern attracted their share of the tourist business. The hotel at Silverton and the inn at Monte Cristo were almost always filled to capacity. Guide services were available for the many scenic hikes and climbs in the region, and the Hartford Eastern did a thriving business. An informal ski tournament was held in Glacier Basin on July 4 and 5. No prizes were handed out; the only trophy was the joy of competition.

The mining era had given way to the tourist boom, but the Boston-American purchased or leased additional claims and continued its activities during 1920. The tramway was completed and most of the machinery installed in the new concentrator. The company still alleged it had 120,000 tons of ore blocked out and ready to mine; it further stated that 18 carloads had been shipped and that the returns were in high figures. Later in the year, however, the Boston-American Mining Company began to run short of capital to operate the mine. The concentrator, built to handle 100 tons per day, never processed a pound of ore. The tramway transported nothing, and the powerhouse, located about a quarter mile below Monte Cristo, provided only enough power to light the bunk and cook houses.

A small force of men was present, however, doing maintenance and assessment work on the property. The chill air heralded the coming of fall, and the Boston-American decided to keep a crew at the mine throughout the winter. Four men were to stay at Monte Cristo, subsist on stored provisions, and extend the crosscut tunnel, already nearly 3,000 feet long, farther into Toad Mountain. After the last tourist left, the clanging of drills and blasting of dynamite were the only man-made sounds heard in Monte Cristo. The snows came, and by December the trains did not go beyond Silverton. One of the four miners remaining at Monte Cristo was Joe Cook, who had moved to the town with his family in 1902, when he was seven years old. Because he had grown up at the mining camp and had lived through several of its boom and bust cycles, Cook had naturally accepted the harsh life and adapted himself to it. Now, at 25 years of age, he was a seasoned miner, one of those destined to spend an isolated Christmas at Monte Cristo.[1]

One day about this time Cook and his three companions were sleeping after working in the mine. The snow had fallen heavily during the day and through the night, and when the men awoke the next morning they discovered that an avalanche had carried away the head-house, foundry, tramway, and all their tools and dynamite. Everything lay buried under tons of snow on the flat below.

The crash of that slide sounded the death-knell of organized mining at Monte Cristo. With their tools gone, the four elected to abandon mining activities and return to Puget Sound for the remainder of the winter. After a week's preparation, they left Monte Cristo and hiked the 14 miles to Silverton. The trip out was uneventful; the snow was firm, and with everyone wearing snowshoes, they covered the distance quickly.

No organized attempt at productive mining in the Monte Cristo district was ever again attempted. The miners had relinquished the mountains to a new breed, the recreationist, who came to seek a different type of wealth.

CHAPTER XV

1921-78

AN ALPINE RESORT

The Ruckers could not fail to notice the increased tourist business that the Hartford Eastern line had experienced during its five years of operation. The hotel at Silverton had also been a success. But, by 1921, they realized that the tourist of the day was rapidly becoming more sophisticated than he had been in the past. Rude hotels in picturesque mining towns were fine for a short stay, but something more was required to attract vacationers. They demanded comfortable housing, as well as golf courses, tennis courts, a choice of easy or difficult hiking trails, and other diversions.

Fortunately, the Ruckers had a location where just such a facility could be built. About four miles beyond Silverton toward Monte Cristo, the railroad right-of-way crossed a mile-wide valley near the base of Big Four Mountain. Here the land was flat, the view splendid. No danger of avalanche existed, since the precipitous mountain slopes stood well away from the site. The place had been called Camp Glacier for years, because the snowfields at the foot of Big Four Mountain were packed to ice-like hardness.

After the spring thaw of 1921 melted the snow, the Ruckers moved men and materials to Camp Glacier and began the development. They did not attempt to economize because they intended to create a major tourist attraction to augment business on their railroad; in fact, $150,000 was expended in the construction of an imposing mountain lodge, cabins, golf course, tennis courts, man-made lake, and tent cabins for the more robust (or less wealthy) vacationers. Perry Creek was harnessed to generate electricity to provide light and heat. All the buildings (including the more spartan tent cabins) had hot and cold

237

The Big Four Inn, completed on July 2, 1921, hosted thousands of visitors over the years until its demise in 1949. Gas car number 100 rests on the Hartford-Eastern tracks awaiting the evening trip back to Hartford. Big Four Mountain, almost stripped of snow by the summer's heat, rises behind the hotel.

running water. The big lodge consisted of 35 sleeping rooms plus a spacious lobby and recreation room equipped with a large double fireplace.

The tailrace of the Pelton wheel which provided the electricity was dammed to form shallow Crystal Lake, thus adding a bit of charm to the valley setting. The nine-hole golf course, surrounded by the tent cabins, was located between the inn and Big Four Mountain. The trail to the ice caves was planked and crossed over the Stillaguamish River on a good suspension bridge. The Ruckers rushed everything to completion as quickly as possible in order to take advantage of the summer business. In fact, putting and bowling greens were still under construction when

Big Four Inn opened on Saturday, July 2, 1921, to a public eager to savor the delights of the alpine retreat.

Spring arrived somewhat later at Monte Cristo than at Big Four, and with it returned John Andrews, Illinois resident and stockholder in the Boston-American Mining Company. During his 1919 visit, Andrews had decided to come back to the Cascades. When he discovered that Dr. Cassiday was going out of business and wanted to sell the Casscrest Inn, he quickly took advantage of the opportunity and purchased the place. Thus Andrews, a bachelor with few family ties in the Midwest, became a Washington resident.

Andrews renamed the hotel the Monte Cristo Inn, but he retained the staff left over from Cassiday's operation. "Aunty Tam," the cook, who had worked for the doctor during the summer of 1920, stayed on, but when the season was over she announced she would not be able to return in 1922, and a new cook had to be found. Because Andrews had a quick and ready humor and a gentle charm that delighted everyone who stayed at the establishment, the inn prospered, although he was still a neophyte in the business when the summer ended. Of course he had stiff competition from the Big Four Inn, only nine miles down the tracks, but his advertisements implored tourists to be sure and go to "the end of the line." Unlike the miners, who had come to Monte Cristo to wrench fortunes from the mountains, Andrews blended with and complemented the hills, as though they had been meant for each other.

The year proved to be a good one for the railroad and both inns (Big Four and Monte Cristo) as the new mobility of the leisure-seeking American populace carried people farther from their normal haunts. Word of the region's glories soon spread throughout the state—in fact, all over the world. Thus a tradition was born: anyone of note who visited Big Four Inn was expected to sign his name on the lobby walls. As a conseqence, they soon became a veritable who's who of notable personages.

While productive mining had ceased, a small amount of prospecting occurred through 1921 and beyond, and the Boston-American Mining Company continued to pay taxes on its patented claims and do assessment work on the unpatented ones. The company did not ship any ore, but the mining activities gave an aura of authenticity to the region, and the inquisitive tourists actually glimpsed miners at work from time to time. Indeed, the Monte Cristo Inn played host to prospectors as well as tourists.

In the 1920s gas cars dominated the tracks of the Hartford Eastern Railroad. Winter often made the way difficult or impassable. Snow plastered to the front of this galloping goose has reduced visibility to zero, requiring its removal by hand. The driver, broom in hand, attends to this task as a curious passenger peers from the rear of the vehicle.

When snow closed the facilities at Monte Cristo, the railroad's gas cars limited service to Big Four Inn, to which point the tracks were kept open during the winter. The fact that Big Four Inn operated throughout the year attracted winter sports enthusiasts to the area.

A new cook arrived at Monte Cristo in the spring of 1922, in response to Andrews' advertisements. During the summer the "galloping geese" delivered load after load of customers eager to experience the solitude of the mountains. With the Monte Cristo Inn operating on a regular schedule, the post office, which had been closed for ten years, reopened for the summer, and letters and post cards once again bore the Monte Cristo imprint. Andrews was acting postmaster, as well as mayor, town clerk, et cetera. And thus the years went by, each summer blending into the one preceding, while the beauties of Monte Cristo were enjoyed by travelers who journeyed to the inn.

When the 1924 tourist season began, one of the first gas cars to arrive at Monte Cristo carried a petite 15-year-old girl named Dorothy Reid. She and her family had first heard of Monte Cristo from her brother. Crawford Reid had been eighteen years old when, during the summer of 1919, he worked at the Waldheim camp near Silverton for the United States Forest Service. During the next three summers he was the ranger at Barlow Pass. His daily routine consisted of hiking to Monte Cristo in the morning, returning to the pass for lunch, then walking to Big Four in the afternoon—a distance of eighteen miles. On Thursdays, he patrolled to Goat Lake, a sixteen mile round trip. Reid was completing a course in electrical engineering when he spent the winter of 1923-24 at Monte Cristo, helping James Kyes paint the Monte Cristo Inn and repair the foundation and front porch. The Boston-American hydro-power plant, located a half mile down the Sauk River from Monte Cristo, had been idle since 1920 when mining had been abandoned. During that winter stay, Reid put his electrical engineering schooling to practical use when he repaired the machinery and started up the powerhouse generators. As a result of his efforts, the hotel, cookhouse, and Riddle residence were illuminated by electricity, and several street lights brightened the village at night. Reid's vivid descriptions of the area in which he had worked caused the whole family to visit Monte Cristo in the summer of 1921.

Although Dorothy Reid was only twelve years old at the time, the thought of returning dominated her thoughts the next few years, and

Dorothy VanNorman Photo
John Andrews and Dorothy Reid (VanNorman) on the front porch of the Monte
Cristo Inn (Royal Hotel) in the summer of 1927. Dorothy worked as John's secretary
and guide, leading many visitors into the intimate niches of the surrounding mountains.
Notice the collection of walking sticks and alpenstocks in the background.

now, in 1924, her wish was granted. She was employed by Andrews at the Monte Cristo Inn, working as his secretary. She quickly explored the cirques, basins, and lakes surrounding Monte Cristo, and thus became a guide, taking visitors into the alpine regions. She was always ready, with cup and camera strapped to her side, to lead whoever wanted to see the sights and revel in the splendors of the hills.

Life at Monte Cristo during that and subsequent summers was pleasant and exciting, highlighted by the visits of people from nearby camps. One such person was Tina Vert, a silver-haired lady employed as a cook in a mining camp near Mineral City. After her day's work was finished, she often hiked over Poodle Dog Pass and down into Monte Cristo to visit the townsfolk. Then she blithely hiked back over the pass in order to attend to her job the following day. That was a 1,500-foot climb and a four-mile hike each way. The term "recreation" apparently had a different meaning then than it does today.

James Elsworth Kyes was another frequent visitor to Monte Cristo. His father, James Kyes, had played an important role during the town's mining years. Jimmy, who had been raised in the village, was familiar with and loved every valley and peak. He was scarcely old enough to remember the mining days, but in his mind's eye he could still see the tramway where it crossed Mystery Hill, envision the buckets moving slowly "on that streak of black," hear the screeching of the ore cars, the ceaseless roar and whir of the concentrator. Jimmy Kyes and Dorothy Reid soon discovered that they had common interests, because they shared each other's keen affinity for the wilderness. They were often seen hiking or climbing together in the high alpine terrain.

After Aunty Tam left the Monte Cristo Inn, a new cook had been hired each year to fill that role. Two of the replacements had been single, and they had done their best to end Andrews' bachelorhood, without success. Then, in the spring of 1925, Estella Fish arrived on the Ruckers' gas car. The new cook was a strong, gentle woman who competently set about the tasks at hand. Andrews looked upon her as more than a cook and hostess: she was the woman for whom he had been searching. At their wedding the minister asked Andrews why he had waited so long to escort the charming lady to the altar. He answered with his characteristic good humor and quick wit: "If it turns out that she is the right one, she was worth waiting for, and if she isn't the right one, I won't have so long to live with her." As it turned out, she was

John and Estella Andrews in the early forties. John arrived in Monte Cristo in 1921 to operate the hotel. Estella answered his ad for a cook a few years later, and the two were subsequently married. They were host and hostess to hundreds of tourists at the Monte Cristo Inn during the late twenties and early thirties.

the right one, and they lived together until both were in their 90s, just short of their golden anniversary.

Estella also brought to Monte Cristo an adult son. Like those around him, Russell Fish was enchanted by the splendor of his new surroundings. He became acquainted with Jean and Edith Bedal, who operated a pack train in the Sauk River district and occasionally made their way

J.A. Juleen Photo

The Bedal Girls, Edith and Jean, with their pack animals at the headquarters building of the Penn Mining Company just below Goat Lake. Raised at Orient, where the South and North forks of the Sauk River join, the girls became leading packers in the valley.

into Monte Cristo. They had been raised at Orient, where the two forks of the Sauk joined, and had attended school at Monte Cristo during their younger years. Their mother, a Suiattle Indian, had taught the girls a deep respect for the land; their father, a Frenchman, had instilled in them a keen business sense. As a result, the sisters were among the leading pack train operators in the area. Fish became engaged to Jean Bedal, and marriage soon followed. In the early 1930s they ran the old Boston-American cookhouse as a lodge for tourists, miners, and other travelers.

The ten year lease under which the Ruckers operated the Hartford Eastern Railway Company expired in the spring of 1925, and they negotiated with the Northern Pacific to secure an agreement for future control of the railroad. On October 1, 1925, the Northern Pacific, anxious to sever all ties with the Monte Cristo branch, signed a warranty deed which conveyed title to the Hartford Eastern of the right-of-way from Hartford to Monte Cristo. The Ruckers now owned their railroad outright.

By 1925 a new stop had been established along the line. The Sah Hah Lee Campfire Girls' camp had been constructed about a mile above Big Four Inn, at the base of Mount Dickerman. The building, a shake-sided lodge, was typical of retreats of that day, and provided an idyllic setting for outdoor activities. The Boy Scouts were not lacking facilities either, because a Scout camp was located at Lake Kelcema, about two miles up Deer Creek, above Silverton. Everyone appeared to be seeking his share of pleasure from the Cascades.

As the years went by, summer followed summer, and tourists flocked into the mountains on the little gas cars. John and Estella Andrews played host and hostess to thousands over the years, and Dorothy Reid escorted the more hardy visitors into the intimate niches of the mountains. Glacier Basin was her favorite place, and she introduced people from the world over to the magic alpine valley, to its crags, glaciers, snowfields, and cascades.

Not everyone was content to spend merely a week or two in Monte Cristo. Garda Fogg was one of those who desired to become part of the old town. She was a Mountaineer who had first glimpsed Monte Cristo in 1911 after hiking from Index across Poodle Dog Pass. On that occasion she did not descend to the town, but spent the night in the abandoned Eldorado mine cabin. Over the years, however, Garda

J.A. Juleen Photo

The Sah Hah Lee Campfire Girls retreat located a mile above Big Four Inn on the Hartford Eastern line. Here girls from Everett and other cities came to escape the clangor of civilization at the base of Mount Dickerman.

became haunted by the memory of what she had beheld from Poodle Dog Pass in 1911. Finally, in the spring of 1924, she wrote to Andrews, inquiring about room and board for her mother and herself that summer. As a consequence, Garda made her first trip into the old town. Once she had seen the community first-hand, she realized she would never be satisfied with just visits to the hotel.

She had a fine cabin built in 1926 on Dumas Street, near the spot where the old Glacier Saloon had stood, and from that time on the village was "her place" and she was later dubbed the "mayor of Monte Cristo." Assisting in the cabin's construction was a teen-age lad whose family had become almost synonymous with Monte Cristo. Montana Kyes, youngest ·of the family's children, was following his father's footsteps and helping build the town's history. He worked as a novice carpenter that summer, and his handiwork still stands in 1978, more than a half century later.

Shortly after the completion of Garda's cabin, Martin Johnson began building his own just up the street. He used surplus lumber packed down from a ruined lookout near Silver Lake. The new construction was not on the grand scale of the original Monte Cristo, but it gave a

Frank Peabody in later years standing on the front porch of the Monte Cristo Inn (Royal Hotel). One of the first prospectors to stake a claim in the valley, he is buried in the Monte Cristo townsite with his wife, Kittie.

new impetus to the activity. Shortly afterward, however, Johnson sold his cabin to Frank and Kittie Peabody, and left to take the job of care-taker at Big Four Inn. Peabody was now advanced in years, and he brought his nurse with him. Kate Knowlton had been a nurse during the war, and she was now Peabody's private attendant. Like others be-fore her, she quickly became attached to the locale and hiked to remote valleys and peaks. Peabody died in 1930, and his ashes were buried beside a huge boulder near '76 Creek, just below the spot where he and Joseph Pearsall had staked the first claim on July 4, 1889. The monu-ment is now appropriately called "Peabody Rock." Even in death, the prospector was not to be separated from this place that he loved. After his death, his wife and Kate continued to spend their summers at Monte Cristo, staying in the little cabin on Dumas Street.

Unfortunately, the prosperity which had fostered this onrush of af-fluent visitors proved to be largely false, the 1929 stock market crash marking the beginning of the great depression of the 1930s. With money resources rapidly drying up, people were no longer able to spend funds for mountain vacations because survival itself had become a prob-lem. Of course Monte Cristo had weathered depressions before, but this time no life-giving Eastern capital flowed in, and the economy deteri-orated rapidly. Since 1926 the Hartford Eastern had been operating at a deficit, which, by 1928, totaled $139,803. With the depression closing in around them, the Ruckers lost more money each year, and the number of passengers on the line dwindled.

By 1932 Monte Cristo had been almost abandoned by the tourists who once thronged to the inn. Dorothy Reid had left after 1930, Jimmy Kyes was an officer in the United States Navy, and John and Estella Andrews entertained fewer and fewer visitors as the decade began. The burden imposed by the railroad's operation on the Rucker brothers' other enterprises became too much of a strain, and in early 1933 they petitioned the Interstate Commerce Commission to allow them to dis-continue the Hartford Eastern Railway.

The final chapter came to a close on April 12, 1933, when the I.C.C. authorized the line to discontinue operations. Regular service was never again restored into Monte Cristo. With no transportation, the hotel business came to an abrupt halt and a new period of isolation began.

The railroad was gone; at least regularly scheduled service had been discontinued. Motor car, bus, and truck travel was commonplace into

Dorothy VanNorman Photo
*The operation of the Hartford-Eastern Railway posed problems just as the earlier rail-
way companies had experienced. Here, a derailment has badly smashed the gas car, and
a steam locomotive is being brought from the rear to assist in rerailing it. Rocks or
other debris which could be around every turn made the trip up the rails hazardous in
places.*

Granite Falls and Robe by 1933, so the Ruckers abandoned the railroad
from Hartford to Robe, thus eliminating the problem-ridden Stillaguamish Canyon. However, they continued to run the gas car from
Robe to Big Four Inn, in order to obtain supplies and customers for
their mountain retreat. Supplementing the periodic service provided by

A converted motor car headed toward Granite Falls about to enter tunnel number three. Flanged wheels replaced rubber tires, allowing the vehicle to ride the rails of the Hartford Eastern line.

the gas cars, the residents of Silverton contrived several makeshift gasoline speeders and trailers to make necessary trips for supplies.

Except for an occasional speeder, Monte Cristo saw no traffic on the line. The pack train was the main source of transportation into and out of the resort. Russell and Jean Fish remained at Monte Cristo, using their pack train to haul in supplies from time to time and to transport visitors to their lodge in the old Boston-American cookhouse. The Fishes served as Monte Cristo's caretakers, hotel operators, and suppliers. The true Monte Cristo buffs blithely disregarded the isolation and spent a great deal of time in town during the summers. Garda Fogg, Kittie Peabody, Kate Knowlton, and others made their way to their cabins and properties the best way they could to enjoy the solitude.

During the summertime Silverton residents used their gas speeder to make the jaunt to Big Four Inn to attend the festivities often held during the evenings. One of Silverton's "characters" was Charlie Weishedel, a man who, due to his unsavory ways, was popularly known as "Carp." He was always present to mooch a ride on the speeder when it left for the inn. One afternoon several of the men decided that "Carp" had to be taught a lesson. The men waylaid Weishedel just before leaving for Big Four, and dragged him, kicking and bellowing, to the railroad yards. Since he sported a full set of chin whiskers, the men clamped him to one of the railroad switches by closing the switch points on his beard, then left him there while they headed for the merriment at Big Four. Weishedel was left kicking and roaring, fouling the air with his imprecations. But he was securely fastened to the rails until, by cutting off much of his beard, he managed to free himself, long after the speeder was out of sight.

The era of gas cars and speeders ended in 1936 when the rails were torn up from Granite Falls to Barlow Pass and shipped to Japan, whose rapidly expanding industrial development brought high prices for the scrap metal. The old right-of-way was converted into a gravel road, and by the spring of 1937 one could drive an automobile into Sah Hal Lee girls camp, a mile beyond Big Four Inn. This new means of access freed the area from its isolation, and visitors once again flocked to the inn. The auto trip lacked the quaintness of the ride on the "galloping goose," but people could now come and go whenever they pleased.

The Civilian Conservation Corps constructed the long-sought road over Barlow Pass and down the Sauk River to Darrington in 1938 and 1939. This opened the country considerably, and tourists and loggers alike could now gain access to more remote areas than ever before.

Eventually the road became know as the "Mountain Loop Highway."

The situation in Monte Cristo remained relatively unchanged, however, except that the Fishes now had to pack their supplies only from Barlow Pass. But access was not to be denied Monte Cristo. The world situation in 1941 had prompted the United States to mobilize itself against another overseas threat, and Congress made funds available for construction of roads into areas which might produce war-critical materials. Monte Cristo, with much of its ore still in the ground waiting to be mined, qualified for just such a road. With government aid, the rails from Barlow Pass to Monte Cristo were removed, and the present-day gravel road constructed. Thus one could, by 1942, drive his car into Monte Cristo and spend the day in recreation where miners had once toiled laboriously.

Because their pack train was no longer needed to sustain Monte Cristo, the Fishes sought different pursuits, but each summer they leased the Boston-American cookhouse to other persons who ran the operation, providing shelter to travelers, and to the people who drove their cars into Monte Cristo. Garda Fogg regularly stayed at her cabin when she came to roam the hills and valleys; Kittie Peabody, advanced in years, was an occasional visitor, always accompanied by her nurse, Kate Knowlton.

The house built by "Doc" Welch and James Kyes for Charles A. Riddle, generally acknowledged to be the most elegant home in Monte Cristo, had been sold to the Swain family. On the night of July 26, 1944, the family went for a short walk but left a log burning in the fireplace. Unfortunately, the spark screen had not been placed before the fire, and an ember landed on the carpet, igniting the house and burning it to the ground.

The old Monte Cristo Inn was not faring well after years of neglect. The ravages of winter, time, and vandals had left their mark. The structure, built by Cohen and Sheedy at the turn of the century, had been named, in succession, Rockefeller House, Royal Hotel, Casscrest Inn, and Monte Cristo Inn. Now, because it was crumbling and considered dangerous, the Forest Service pulled it down, where the remnants lie today along Dumas Street—an ignominious end to a once grand establishment.

Kittie Peabody died in 1946. She, too, was cremated, and her remains buried next to her husband's at Peabody Rock. Kate Knowlton had a

Philip R. Woodhouse Photo
The bronze plaque that marks the final resting place of Frank Peabody, one of the original pioneers of Monte Cristo, and his wife, Kittie. Their ashes are buried at the base of this rock, near the spot where the first claims had been staked in '76 Gulch.

bronze plaque placed on the rock to mark the grave of one of Monte Cristo's first prospectors, and that of his wife. (Joseph Pearsall, the other "original discoverer" of Monte Cristo, was last known to be in the Klondike in 1902, but he was never heard from again.) Kittie Peabody left all her Monte Cristo property to Kate Knowlton, who had become known as "Timberline Kate" because of her activities at the mines. The property amounted to 17 mine claims, several town lots, and the cabin. She actively continued her interest in the mines and became well known to frequent visitors.

During the summer of 1948, Arthur Van Norman and his wife, the former Dorothy Reid, drove to Monte Cristo. With her husband and children, Dorothy took a long, nostalgic walk through the old townsite, and noted how much it had changed since she had guided tourists to the scenic areas nestled among the crags. On this trip she met Mr. and Mrs. Del Wilkie, who were also quite enthusiastic about the scenery. Wilkie was negotiating to buy the Boston-American cookhouse from John Andrews with the intention of operating it as a tourist lodge. He purchased the structure and surrounding land in July, 1951, and with his wife, Rosemary, operated the building as a lodge for many years.

During World War II, Big Four Inn served as a rest center for the United States Coast Guard. By the war's end the building was beginning to fall into disrepair, but it was reopened as a tourist hotel. On September 6, 1949, the building caught fire and was destroyed. The 28-year-old wooden structure burned like kindling. The concrete sidewalks and double fireplace, with its chimney, were all that remained of the once elegant resort, and today they mark the location of the buildings.

During the summer of 1951, Ed and Enid Nordlund erected a small cabin on the lower end of Dumas Street, just below Garda Fogg's place. Lumber and other supplies were plentiful, because many of the wrecked buildings in the town still contained useable material, free for the taking. Thus, the little Nordlund cabin became a potpourri of Monte Cristo history, with timbers from the concentrator, window frames from the old assay office, and a door from the Monte Cristo Inn. Enid had first visited Monte Cristo on August 5, 1924, and her heart never left. Now the Nordlunds had their own cabin, heated by a wood burning cook stove, where they could return after a long day's hike through the hills.[1]

Del and Rosemary Wilkie renovated the lodge and built several cabins around the parking area in front of the main building. The cabins also became a collective construction history of Monte Cristo. Like James Kyes, Del Wilkie was a "jack of all trades," and he quickly recycled the wreckage of the ruined town buildings into cabins for weekend visitors. The old Pelton wheel and generator which had supplied power to the Monte Cristo Inn was removed from the basement of the inn's ruins and housed in a new building to provide power to the lodge and cabins. A Diesel-powered generator was added, and the Pelton wheel used only for back-up power. The wheel remains in the same place today (1978) and, using the water diverted from '76 Creek, still supplies power to the lodge and cabins.

A young man went to work for Wilkie in the summer of 1953. Ron Van Norman, Dorothy's son, served as general handyman at the resort. He received no pay, but the room and board were free, and the experience invaluable in shaping a growing lad. He carried on the family tradition at Monte Cristo during the summers of 1953, 1954, and 1955.[2]

The last remaining structure of the Comet Bunker prior to 1958. In that year, this bunker which was visible from the town, collapsed.

"Timberline" Kate Knowlton joined Frank and Kittie Peabody in eternal rest in 1955. No longer would she be seen at her mines, her silver hair glinting in the sunlight. Three years later, on June 30, 1958, the final remaining vestige of the Comet mine's ore bunker collapsed during the night. The last mine building was gone. Ever since the Wilmanses had constructed it in 1894 it had stood outlined against the snowfield on the side of Wilmans Peak, 2,750 feet above the town, for all to see. Now it, too, had vanished.

In the summer of 1962, a group of people gathered at Monte Cristo on Dumas Street, at the spot where the Monte Cristo Inn once stood. Eulogies were read, and a bronze plaque that had been placed atop a small concrete pillar was unveiled. The plaque was a gift from the men of the United States Naval Academy, where Jimmy Kyes had received his military training. Jimmy, one of Monte Cristo's "native sons," had been commander of the destroyer *Leary* during World War II, when it was torpedoed and sunk by the Germans. While the ship was sinking, Jimmy gave his life preserver to another member of the crew, and he was never seen again. The plaque was Annapolis' way of remembering, of honoring a comrade in arms. Near the plaque stands a stately subalpine fir, surrounded by a white picket fence. When it was a tiny seedling, the tree had been carried down from a high meadow by a very young Jimmy Kyes and planted in the garden of the Monte Cristo Inn when that establishment was called the Royal Hotel. Today it stands as a living memorial to the war hero.

In the fall of 1963, the Wilkies sold their holdings at Monte Cristo to a corporation consisting of four Seattle and Everett men. They planned to rebuild the town with the expectation that it would become a ski and tourist resort. The developers made elaborate plans, and for a while it

Philip R. Woodhouse Photo
The bronze plaque dedicated to the memory of Jimmy Kyes. It stands on a concrete pedestal in the front yard of the old Monte Cristo Inn on Dumas Street.

appeared as though Monte Cristo was once again about to rise from its ashes like the proverbial phoenix. But personal tragedies to two of the corporate members took the spark out of the organization and the plans never materialized. During its ownership, however, the corporation leased the lodge on a yearly basis to the George Hill family, then the Glen Heimers, who greeted guests warmly during the summers of 1964-66.

Garda Fogg sold her cabin in 1966 to Esta Finney who, with her two children, spent many a summer visiting at Monte Cristo. During an early inspection of the cabin, Esta commented to Garda about how the cabin's interior was cluttered with the year's accumulation of miscellaneous odds and ends. Garda's reply was characteristic of her ability to be outspoken: "You're looking at the mud when you should be looking at the sky."

In 1966, Al Reiser and his sons, owners of the O & B and Boston-American mines, reopened the latter's tunnel, which had collapsed in the late 1930s.[3] The following year a new corporation purchased the holdings of the former and planned great accomplishments at Monte Cristo. A decade later, however, none of the plans had materialized, but the George Budge family and Bob Hamlin, together with others, leased the Boston-American cookhouse during the summers and kept it open for tourists. About this time the last bunker of the Boston-American concentrator collapsed, thus removing another landmark from the townsite.

A Canadian firm became interested in the Mackinaw mine on Weden Creek in the winter of 1969, and considerable exploration work was done. Although nothing was produced, the rumors of new veins began to sound like the days of old.

When the summer of 1973 melted the winter snows from Monte Cristo's hills, visitors noticed that one more link with the past was gone. For eighty years, ever since the Wilmans brothers built the Comet tramway high on Wilmans Peak, its four cables had been visible from Monte Cristo each morning. Illuminated by the sunlight against the shadowed crags, they had looked not unlike a spider's thread. One cable had remained after the other three had fallen—and, glistening in the sky, had pointed the way to the mine. Now it, too, had disappeared.

Today Monte Cristo reveals little of its past activities. What nature has not removed, man has, and the casual visitor is hard-pressed to find

Dorothy VanNorman Photo

The Boston-American concentrator built by James Kyes when he was the superin-tendent for that mining company. Although the machinery had been installed, and grand plans for production announced, the mill never processed an ounce of ore.

any evidence of the faded glories. But nature has a way of reclaiming its own very quickly in the Cascades. Joe Cook, one of the last active miners in Monte Cristo, his grandsons and his schoolteacher (the former Miss Rice) visited the ghost town in the late 1960s. They stood at the spot where the schoolhouse had been, and there lay a window frame, once part of the building, with a tree sixteen inches in diameter growing through it. Cook noted that that was the first time he had ever felt old, time had passed so swiftly.

Philip R. Woodhouse Photo
Little remains of the tramway tension station atop Mystery Hill. Because of their size, the brake wheels remain where they were placed in 1893. This picture, taken in 1975, provides a view past the wheels to the opposite side of Glacier Basin where the upper terminal was located. Ore, mined at the upper end of the tramway, was carried across the basin to this station then down to the concentrator near the town.

EPILOGUE

But what of the future? Many people agree that Monte Cristo, or the mountains nearby, still holds enough mineral wealth to be worth mining. One concern, the Bren Mac Company of Canada, has blocked out a lode of copper-tungsten ore in Vesper Peak near Big Four Mountain which it plans to mine over a period of 25 years. The only remaining hurdle to be leaped before the operation can begin is the filing and approval of an environmental impact statement, a device that did not trouble the old miners. But this is not a boom like those which have gone before, because an enormous amount of money and effort have been spent to ascertain the size and shape of the ore body, and productive extraction of the low-grade ore would almost certainly be a long-term operation.

The company's plans originally called for tunneling from the Williamson Creek side of the mountain to strike the body of ore at the lowest possible elevation. But Williamson Creek flows into the Sultan River and thus into Spada Reservoir, which provides some of the water to Everett. Naturally, Everett—the city that once processed the Monte Cristo ores—was not too enthusiastic about the possibility of drinking mine tailings and chemicals from Vesper Peak, and threatened to bring lawsuits to prevent this happening. The Williamson Creek tunnel plan was then abandoned in favor of a longer passageway to be bored for two miles from the South Fork Stillaguamish beneath Sperry Peak into the lode. The tunnel would be twelve feet high and twenty feet wide, and would allow a double-track railway to provide access to the mine.

At the tunnel entrance, the usual headhouse, bunkhouse and concentrator would be built. But what of the mine and mill tailings? After

Philip R. Woodhouse Photo
The author inspects a long-abandoned explosives shed, located 250 feet beneath the
floor of Glacier Basin. Compressed air pipes frame the scene in the number three tunnel
of the Mystery Mine.

extracting the mineral content of the ore, the flour-fine tailings would
be mixed with water and piped to a logged-off area above ill-fated
Tunnel No. 7, where a retaining dam would allow the slurry to settle.
The water, thus separated, would be piped back to the mine to be
reused. Such a "closed cycle" would prevent the usual water pollution
of the area in which the facility is located. While it is doubtful that

Philip R. Woodhouse Photo

When a lensatic body of ore was encountered, a stope, like the one seen above the tunnel in this picture, was begun. As ore was removed, wooden platforms were built and ore chutes constructed to control the movement of the minerals to the lower tunnel. Stoping continued until the last of the ore had been removed. In some instances stopes and chutes were built hundreds of feet up into the vein. This scene is deep beneath Mystery Hill in the number three tunnel of the Mystery Mine.

Monte Cristo would be much affected by this operation, Silverton would probably prosper, for it it ideally situated, lying half-way between the mine site and the settling basin. In late 1977, the Bren Mac

Company was still working out the environmental problems of its proposed operation.

Of more immediate impact to Monte Cristo would be a reopening of the Mackinaw mine on Weden Creek. If the proper economic conditions dictated, the nickel-copper ore could again be extracted from this mine. In 1969 a Canadian company did exploratory work in the mine, but no production was attempted. If the mine were reopened, Monte Cristo, only three miles up the road, might once again become a boom town.

Almost every year rumors can be heard of people discovering veins never before found at Monte Cristo. Occasionally the old tunnels are prospected and tight-lipped men leave the area without revealing what riches (or lack of them) they have uncovered in the hills. Perhaps, however, the future of Monte Cristo does not lie in mining but in the tourist trade which has been its mainstay for the last half century.

In the 1960s, Washington sought an attraction to bolster the state's tourist industry. Three themes, each capitalizing on the state's history, were considered—logging, fishing, and mining. Only one of the three would ultimately be chosen to be developed into a major tourist facility. Monte Cristo had been selected to be developed if the mining theme was picked by the state. The town would be reconstructed along the lines of Virginia City, Nevada, or Barkerville, British Columbia, to entice visitors to Washington, as those towns attract people to their respective locales.

As fate had it, an economic downturn in the late 1960s and early 1970s doomed the plans and the idea was shelved. But the possibility still exists for Monte Cristo to be developed into a replica of what it once was—an old mining town accessible only by steam railway. Tourists could drive to Silverton, park their cars at Deer Creek, then board the train for the fourteen-mile rail trip to Monte Cristo. The town could be rebuilt, complete with aerial trams and mine buildings all in place, and less robust visitors could ride on an aerial tram to the top of Mystery Hill (now called Mystery Ridge) where they could view Glacier Basin and the surrounding peaks. A mine could be opened for tours, and dinners and lunches could be obtained at the Royal Hotel, along with rooms for the night or week.

The corporation that purchased some of the land at Monte Cristo in 1963 had intended to convert the place into a ski resort. This possibility seemed unlikely because the avalanche hazards are legendary, both in the basins and along the road to the town. Several European experts who visited the area during the 1960s referred to it in similar terms regarding skiing: "avalanche basin" they named Monte Cristo, with good reason. Ted Knightlinger, then head of the Washington State Tourist Bureau, said it well when he questioned whether skiers, who were not too plentiful at Mount Pilchuck, would drive an additional 25 miles up a narrow, icy road to reach Monte Cristo.

The suggestion has been made by some of the current owners that the Forest Service purchase all the private land and annex the valley to a nearby wilderness area. This would be a formidable task, however, because clear title to the hundreds of claims and town lots would be extremely difficult to obtain, many of the transactions having been obscured by the passage of time. The title to any land the government wishes to acquire must be completely free of future claims. To accomplish this would be time-consuming and difficult, although perhaps not impossible.

Or Monte Cristo could continue as it has, changing in concert with the times and attracting people who return year after year because "something" keeps drawing them back.[1]

NOTES

CHAPTER I

1. Most published accounts of the discovery describe a more dramatic event. They tell of Peabody and Pearsall together sighting the glittering band from either Silver Tip Peak or the meadows near Silver Lake. The recitations usually depict one of the men jumping up and down in excitement and exclaiming, "It's rich as Monte Cristo." This story, however, cannot be substantiated.

All printed versions dated after 1897 refer to this "instant naming." The few portrayals written prior to 1897 give Pearsall sole credit for having made the discovery. John MacDonald Wilmans' reminiscences refer to "Pearsall, who was the discoverer of it," while Hodge's narrative describes Pearsall's climb of Hubbart's Peak. The question arises: Why is 1897 the turning point in the reports of the discovery?

Pearsall was a restless, adventurous individual who traveled to wherever gold was being prospected; Peabody was a more domesticated person, known for his tall tales. In 1897 the Klondike beckoned men to the Far North to seek their fortunes, and Pearsall left the Cascades to answer the challenge, apparently never to return. This left Peabody to tell the story of the discovery as he saw fit, with no one to refute him. Thus Peabody appears to have involved himself in both the finding and naming of the place when, in reality, he did not take part in either.

Regarding the naming, the reader may reference Note No. 1 in Chapter II. The actual date of the discovery is clouded by the passage of time and the lack of records. In the telling and retelling of the tale, it has been erroneously placed on July 4, 1889. The mining records at the Snohomish County Courthouse clearly record the fact that the first *claim* was located on July 4, 1889, and was therefore called the Independence of 1776 in honor of that holiday. Since this was accomplished on the third journey into the area, the discovery obviously had to have been made at least a month earlier, and most likely earlier still.

2. Most prospectors did not carry surveying instruments with them, nor were they surveyors. Consequently, the process of plotting the land they were claiming generally consisted of pacing off the boundaries. The prospector selected a corner to be the starting point of this process, and drove a stake into the ground or built a rock cairn to mark the spot. The twenty-acre plot was then paced off and recorded.

A typical claim record would thus read: "From a rock monument (cairn) 750 paces NW'ly to a driven stake, then NE'ly 1500 paces to a prominent tree stump, then SE'ly 750 paces to a driven stake, then SW'ly 1500 paces to the starting monument." Often a claim corner lay in an inaccessible location, which led to some indistinct and humorous location records. Such a claim might have read: "From a driven stake approximately 750 paces SE'ly to a point somewhere beyond the stump on the edge of the cliff, then NE'ly approximately 1500 paces to a point opposite a large prominent boulder in the rockslide, then NW'ly approximately 750 paces to a rock monument, then SW'ly 1500 paces to the starting stake."

The country in which these claims were made was quite precipitous, and the prospectors experienced difficulty in establishing the length of a pace as well as the corner markers. This often resulted in overlapping and contested claims which required a rigorous survey to settle. Pity the surveyor who had to locate those points out in space "somewhere beyond the stump on the edge of the cliff."

Once the ground had been paced and "staked" at the corners, the prospector recorded the data on a sheet which he carried for this purpose. He dated the claim form, noted the time of the discovery, and posted a copy of this sheet, usually on the starting stake or cairn, in an inverted tobacco tin or other container. This was extremely important in case the claim was contested by another party. The claimant then had to travel to the local county seat and record the location with the auditor as quickly as possible to make it a matter of record. Prior to any large-scale sales of land so plotted, the owners generally had the area surveyed to establish the boundaries more exactly. When the first surveys were made at Monte Cristo no accurate maps of the locality existed and a system of "mineral monuments" was established in '76 Gulch, Glacier Basin, and near the townsite, from which all the claim surveys were referenced—i.e., "fourteen hundred feet north 53 degrees west from mineral monument number three," et cetera.

3. A man named George Walker made an independent locating expedition into '76 Gulch near the end of summer. On September 19, 1889, he located the Uncle Sam adjacent to the '75 on '76 Creek. This event was recorded with the county auditor in Snohomish City on September 25. On October 14, Mac Wilmans, Peabody, and Pearsall, together with Thomas Ewing and George

Grayson, purchased Walker's interest in the property for the sum of $1,000.
This action left them in exclusive control of all the properties in the '76 Gulch
and Glacier Basin area.

CHAPTER II

1. The note in Chapter I describing the popular account of the discovery also
mentions one of the men waving his arms and esclaiming, "It's rich as Monte
Cristo." However, careful study of the data at hand indicates the naming did
not occur until the summer of 1890. Mining records in the county courthouse
detail the staking of each claim, giving the time and location of each property.
All claims had their mining districts listed in the description of their locality.
But, throughout 1889 and the early part of 1890, the claims at Monte Cristo
were noted as "located in an unnamed region" or "located in an unnamed
valley to the north of Silver Creek." Then, on June 21, 1890, the county
auditor recorded the site of the Sidney claim, which had been located on June
16, as lying in the Monte Cristo Mining District. This was the first time the
name appeared in the official records.
    In articles written after this date, the newspapers referred to the Monte
Cristo district rather than to an unnamed region, which they had done previously. Sam Strom states in his diary that Fred Wilmans told him the account
of the naming which appears in this book. Of all the stories, this version
probably comes the closest to the truth. Strom's statement places the event in
the early summer of 1890, which coincides with official records and newspaper
articles on the subject.
2. See Note 3, Chapter III

CHAPTER III

1. Today it would be a much easier task to set up a sawmill in such a remote
location because power would be transmitted by electric cable, thus requiring
only the transporting of a motor and a modern, lightweight saw to the site.
2. The name Blewett may be familiar to the reader. Edward Blewett was active
in mining enterprises throughout the state, particularly in the Wenatchee
Mountains. The old town of Blewett (now gone) and Blewett Pass were named
for him. During his involvement in Monte Cristo he returned to Blewett, near
the base of Culver Gulch, and built a twenty-stamp mill at that site. In 1977 the
remains of the old bunker and mill could still be viewed from the highway
crossing Swauk Pass (called Blewett Pass on highway signs), near the state
historic site called the Old Arastra.
3. For years the local newspapers carried reports and statements of experienced

mining "experts" which extolled the wealth lying in the Cascade Mountains waiting to be picked up off the ground. Taken as a whole, the remarks quickly become a monotonous drone filled with misleading statements: "It lies right out on the surface and you have only to shovel it up"; "richest mineral region in the world"; "even richer results than were anticipated"; "a mining excitement never before known in this country." Perhaps one statement explains the others: "There is nothing that appeals to the mind of men so strongly as the chance of finding gold and silver ore."

The entire region was caught up in a "gold fever," and the newspapers did their share to maintain the momentum of this malady. After reading these accounts, many sane, sober persons grabbed pick and shovel and, with the gleam of gold in their eyes, headed for the hills. With few exceptions, they were blinded by ambition and could not see the gold for the rocks. Most returned broke and disillusioned by their experiences. A few, however, did make strikes of minerals and managed to find buyers for the properties. They sometimes returned relatively wealthy and swelled the glowing reports which filled the newspapers. The accounts of those who had lost everything were not newsworthy, and thus never reached the presses.

CHAPTER IV

1. A popular legend tells the tale of seven Chinese coolies and a locomotive that were buried in the collapse of Tunnel No. 7. The story loses credibility when compared with the facts. At the time of the accident the rails for the Monte Cristo line were on a ship making its way around Cape Horn, and the bridges for the two major crossings of the Stillaguamish were not completed. A locomotive could not, therefore, have been in the tunnel. Moreover, construction crews never ran locomotives into unfinished tunnels because the consumption of oxygen, together with the release of fumes by the boiler fire, would suffocate everyone.

With regard to the other portion of the legend, coolies were never employed during construction of the line. The railroad was built by immigrant labor, but the men were mostly Italians, not Chinese, because about two decades earlier a bloody racial war in Washington Territory had resulted in the banning of Chinese laborers from Snohomish County.

The narration of the collapse in this book is based upon an article in *The Coast Magazine* for May, 1902. The account is the most plausible rendering available and coincides with newspaper versions of the event published in 1892.
2. The road up the Sauk River was ultimately finished, but the Stillaguamish road was completed first, and the equipment was shipped to Monte Cristo over this route.

3. This is the figure that John MacDonald Wilmans gave in his reminiscences, but a more accurate calculation would indicate that they lost closer to $360,000.

CHAPTER V

1. A letter from C.H. Taylor, company auditor, to Joseph L. Colby, president of the Monte Cristo Mining Company, dated March 27, indicated that deeds to certain lots in the government townsite had been drawn up in the names of George Blake, Joseph Pearsall, and McDevitt and Blake, to be delivered to them as gifts from the company.
2. An interesting comparison may be made between this rather lengthy, detailed report and the statements given to the press. Compare, for instance, the abandonment of tunnels on the Emma Moore and '76 claims, which were related in the report, with Alton L. Dickerman's statement to the *Everett Herald* on October 6, 1892: "In almost every case, in fact I believe without exception, the mines have developed in value with every foot of tunnel that has been driven—the Pride of the Mountains, '76, Rainy, Mystery and Emma Moore, in particular, showing up fine bodies of ore beyond even the surface indications."
One must pause to wonder who was trying to mislead whom.
3. Amid this frenzied construction activity, a tragedy occurred at Monte Cristo on August 18, when James Lillis, one of the original prospectors with C.H. Packard's group, was severely injured by falling rock while working at the Summit mine claim. He died the next day of his injuries. His passing was quickly forgotten, however, as the struggle to wrench wealth from the ground continued unabated.
4. In 1978, 85 years later, this machinery still lies where it was placed in 1893—mute testimony to the skill and determination of the pioneer engineers.
5. The Colby-Hoyt syndicate came to the Pacific Northwest with a certain amount of naivete regarding the climate of the area. The men erroneously assumed it was milder than it often turned out to be, thus they were somewhat rudely shocked by the nature of the winter of 1892—93. In fact, Monte Cristo may have enjoyed a milder winter than Everett did, if one takes literally the comments of C.H. Taylor, auditor of the Monte Cristo Mining Company. In a letter dated January 31, 1893, Joseph L. Colby, president, he stated:

The theory that the shores of Puget Sound have a semitropical climate, received a rude shock last night. The mercury fell with a dull sickening thud to the neighborhood of 5 degrees below zero. It is reported all the way from zero to 15 below, and although I do not see a thermometer, I think it safe to say it was 5 below . . . . In all events it was cold enough to demonstrate the necessity for having some means of thoroughly heating your house, and I hope your architect will bear it in mind.

6. The line was, in fact, the first Pacific slope railroad to be equipped with the new, improved M.C.B.—Master Car Builders—knuckle-grip couplers which are standard on virtually all railroads in the United States today.

CHAPTER VI

1. The process whereby the ore was reduced to useable metals by the Everett plant was thoroughly explained by Milnor Roberts in the 1901 Annual Report of the Washington Geological Survey.

2. An article in the May, 1902, issue of *The Coast* described the mill's operation in layman's terms.

CHAPTER VII

1. The wages earned in 1895 may seem terribly low, but if one takes into account the prices of commodities and the way of life at that time, the buying power of people employed at Monte Cristo will be seen to be comparable to that made by persons in the same jobs today. However, the miners worked under conditions far more severe and dangerous than do their modern counterparts. Nor did they receive fringe benefits; the men had to provide all such service for themselves and their families.

Moderating the negative features of the work was the fact that many necessities which we pay for today were free for the taking at Monte Cristo. One could cut firewood, hunt game, collect berries and greens, and most of the people made their clothes. This factor reduced their dependency on wages to provide a living. Later, in the early part of the twentieth century, when hunting, fishing, and timber cutting were regulated, this way of life ended and was replaced by one characterized by almost total dependency on the earned wage.

CHAPTER VIII

1. This area, called the "sink hole," continues to plague county road crews today, just as it did the railroad section gangs in Monte Cristo's heyday.

CHAPTER IX

1. No copies of the *Monte Cristo Mountaineer* are available today, but many items were reprinted in other newspapers, particularly the *Everett Herald*.

2. The reader may want to compare the floods of 1892, 1896, and 1897 with those which occurred during 1964, 1975, and 1977. Each time the region is subjected to a flood of this destructive nature, it is hailed as a 100-year or a 1,000-year flood. This implies that such occurrences are unusual. The records indicate, however, that they are regular, normal phenomena on the western slope of the Cascades. In fact, they were so well known in the 1890s that many farmers on the lowlands—particularly Ebey Island—built special barns having second-story stalls for cattle and other animals. When floods threatened, the men simply drove the cows up the ramps to the elevated refuges to wait out the storm.

CHAPTER X

1. Much of the arsenic plant's machinery was ultimately moved to the Tacoma smelter. In 1978, that facility, at odds with the Environmental Protection Agency, continued to produce arsenic trioxide from ores laden with the controversial substance. The process has changed little through the years, and today the plant extracts almost all the arsenic trioxide derived from ore in this country.

CHAPTER XI

1. This comment reflects the sometimes bitter rivalry between cities and localities which was prevalent at the turn of the century. The newspapers of Everett repeatedly accused their counterparts in Seattle of claiming dominance over all railroads, roads, waterways, mines, or other enterprises in the region. Individual cities made strenuous efforts to attract business rather than allow a rival city to "capture" the prize. Of course in the 1890s good roads and automobiles were nonexistent between the closest towns, and the cities were sociologically as separated as though they were on different continents.

CHAPTER XIII

1. Otto's son, Elof Norman, who grew up in Monte Cristo but now lives in Everett, has written a charming account of what life was like at the turn of the century in a mining town high up in the Cascades. See *The Coffee Chased Us Up*, published by The Mountaineers in 1977.
2. Spurr's report on the mineral resources of the Monte Cristo Mining District described the ore deposits as having been formed by waters which leached minerals from the native rock and redeposited them in joint planes. The aqueous solutions thus formed would descend only to the level of the prevailing water table, where they would cease their vertical movement. If this was true,

Spurr reasoned, the ore deposits of Monte Cristo would not persist very far below the surface, because the water table was rather high in this area of heavy rainfall. The result would be shallow ore deposits which would be less mineralized with increasing depth. The experience of miners at Monte Cristo had reflected this conclusion. They drove many exploratory tunnels into what appeared to be rich surface leads, only to find the ledges pinched out to nothing 25 to 100 feet below the outcrop.

Many local business people had accused Spurr of giving the Monte Cristo region a "black eye," with consequent curtailment of investment funds that otherwise might have been spent to develop the properties. In 1908, after thinking further on the subject, and refining his analysis, Spurr published a partial retraction of his original conclusions. He stated he now believed the Monte Cristo lodes to have been primary fissure veins, modified by water action. Such a conclusion necessarily conceded that mineralization could continue at great depths, far below the local water table.

The primary source of Spurr's error in the analysis of the Monte Cristo ore deposits resulted from lack of understanding a phenomenon known as secondary enrichment, a process whereby descending waters and rising hot solutions concentrate minerals along primary fissures in the rock structure. Much of the knowledge of geologists who investigated the Monte Cristo minerals in the early days was based upon studies of ore deposits in the Midwest and Rocky Mountains. The Rockies are about sixty million years older than the Cascades, and the geologists' attempts to apply knowledge gleaned from the older mountains failed at Monte Cristo. Secondary enrichment had been in progress sixty million years longer in the Rockies than it had in the Cascades; thus ore in the Rocky Mountains increased in value with depth, because the enrichment process had slowly concentrated it far below the surface. Geologically speaking, relatively little time had been available for this process to occur in the Cascades; consequently, the range contained almost no secondarily enriched deposits of any size.

The pioneer geologists assumed that what was true in the Rockies was also true in the Cascades, and drew many erroneous conclusions. When they sampled the rich surface deposits, they mistakenly concluded that the veins would increase in value with depth. At Monte Cristo, the opposite was generally true. The best producing mines were all utilizing surface deposits and seldom found it economical to stope ore farther than 500 feet below the outcrop. When Spurr returned to Monte Cristo in 1909, he had gained considerable knowledge that he had lacked in 1900, and this factor influenced him to modify his conclusion.

CHAPTER XIV

1. Joe Cook still (in 1978) lives in Everett and works part time as an automobile mechanic. Although past 80 years of age, he remains alert, and can clearly recall events of the distant past.

CHAPTER XV

1. The writer of this book spent many post-hike dryouts in the warm, friendly cabin with its memorabilia from the mining days, and thereby received his initial inspiration to seek out the history of Monte Cristo. He was encouraged in this by Ed and Enid Nordlund who offered considerable assistance during various phases of the project.
2. During the summers of the early 1960s, Walt Meglasson worked for Del Wilkie at Monte Cristo under the same circumstances. He interested the writer of this book in the Monte Cristo area, and later introduced him to the Nordlunds, who were instrumental in furthering his interest in the region's history. Meglasson also began the search for the source data upon which this book is based, which the writer has carried to completion.
3. The writer of this book made his first trip into the depths of Toad Mountain in 1966, and he felt as if he had been given an eerie passport to the past when he observed the names James Kyes, Dan Cook, and Elsworth Cook, together with the date 1918, printed on the wall of the mine. The signatures had been made with smoke from carbide lamps when Jimmy Kyes was twelve years old, and were clearly readable 48 years later.

EPILOGUE

1. The writer is one of those persons who finds it difficult to describe the ''something'' which attracts him to the old townsite and its attendant scenery. Despite numerous visits to the place, new discoveries can always be made, or old ones observed in a new light or in different weather. Whatever beckons him to Monte Cristo is more than the natural beauty; it is almost as if some mysterious inner meaning or peace is about to be revealed amid the splendor of the alpine meadows, the mountains, and the tunnels which pock them. He has, obviously, succumbed to the Lorelei of Monte Cristo, and to return is almost like making a trip home.

APPENDIX 1

THE MONTE CRISTO CONCENTRATOR

("From Ocean Shore to Mountain Crest and Back Again in a Day," *The Coast*, May, 1902)

As the ore of this district is of a character adapted to concentration, let us pass through the mill and see what it is and how it is done. From the two mines of the Monte Cristo Mining Company—the Mystery, one half mile away, and the Pride, one mile away—the crude ore is carried along upon two overhead tramways which have a daily capacity of 400 buckets each containing 700 pounds of ore. These buckets dump their loads at the terminal building one-fourth of a mile from the mill. Here it is passed through grizzlys (course screens) and all the ore coarser than six inches is put through a large gauge crusher which is run by an electric motor and broken to the desired size.

From the terminal building in cars holding two tons the ore is hauled one-half mile along a track beneath a shed to the concentrator, where it is dumped into bins holding 100 tons each.

The principal of concentration is, that by gravity the mineral and the stone, or silica, is separated. Hence, the entire process is carried on by water through a series of mechanical apparatuses, the stone being washed away in what is called the "tailings," and the mineral bodies, the "concentrates," being gathered together.

A flume brings the water from Seventy-six creek a mile away, a thousand gallons of which are used every minute that the mill operates.

A steam engine of 150 horsepower runs the mill; also, a 500 volt dynamo which operates a motor for compressing air for the drills at the mines; and another dynamo which gives light to the mill and camp.

From the bins the ore is fed through a crusher and then passed through a set of rolls, after which it is elevated by a system of buckets one hundred feet and fed automatically through four screens to be sized in grades from eight to two millimeters.

277

The ore over seven millimeters is caught on three jigs, which have three products—concentrates, middlings and tailings. That under seven millimeters is carried to a hydraulic classifier of three compartments, where it is separated and concentrated for the next three jigs.

The middlings are passed through another set of rolls and elevated 65 feet where they are sized on a two millimeter screen, passed on to an hydraulic classifier and fed on three jigs, called "slime jigs," where they are shaken and washed and the ore concentrated.

The muddy overflow from all the classifiers is run into settling tanks and from them the mud is fed to pass over four large round revolving tables across which water is constantly running. The product of this machine is concentrated ore, middlings and tailings. The tailings are run out into the gulch, but the middlings are fed to five vanners, where they are concentrated.

From the jigs, the round tables and the vanners the concentrated ore is taken through launders to bins, where it lies to await shipment to the smelter. This ore carries gold and silver in the ratio of two to one. Extreme care is constantly exerted to gather all the precious mineral and lose as little as possible in the tailings. The plant is under the management of John P. Christopher, with L. Bilodeau superintendent of the mill.The concentrator is a double plant and has a capacity of 300 tons of ore daily.

While this article describes the mill's operation accurately, it alludes to several features which were not present in early 1894, but which were added at later dates: the large gauge crusher at the tram receiving terminal was originally operated by a steam engine, and the 500 volt and lighting dynamos were not yet installed in the concentrator. After reading the descriptions of the concentrator operation, even the non-technically oriented reader can appreciate the complexity involved in extracting metals from the raw ore.

APPENDIX 2

MONTE CRISTO CHRONOLOGY

SPRING, 1889   Joe Pearsall discovers a valley lying north of the headwaters of Silver Creek.

JULY 4, 1889   First claim, the Independence of 1776, staked in '76 Gulch.

SUMMER, 1890   The name "Monte Cristo" selected for the area. The first cabin built in '76 Gulch.

SPRING, 1891   Construction of a road up the Sauk River from Sauk City to Monte Cristo begun.

SUMMER, 1891   First railroad surveys begun. Barlow Pass discovered.

DECEMBER, 1891   Colby-Hoyt syndicate, using, in part, John D. Rockefeller's funds, buys into the Monte Cristo mines.

SPRING, 1892   Construction of the Everett and Monte Cristo Railroad begun. The first topographic map of the Monte Cristo area completed.

SEPTEMBER, 1892   Tunnel no. 7 on the Everett and Monte Cristo right-of-way collapses.

NOVEMBER 2, 1892   First rails for the railroad arrive in Everett, via Cape Horn.

NOVEMBER 18, 1892   First destructive flood washes out railroad.

FEBRUARY 27, 1893   Monte Cristo town plat filed.

MAY, 1893   Everett smelter ready to process ore.

JUNE, 1893   First plans laid for construction of the Monte Cristo tramways.

LATE SUMMER, 1893   United Concentration Company's concentrator at Monte Cristo begun.

SEPTEMBER 6, 1893   First scheduled train reaches Monte Cristo.

SPRING, 1894   Wilmanses Comet Mine tramway in operation.

EARLY AUGUST, 1894   United Concentration Company's tramways operating.

279

SUMMER, 1894   John D. Rockefeller seizes control of the Everett Land
                      Company.
AUGUST 1, 1894   Frederick Gates arrives in Everett to investigate and
                      manipulate Rockefeller's interests.
AUGUST 20, 1894   The concentrator at Monte Cristo starts the treatment
                      of ores.
FALL, 1894   Owners of many of the mine claims at Monte Cristo
                      seek, and are granted, patents.
SPRING, 1895   Frederick Gates begins reorganizing Monte Cristo
                      companies on Rockefeller's behalf.
SUMMER, 1895   Labor troubles develop at Monte Cristo.
FALL, 1895   Wilmanses Golden Cord Mine leased to other
                      operators.
FALL, 1895   O & B Mine started on Toad Mountain.
WINTER, 1896   Air drills in use in the Mystery Mine.
SPRING, 1896   O & B Mine bankrupt.
SUMMER, 1896   Mystery no. 3 Mine tunnel bored beneath Glacier Basin.
FALL, 1896   Floods do great amount of damage to the Everett and
                      Monte Cristo Railroad.
SPRING, 1897   All mines running with record output. The Wilmanses
                      once again control the Golden Cord.
SUMMER, 1897   Record mine output. The upper terminal of the Pride of
                      the Mountains tramway moved down the mountain to
                      the "New Discovery" tunnel.
NOVEMBER 19, 1897   Railroad wiped out by massive floods in the canyon of
                      the Stillaguamish and elsewhere.
DECEMBER 11, 1897   Frederick Gates announces the railroad will not be
                      rebuilt.
JANUARY 7, 1899   Rockefeller gains controlling interest in the Monte
                      Cristo mines and attendant companies.
SUMMER, 1900   Railroad service restored to Monte Cristo. The railroad
                      is reorganized and the section between Everett and
                      Snohomish sold to the Northern Pacific.
FALL, 1900   Mystery and Pride of the Mountains tunnels are
                      connected underground.
1901   Josiah E. Spurr publishes the definitive and controversial
                      report on the ores of Monte Cristo.
JULY 14, 1901   The first excursion run to Monte Cristo using open
                      observation cars.
FALL, 1901   Ore transported down the "45" tramway to the
                      railroad near Silverton.
SEPTEMBER 16, 1902   Railroad sold to the Northern Pacific.

MID-SEPTEMBER, 1903 The smelter and the Monte Cristo mines sold as a package deal to the Guggenheim smelter trust (ASARCO).

DECEMBER 3, 1903   Monte Cristo mines closed by ASARCO.

SPRING, 1904   Excursions into Monte Cristo discontinued.

JULY, 1905   Reshoring of tunnel no. 4 in the canyon of the Stillaguamish undertaken to forestall a collapse.

AUGUST 11, 1905   Wilmans brothers return to Monte Cristo, after a long absence, and buy the mines from the Guggenheims.

FALL, 1906   Samuel Silverman buys the mines at Monte Cristo from the Wilmanses.

MAY 31, 1907   The first carload of ore from Monte Cristo in four years shipped to the smelter.

FALL, 1907   The mines at Monte Cristo again closed.

OCTOBER 31, 1908   The last scheduled train for several years leaves for Monte Cristo.

1909   Josiah Spurr, in a report written after an extensive inspection, rejects plans to reopen the mines.

WINTER, 1910   Heavy snows crush many buildings at Monte Cristo

SUMMER, 1911   Tunnels no. 2 and no. 4 removed in the canyon of the Stillaguamish.

FEBRUARY, 1913   The Public Service Commission orders the Northern Pacific to reopen the railroad into Silverton.

SUMMER, 1913   Boston-American tunnel begun at the base of Toad Mountain.

JULY 21, 1913   The first scheduled train since 1908 reaches Monte Cristo.

SPRING, 1915   The Ben Lomond Mine (Rainy) goes bankrupt.

MAY 11, 1915   The Rucker brothers obtain a lease for the operation of the railroad, and establish the Hartford Eastern Railway Company.

WINTER, 1915   Massive snows crush most of the remaining buildings at Monte Cristo.

JUNE 17, 1916   The Ruckers reinstate observation car excursions on the Hartford Eastern.

OCTOBER 19, 1916   The Boston-American company announces the locating of the O & B ledge at a depth of 1,500 below the surface outcrop.

FALL, 1917   The Boston-American cookhouse and bunkhouse completed.

SUMMER, 1918   The Mountaineers' outing to Monte Cristo undertaken.

SPRING, 1919	The Royal Hotel at Monte Cristo renamed the Casscrest Inn and operated by Dr. F.F. Cassiday.
LATE WINTER, 1920	The Boston-American tunnel in Toad Mountain abandoned; the last active mining ceases.
SPRING, 1921	John Andrews opens the Casscrest Inn and changes the name to the Monte Cristo Inn.
JULY 2, 1921	Big Four Inn opened to the public by the Ruckers.
OCTOBER 1, 1925	The Ruckers buy the Hartford Eastern right-of-way from the Northern Pacific Railway.
APRIL 12, 1933	Scheduled service on the railroad discontinued.
SUMMER, 1936	The rails are torn up, and an automobile road constructed from Robe to Big Four and Sah Hah Lee Camp.
1938-39	Road over Barlow Pass constructed by the C.C.C.
1941	The gravel road into Monte Cristo constructed.
JULY, 1951	John Andrews sells the Boston-American cookhouse to Del Wilkie.
SUMMER, 1962	The Kyes memorial is dedicated.
FALL, 1963	Del Wilkie sells the lodge to the first corporation.
SPRING, 1967	The second corporation purchases the lodge from the first corporation.
WINTER 1972-73	The last tramway cable falls.

APPENDIX 3

PLACE NAMES

BARLOW PASS	After M.Q. Barlow, the original surveyor and locating engineer for the Everett and Monte Criste Railroad.
BIG FOUR MOUNTAIN	After the big number four which forms in the snowfield on its side as viewed from Monte Cristo.
BIG FOUR INN	After Big Four Mountain.
BOSTON-AMERICAN COMPANY	Named the American Mining Company by H.D. Cowden, president, but added the name Boston after the reorganized company's treasurer in 1913.
CADET PEAK	After the Cadet claim near its summit.
CASSCREST INN	After the Cass Crest Mine.
CASS CREST MINE	After Dr. F.F. Cassiday, who owned and operated it.
COMET MINE	Named, because of its altitude, at the whimsy of its locator.
MOUNT DICKERMAN	After Alton L. Dickerman, consulting geologist for the Monte Cristo Mining Company.
EVERETT	After Everett Colby, son of Joseph Colby, one of the town founders.
GLACIER BASIN	After the hanging glacier on the south wall of the basin.
GLACIER CREEK	The creek flowing from Glacier Basin.
GLACIER FALLS	The falls over which Glacier Creek flows.
GOAT LAKE	Orginally called Ouliette Lake, but changed to Goat lake due to the many mountain goats

in the area. The creek which drains the lake is still called Elliott Creek (phonetically) after the original name.

GRANITE FALLS — After the falls on the Stillaguamish River.

IDA GULCH — After the Ida claim above the head of Goat Lake.

IDA PASS — After the Ida claim above the head of Goat Lake.

KYES PEAK — After James Kyes and his family.

MONTE CRISTO — After Alexander Dumas' book, *The Count of Monte Cristo*. Deliberately named to conjure up visions of great wealth.

MONTE CRISTO PEAK — After the town's name.

MYSTERY HILL (RIDGE) — After the Mystery claim on its side.

O & B MINE — After the original locators, Oliver McLean and Ben James.

POODLE DOG PASS — After the Poodle Dog claim in the gulch just below the pass.

PRIDE OF THE MOUNTAINS — Named at the whimsy of the original locators.

PRIDE OF THE WOODS — Named at the whimsy of the original locators.

PROSPECTOR PEAK — After the original prospectors at Monte Cristo.

RAINY MINE — After the prevailing weather in the area.

ROBE — After Truitt K. Robe, early pioneer.

SAH HAH LEE CAMP — From the Chinook jargon meaning, roughly, heaven.

SILVER LAKE — After Silver Tip Peak, in whose cradle it lies.

SILVER TIP PEAK — After the long-lasting patch of snow near the summit which makes the peak appear to be tipped with silver.

SILVERTON — After the silver ore. Originally called Camp Independence, but the name was changed so not to confuse it with Independence, Missouri.

SPERRY PEAK — After A.D. Sperry of Silverton.

TOAD MOUNTAIN — After the toad-shaped rock on the side of the mountain which appears to be attempting to leap to the summit.

WEDEN CREEK — After O.N. Weedan (or Weeden), an early prospector.

WILMANS PASS — After John MacDonald Wilmans and Fred

	Wilmans, the first investors in the Monte Cristo area.
WILMANS PEAK	After John MacDonald Wilmans and Fred Wilmans.
'76 CLAIM	Located on July 4, 1889, and originally named the Independence of 1776, but quickly shortened to '76.
'76 GULCH (Basin)	Named for the claim on its flank.
'76 CREEK	After the gulch from which it flows.

APPENDIX 4

GLOSSARY OF TERMS

ADIT	The entrance of a horizontal mine tunnel.
AERIAL TRAMWAY	A method of transporting materials by means of suspended cables and buckets.
ARGENTIFEROUS	Containing silver.
ASSAY	The chemical analysis of an ore to determine, quantitatively, what values of metals it contains.
ASSESSMENT WORK	The annual work required by the government as proof that a mine claim is not lying idle. $100 per year is usually considered adequate.
AVALANCHE	A snow slide.
BAILER, COMPRESSED AIR	Also called an ejector or eductor; a device whereby a blast of compressed air is used to generate a suction for the pumping of a densed fluid (water).
BALLAST	In railroading, the crushed rock tamped between and under the ties to create a firm roadbed.
BLEICHERT TRAM	A specific type of aerial tramway, patented by Adolph Bleichert; uses a stationary carrying cable from which the car hangs, and rolls along, on wheels. A second, or traction cable, is clutched to the car to serve as the moving force.
BLOCKING OUT	In mining, the boring of tunnels or other activity, to define a body of ore at its known extremities. Generally done prior to any commitment to production.
BULL WHEEL	The wheel around which the moving cable of an aerial tramway passes at one of the terminal stations.
CIRQUE	The head of a glacial valley, where the glacier has carved a bowl-shaped hollow.

CONCENTRATOR	A mill where the ore is crushed and the lighter non-metallic material is separated from the heavier metallic pay dirt.
CONSIST (NOUN)	With the accent placed on the first syllable, the makeup of a train.
CORLISS ENGINE	A steam engine using a rather complex but very efficient valve train.
CROSSCUT	A horizontal mine tunnel not bored along the vein.
CRUSHER	A device to reduce the raw ore particles to a smaller size determined by the design of the mechanism.
DIP	The angle at which a vein of ore is tilted from the horizontal.
DORE BARS	The result of the smelting process. The bars consist of gold and silver of rather high purity, from which these metals are refined.
DYNAMO	A direct current electric generator.
FLANGER	A device attached to the pilot of a locomotive to clear ice and snow from the inside of the rails to make way for the wheel flanges.
GAD	A pointed metal bar used to wedge and break pieces from an ore vein.
GALENA	The sulphide ore of lead.
GANGUE	That portion of the ore containing no mineral, separated from the ore during concentration.
GIANT POWDER	A mixture of nitroglycerine and a substance similar to black powder, formed into sticks, and used in hard rock blasting.
GOSSAN	A hydrated iron oxide formed by the contact of veins of sulphide ores with the atmosphere. This formed an "iron hat" over the vein which differed in color from the surrounding rock, and was used by the early prospectors to locate these veins.
GRIZZLY	A coarse screen through which the raw ore is passed. That which passes through goes to the concentrator, and that which does not is run through a pre-crusher to reduce its size.
GRUBSTAKE	An agreement whereby a person buys the supplies and food (grub) for another person with the understanding that he claims all mineral strikes for the provider of the grubstake.
GYRATORY CRUSHER	A rock crusher which uses a vessel in the shape of a

cone, inside of which is located another conical shaped device roughly the shape of a child's top. The internal piece is pivoted at the bottom, and is slowly "gyrated" at the top, crushing the ore between it and the conical vessel.

HALLIDIE TRAM
A specific type of aerial tram, similar to a ski lift, in which the supporting and moving cable are one in the same.

HOWE TRUSS BRIDGE
A bridge using a lattice work of wood to carry the compressive stresses, and steel bolts to carry the tension. On the deck span truss, the train travels over the top of the trusswork, and on the through span truss, the train travels through the trusswork.

LEDGE
In mining, the vein of ore, particularly if it is nearly horizontal.

OUTCROP
The point at which the vein becomes exposed on the surface.

PATENT
In mining, the deed to the land itself, as differing from the claim, which only conveys the mineral rights.

PELTON WHEEL
An impulse water turbine, which uses a powerful stream of water played against wheel-mounted buckets to rotate the wheel.

PUNCHEON
The split planking used in early pioneer road construction.

RAISE
In mining, a tunnel bored upward from below.

RE-SHOPPED
Refurbished.

REVERBERATORY
A smelting furnace in which the flames are deflected downward off the roof.

ROASTING
In ore processing, the process where the ore is heated, just short of smelting, to drive off impurities such as sulphur and arsenic.

ROLLS
A type of ore crusher using two large rollers rotating almost in contact with one another. The ore is dropped between the rolls and crushed.

SCREENS
Wire mesh or perforated steel plates used to classify or separate particles of a specific size or smaller from the rest of the ore.

SHAFT
A vertical tunnel dug, generally, from the ground surface downward.

SHOO-FLY CURVE
In railroading, a curve built around an obstacle such as a collapsed tunnel or washed out bridge.

SMELTER	A plant containing the smelting ovens in which the base ore is reduced to its metallic content.
SPEEDER	A small, motor powered railway car, generally carrying one or two people.
STOPE	A mining cavity created when the ore is removed from the vein. It follows the contours of the vein and is irregular in shape.
STINGER	A very thin vein.
SULPHIDE ORE	An ore containing one or more metals and the element sulphur. Thus the sulphide ore of lead is galena, of iron is pyrite, of zinc is zinc blende, of iron and copper is calcopyrite, and of iron and arsenic is arsenopyrite (mispickel).
SWITCHBACK	A method by which a railroad gains altitude without gaining distance. The train is stopped, a switch thrown behind it, and the train is then backed up a grade. A switch is then thrown in front of the train, and it is moved ahead, now on a higher elevation than before.
TAILINGS	The result of the concentration process. The fine particles of gangue which have been removed from the ore.
TRAM	Short term for an aerial tramway.
TRAMWAY	An aerial tramway.
TUYERES	The air inlets in a blast furnace.
VANNER (FRUE VANNER)	A large, flat table, rectangular in shape, that is tilted slightly from the horizontal along its long axis to allow water to flow from one side to the other. Small strips of wood or other suitable material are fastened parallel to the long axis every few inches causing the water to flow down the table in many small cascades. The entire table is continuously shaken from side to side in an oscillatory motion. The flour-fine ore, mixed as a slurry with water, is introduced at the high side of the table. The motion of the water and the table allows the lighter gangue to flow over the strips and be washed away with the tailings, while the heavier mineral is trapped by the strips. The troughs above the strips are periodically "scraped" to recover the mineral.
VEIN	The mineralized fissure along which the minerals of the area have been deposited and concentrated.

WHALEBACK   A type of steamship, built somewhat like a submarine, with its decks constantly awash in the seas, and the control house and crew's quarters standing above it on pillars.

WINZE   A vertical mine tunnel connecting two or more levels, with all its winding machinery underground.

WYE   The letter Y. In railroading, used to describe a pattern of switches which, when viewed from above, resemble the letter Y. The device allows a locomotive or cars to be turned around without the use of a turntable.

BIBLIOGRAPHY

BOOKS

Adams, Kramer. *Logging Railroads of the West.* Seattle: Superior Publishing Company, 1961.

An Illustrated History of Skagit and Snohomish Counties. Chicago: Interstate Publishing Co., 1906.

Clark, Norman H. *Milltown: A Social History of Everett, Washington.* Seattle and London: University of Washington Press, 1970.

Gray, Henry L. *The Gold of Monte Cristo.* Seattle: Henry L. Gray, 1969.

Nevins, Allan. *John D. Rockefeller: The Heroic Age of American Enterprise* (two volumes). New York: Scribner's, 1940.

Poor's Manual, Railroads of the United States. New York: H.V. and H.W. Poor, editions of 1901, 1902, 1929, 1930, 1931, 1932, 1933, and 1934.

The Mines Handbook. New York: Stevens Copper Handbook Co., 1916 (Vol. XII), 1918 (Vol. XIII), 1920 (Vol. XIV).

The Trenton Iron Co. *Wire Rope Transportation in All its Branches.* New York: Cooper, Hewitt & Co., 1896.

Whitfield, William. *History of Snohomish County.* Chicago: Pioneer Historical Co., 1926.

Wilkie, Rosemary. *A Broad Bold Ledge of Gold.* Rosemary Wilkie, 1958.

ARTICLES IN BOOKS AND MAGAZINES

Fergusen, E.C. "Beginning of Snohomish County," *The Coast,* Vol. 16 No. 5 (November 1908).

"From Ocean Shore to Mountain Crest and Back in a Day," *The Coast,* Vol. 3 No. 4 (May 1902).

Fuller, H.A. "Points of Interest in the Monte Cristo District," *The Mountaineer,* Vol. II. "War Number" (December 1918).

Hargrave, Margaret D. "The Monte Cristo Outing, 1918," *The Mountaineer,* Vol. 11, "War Number" (December 1918).

Harnett, J.W. "Of the Past and Present in Everett," *The Coast,* Vol. 14 No. 4 (October 1907).

Headlee, F.M. "Mineral Resources of Snohomish County," *The Coast,* Vol. 16 No. 5 (November 1908).

Hodges, L.K. "Mining in the Pacific Northwest," Seattle Washington, *Post-Intelligencer,* 1897.

McIntire, A.W. "Mining Tributary to Everett," *The Coast,* Vol. 14 No. 4 (October 1907).

McRae, John. "History of the Building of Everett," *The Coast,* Vol. 14 No. 4 (October 1907).

Northwest Magazine (Smalley's Magazine). Articles, 1892-97, pertaining to Monte Cristo: April, 1892, Vol. X, Special Number; January, 1893, Vol. XI, No. 1; February, 1895, Vol. XIII, No. 2; August, 1895, Vol. XIII, No. 8; May, 1897, Vol. XV, No. 5.

Roberts, Milnor. "Reduction Plants in Washington," *Annual Report, Washington Geological Survey,* 1901.

Rogers, J.T. "Early Day Reminiscences of Everett," *The Coast,* Vol. 14 No. 4 October 1907).

Sawyer, George E. "The Monte Cristo District," *The Mountaineer,* Vol. 11, "War Number" (December 1918).

Spurr, Josiah Edward. "The Ore Deposits of Monte Cristo," *Twenty-Second Annual Report, Part II,* U.S. Geological Survey, 1902.

The Engineering and Mining Journal. New York: Scientific Publishing Company. Articles, 1892-98, pertaining to Monte Cristo: September 10, 1892, Vol. 54, No. 11; September 17, 1892, Vol. 54, No. 12; April 15, 1893, Vol. 55, No. 15; August 26, 1893, Vol. 56 No. 9; October 14, 1893, Vol. 56, No. 16; December 16, 1893, Vol. 56, No. 25; June 2, 1894, Vol. 57, No. 22; June 30, 1894, Vol. 57, No. 26; September 8, 1894, Vol. 58, No. 10; January 5, 1895, Vol. 59, No. 1; February 2, 1895, Vol. 59, No. 5; August 10, 1895, Vol. 60, No. 6; December 7, 1895, Vol. 60, No. 23; July 11, 1896, Vol. 62, No. 2; August 8, 1896, Vol. 62, No. 6; November 7, 1896,

Vol. 62, No. 19; January 16, 1897, Vol. 63, No. 3; June 26, 1897, Vol. 63, No. 26; July 24, 1897, Vol. 64, No. 4; July 31, 1897, Vol. 64, No. 5; September 25, 1897, Vol. 64, No. 13; January 8, 1898, Vol. 65, No. 2; May 7, 1898, Vol. 65, No. 19; and July 23, 1898, Vol. 66, No. 4.

Whitfield, William. "Snohomish County History," *The Coast*, Vol. 16 No. 5 (November 1908).

NEWSPAPER ARTICLES

Everett, Washington, *Daily Herald*. Articles, 1901-1921, pertaining to Monte Cristo.

Everett, Washington, *Herald*. Articles, 1892-96, pertaining to Monte Cristo.

Port Gardner News (published in Lowell, Washington; predecessor to Everett, Washington, *News*, 1891). Articles, 1891, pertaining to Monte Cristo and Port Gardner Peninsula.

Seattle, Washington, *Post-Intelligencer*. Articles, 1897, pertaining to Monte Cristo.

Seattle, Washington, *Times*. Articles, 1897, pertaining to Monte Cristo; also "Remembrances," by Margaret Callahan, Magazine Section, August 19, 1945.

Snohomish County Tribune. Articles, 1897-1901, pertaining to Monte Cristo.

Snohomish, Washington, *Daily Sun*. Articles, 1889-1899, pertaining to Monte Cristo.

Snohomish, Washington, *Weekly Sun*. Articles, 1889-1899, pertaining to Monte Cristo.

Tacoma, Washington, *Ledger*. Article, June 20, 1895, pertaining to Monte Cristo.

MISCELLANEOUS

Andrews, John. Monte Cristo Inn brochures, 1923, 1924.

Brownell, Francis H. "Remembrances," January 31, 1951.

Dubuar, Paul S. "Scrapbook No. 101." Northwest Collection, Suzallo Library, University of Washington, Seattle, Washington.

Monte Cristo Mining Company. Business letters, 1892-95.

The Mountaineers. Summer outing prospectus, 1918.

Northern Pacific branch line schedules, 1903-1914.

Northern Pacific/Hartford Eastern right-of-way engineering drawings, 1904; revised, 1915.

Spurr, Josiah Edward. Notebooks containing field notes written during surveys taken in 1900.

_____. Report to the American Smelting and Refining Company on economics of reopening the Monte Cristo mines, 1909.

Strom, Sam. "Remembrances," 1936.

United States Coast and Geodetic Survey, 7-½ minute series maps: *Monte Cristo* and *Blanca Lake* quadrangles.

United States Forest Service. "Monte Cristo Historical Tour." Government Printing Office, Region 10, 1975.

Wilmans, John MacDonald. "Remembrances," 1910.

ACKNOWLEDGMENTS

Although it is not possible to name every person and organization that assisted me during the writing of this book, I wish to mention those having a major impact on the project. Everyone who aided me has my deep appreciation, and if any names are missing, it is not due to lack of gratitude. I trust their efforts will be rewarded when they see their suggestions have been utilized in this volume.

Foremost were Ed and Enid Nordlund. The latter graciously allowed me to copy her collection of photographs pertaining to the Monte Cristo area. This, in turn, whetted my interest in the region and spurred me to seek further information. The Nordlunds provided invaluable leads to other sources of data and photographs. Among these were Ellie Loomer, who permitted me to reproduce her assemblage of photographs. Dorothy Reid Van Norman, also located through the Norlunds, let me copy pictures, and she related an interesting personal history of the Monte Cristo area in the 1920s. Joe Cook contributed photographs and told about his experiences in the area from the turn of the century onward.

Walter Meglassen deserves a special note of thanks. He had begun a similar project, but when business matters precluded further work, he turned his information over to me. He had copied every article pertaining to Monte Cristo that had appeared in the *Everett Herald* between 1892 and 1896. Walt also supplied photographs and leads to other sources. The photograph collections of Mr. Bockmeier and Del Stinson were obtained through his efforts.

David Crosson, of the University of Wyoming Western History Research Center, furnished the Josiah E. Spurr photographs and papers

297

which enhanced my geologic understanding of the area; the National Archives made available Spurr's field notebooks. Kim Forman, of the Burlington Northern Railroad, provided drawings of the Everett and Monte Cristo Railroad right-of-way, which allowed the interpretation of many of the photographs as well as giving me a better understanding of the railroad itself. The Snohomish County Auditor's office supplied most of the historic information on the mines and their ownership.

The University of Washington Libraries contributed a great deal of the information used in this book—particularly the Northwest Collection, the science reading room, and the maps, newspaper, and manuscripts departments, all in the Suzallo Library. Photographs were secured from the Northwest Photographic Collection. Mining information was obtained from the Engineering and Mining Library. The Seattle Public Library furnished historic information. The library of The Mountaineers in Seattle was the source of facts about the early climbing and hiking excursions into the area.

This book was merely a collection of data when The Mountaineers expressed interest in publishing a book on Monte Cristo. Through the efforts and encouragement of several Mountaineers—notably Peggy Ferber, Donna DeShazo, John Pollock, and Robert L. Wood—this book came into being. I also wish to acknowledge my gratitude to Robin Lefberg, who prepared the maps and drawings, without which the text would be less meaningful.

PHILIP R. WOODHOUSE

INDEX

299

Philip R. Woodhouse was led to the Monte Cristo region by his complementary avocations of photography and mountain travel. Then his engineering education and training prompted him to research the history of the mines and railroad. For nearly two decades Woodhouse immersed himself in the story—researching newspaper and library files throughout the Northwest, interviewing former residents and their relatives, climbing most of the surrounding peaks, crawling through and measuring every remaining section of the maze of miners' tunnels, and reconstructing the entire railroad on paper. He has taken nearly ten thousand photos, either on site or copying and recreating historic photos from private collections; he has also filmed and produced a documentary on the area.

MOUNTAINEERS BOOKS is a leading publisher of mountaineering literature and guides—including our flagship title, *Mountaineering: The Freedom of the Hills*—as well as adventure narratives, natural history, and general outdoor recreation. Through our two imprints, Skipstone and Braided River, we also publish titles on sustainability and conservation. We are committed to supporting the environmental and educational goals of our organization by providing expert information on human-powered adventure, sustainable practices at home and on the trail, and preservation of wilderness.

The Mountaineers, founded in 1906, is a 501(c)(3) nonprofit outdoor activity and conservation organization whose mission is "to explore, study, preserve, and enjoy the natural beauty of the outdoors." One of the largest such organizations in the United States, it sponsors classes and year-round outdoor activities throughout the Pacific Northwest, including climbing, hiking, backcountry skiing, snowshoeing, bicycling, camping, paddling, and more. The Mountaineers also supports its mission through its publishing division, Mountaineers Books, and promotes environmental education and citizen engagement. For more information, visit The Mountaineers Program Center, 7700 Sand Point Way NE, Seattle, WA 98115-3996; phone 206-521-6001; www.mountaineers.org; or email info@mountaineers.org.

Our publications are made possible through the generosity of donors and through sales of more than 500 titles on outdoor recreation, sustainable lifestyle, and conservation. To donate, purchase books, or learn more, visit us online:

**MOUNTAINEERS
BOOKS**

Mountaineers Books
1001 SW Klickitat Way, Suite 201
Seattle, WA 98134
800-553-4453
mbooks@mountaineersbooks.org
www.mountaineersbooks.org

CPSIA information can be obtained
at www.ICGtesting.com
Printed in the USA
FSHW012032200319
56544FS